Top Secret Tales of World War II

Top Secret Tales of World War II

William B. Breuer

CASTLE BOOKS

Inspiring | Educating | Creating | Entertaining

Brimming with creative inspiration, how-to projects, and useful information to enrich your everyday life, Quarto Knows is a favorite destination for those pursuing their interests and passions. Visit our site and dig deeper with our books into your area of interest: Quarto Creates, Quarto Cooks, Quarto Homes, Quarto Lives, Quarto Drives, Quarto Explores, Quarto Gifts, or Quarto Kids.

ISBN-13: 978-0-7858-1951-6

PO000036

Printed in the United States of America

SUSTAINABLE FORESTRY INITIATIVE

Certified Sourcing

www.sfiprogram.org
SFI-01681

Label applies to text stock.

Dedicated to
EDWARD M. FLANAGAN, JR.
Lieutenant General, U.S. Army (Ret.)
Paratrooper junior officer in World War II
who gained the respect and admiration of
his elite warriors over the years as
he rose to the top in
his profession.

In the high ranges of secret work
[in World War II] the actual facts
in many cases were in every respect
equal to the most fantastic inventions
of romance and melodrama.

Winston S. Churchill

Contents

Part Five—The Tide Turns

Part Six—Allied March to Victory

Introduction

THE HALL OF MIRRORS in the magnificent Palace of Versailles, a mammoth edifice built by Louis XIV in 1661, was bustling with formally garbed delegates from many countries on the beautiful day of June 28, 1919. They had gathered outside Paris for the signing of the peace treaty that concluded what euphoric Allied politicians labeled "the war to end all wars."

It was one of German history's blackest hours, for the victors—mainly Great Britain, France, and the United States—had inflicted harsh terms on the vanquished, including forcing Germany to acknowledge responsibility for starting the four years of bloodshed and carnage known then as the Great War.

With hostile neighbors on all sides, Germany had been virtually disarmed by the Treaty of Versailles. Her six-million-man force had to be slashed to a *Reichswehr* (army) of only a hundred thousand civilian volunteers, and this caretaker force was prohibited from having airplanes or tanks.

Almost before the ink had dried on the peace treaty, a cagey, monocled Old Prussian, General Hans von Seeckt, set in motion a series of clandestine events designed to lead to the rebirth of German military and industrial might. As commander of the Reichswehr, Seeckt, known as the "Sphinx" because of his enigmatic personality, began conspiring to use the authorized hundred-thousand-man force as a cadre for future rapid expansion. Only the best-educated officers and sergeants who had proven themselves to be dynamic leaders and courageous in battle were allowed to remain in the service.

General von Seeckt and his coconspirators in the Reichswehr had to proceed with extreme caution and utilize ingenious deceptions to mask what was really taking place. Many British, French, and American military officers were stationed throughout Germany to make certain that the terms of the Treaty of Versailles were enforced.

Once Seeckt had selected the members of his private club, he made certain that their living conditions were vastly improved, that they had food items not available to civilians, and that their pay was hiked. The general then established a strict routine of sports and other recreational activities that developed strong, healthy soldiers.

Seeckt next created a series of military schools whose "civilian" instructors—in reality high-ranking officers from the Great War—taught sergeants and lieutenants the techniques of commanding entire divisions, in preparation for some future war. Among the eager students was young Erwin Rommel, a platoon leader in the war who was regarded by a superior as "the perfect fighting animal, cold, cunning, ruthless, untiring, incredibly brave."

In 1921, the Old Prussian, without informing the German government, negotiated a clandestine mutual military assistance pact with a highly unlikely ally, the Soviet Union, against whom Germany had fought bitterly during the Great War.

The alliance had been instigated by Nikolai Lenin, the founder of the Soviet Union. Back in March 1917, news of the downfall of Czar Nicholas II had reached Lenin in exile in Switzerland, where he had been trying to foment a revolution. In his impatience to return home, he accepted for himself and his friends the offer by the German Kaiser Wilhelm of a private railroad car to travel to Russia across Germany.

Kaiser Bill, as he was called by the Allies, was confident that Lenin would aid his cause by taking Russia out of the war against Germany. But Lenin's own aim was to make not only Russia but the entire world, Germany included, Communist countries.

Arriving in Petrograd (as St. Petersburg was then called) in April, Lenin called on the Russian masses to join him in overthrowing the moderate government and replacing it with a Communist one. Most of the peasants joined his Bolsheviks, and in October 1917 the government was ousted.

Lenin became absolute dictator. As Kaiser Bill had hoped, he took the huge but ineptly led Russian army out of the war.

Now, three years later, with both the Soviet and German economies in dire straits and inflation galloping out of control, Nikolai Lenin had instructed the Soviet ambassador to Germany, Nucolai Krestinski, to make a discreet approach to General von Seeckt. The result was the secret alliance between the two nations.

If it was not a shotgun marriage, it was certainly one of necessity. The Red Army lacked both professional leadership skills, and military schools for that training. Germany had no airplanes, tanks, or heavy guns, or an air force or a navy.

Under the terms of the pact, German military advisers would secretly assist the Soviet Union in modernizing its army. In return, the Reichswehr would receive periodic clandestine shipments of Soviet-built heavy weapons. At the same time, the cream of the Reichswehr would be sent to the Soviet Union (in civilian clothes) to be trained on the airplanes and tanks being developed there by German armaments experts.

Each year, a third of the annual budget of the Reichswehr went into a curious cartel: the Gesellschaft zur Förderung gewerblichen Unternehmen (the Industrial Enterprises Development Corporation). From its offices, one in Berlin and one in Moscow, it dealt directly with the Soviet government and had several subcontracting branches throughout the Soviet Union.

Men of the hundred-thousand-member Reichswehr trained with dummy tanks constructed of canvas around an ordinary automobile. (National Archives)

The seemingly commercial corporation was a cover for the Reichswehr. Under the direction of the phony firm, aircraft shells, submarines, and poison gas were produced in the Soviet Union and shipped clandestinely to Germany.

At his headquarters in Berlin in September 1921, General von Seeckt set up Sondergruppe R (Special Group R), the cover name for an operation run by selected officers to coordinate the numerous secret German manufacturing and military assistance programs taking place in the Soviet Union.

At the same time, the Old Prussian dispatched one of his key officers, Colonel Oskar von Niedermayer, to the Soviet Union to open the Zentrale Moskau (Moscow Central). Niedermayer immediately began dashing about the immense Soviet Union, wearing civilian clothes and carrying out his function of coordinating all secret German activities in that country.

Colonel von Niedermayer gave special attention to the three immense training bases in remote locales of the Soviet Union that were prepared for the "Black Reichswehr," twenty thousand strong, to conduct extensive and realistic field exercises.

These soldiers were the best and the brightest, destined for eventual high command in some German army of the future. Before leaving for the Soviet Union, each of these soldiers' names was "erased" from the rolls. Theoretically, none of them now existed.

Sent from Germany to the training camps in the Soviet Union under the most stringent secrecy, the men of the "Black Reichswehr" learned the art of war side by side with young Soviet officers, also selected for future high command, from high-ranking German officers. Hermetically sealed zinc containers were used to bring back the remains of German soldiers killed in the rigorous training exercises in which live ammunition was sometimes used.

Another area in which Germany rearmed was her air force. Although the 1919 Treaty of Versailles had directed that Germany destroy all of its combat aircraft and prohibited building more of them, the document made no mention of the use of gliders. So almost as soon as the treaty was signed, scores of active glider-flying clubs sprang up throughout Germany.

Glider flying developed into almost a craze in Germany during the first few years after the Great War. Although the young pilots looked upon their sport as an enjoyable pastime, many others envisioned the clubs as excellent training grounds for power-airplane pilots when the day came that Germany again had an air force. One of the latter was Hermann Goering, who was working in odd jobs as a salesman.

Goering had been a highly decorated fighter ace with twenty-two kills, and he had succeeded Manfred von Richthofen—the famed Red Baron—as a squadron leader after he was shot down. Now, as a civilian in an intolerable postwar Germany, he was bitter about the Treaty of Versailles, and he vowed revenge.

Early in 1922, Captain Edward V. Rickenbacker, America's top fighter ace in the Great War and now an executive with an aviation corporation, was in Berlin on business. Four former German pilots, who had engaged in duels with Rickenbacker's squadron over France, played host to him. One of the four was Hermann Goering.

During a conversation at dinner, Goering told the American, "Our whole future is in the air. And it is by airpower that we are going to recapture the German Empire."

Rickenbacker masked his shock. Only four years after the greatest butchery in history to that time had ended, here was a famous German advocating rebuilding the nation's armed might and going to war once more.

Goering explained precisely how Germany would circumvent the restrictions in the Treaty of Versailles. "First, we will teach gliding as a sport to all our young men," he said. "Then we will build up commercial aviation. Finally we will create the skeletons of a military air force. When the time comes, we will put all three together, and the German Empire will be reborn."

A year later, in 1923, the Allied Control Commission that had been monitoring all German activities since Versailles relaxed some constraints in the treaty to allow the nation to expand its industry, including permission to build a "limited number" of civilian airplanes.

German aircraft manufacturers, delighted to be back in business after being shut down for nearly five years, took a liberal view of "limited number" and began producing hundreds of aircraft of all sizes.

Then, in 1926, General von Seeckt took another gigantic step in his master plan to secretly rearm Germany by creating an illegal "Black Luftwaffe." A special aviation branch, the Fliegerzentrale (Flying Center), was formed with a few squadrons of aircraft converted from civilian use.

Modern aviation equipment and designs were sorely lacking, however, because German industry, hampered by the Treaty of Versailles restrictions, could not provide sophisticated technology. So the Fliegerzentrale, under bull-necked Major Hugo Sperrle, a fighter ace in the Great War, sent "scouts" to several foreign countries to purchase aviation items that were available on the open market. Efforts focused chiefly on the United States, whose industrial and technological capacities were booming.

Sperrle learned from his "scouts" that most of the wanted devices, such as aircraft designs, automatic bombsights, and retractable landing gear, were classified as military secrets by the War Department in Washington and not for sale at any price. Undaunted, Sperrle and other plotters at the Fliegerzentrale decided that what they could not buy, they would steal.

The task of pilfering U.S. military secrets was handed to the Abwehr, Germany's secret service, whose operations had apparently been overlooked by Versailles. Diminutive Fritz Gempp, the Abwehr chief, sent Germany's first postwar spy, thirty-four-year-old Wilhelm Lonkowski, to the United States in 1927. His German passport identified him as William Schneider, a piano tuner.

Before sailing from Bremerhaven, Germany, Lonkowski had been furnished with a "shopping list" compiled by Major Sperrle. Items had been culled from American aviation magazines and trade journals. The scope of Lonkowski's mission would have staggered spies of less robust spirit: as a lone agent, he was expected to steal military secrets from such major corporations as Curtiss Aircraft, Westinghouse Electric, Seversky Aircraft, Fairchild Aviation, and Douglas Aircraft, as well as from the U.S. Army's Mitchel and Roosevelt airfields outside New York City.

Lonkowski soon found that the United States was a spy's paradise. No single federal agency was charged with countersubversive operations, and the United States was the only major nation in the world that had no secret service to ferret out the intentions of hostile powers. Consequently, unmolested and without fear of detection and arrest, Wilhelm Lonkowski rapidly recruited a network of domestic spies and began reaping a harvest of America's military secrets.

Meanwhile, back in Germany, the Sphinx, General Hans von Seeckt, was continuing to use his guile to expand the Reichswehr's clout. Devising a deliberately misleading name, he created the Truppenamt, consisting of sixty of his most capable officers. This group's function was to form a new general staff, which had been outlawed by the Treaty of Versailles.

Seeckt also used evasive means to make sure that Germany would have a large pool of highly trained reserve officers. He achieved that goal by rotating men through the Reichswehr, thereby keeping its strength at one hundred thousand at any given time.

In the early 1930s, when a new leader, Adolf Hitler, told the world that Germany was no longer bound by the Treaty of Versailles and began rapidly to overtly expand its armed forces, it would have a large, motivated, and skilled officer corps, the best in the world.

Meanwhile, halfway around the world from Germany in the late 1920s and early 1930s, Japan was gripped by a secret movement whose goal was a totalitarian state under absolute military control. Numerous covert groups, of which the Black Dragon was the most notorious, advanced the cause through machinations, murders, and mayhem.

In 1927, Japanese military leaders secretly drew up the Tanaka Memorial, a blueprint for armed conquest of the Far East and driving the United States and Great Britain out of the Pacific. The dream of the warlords was called Hakko Ichiu (the Eight Corners of the World under One Roof).

Japan had spent many years preparing for the inevitable war in the Pacific. From boyhood, young men were taught how to engage in armed combat. Schools were operated much like military units. Some of the teachers were army officers who lectured the impressionable boys that it was their duty to die if necessary to help Japan fulfill its divine destiny of conquest.

From 1931 on, each graduating class at the Japanese naval academy was confronted with the final examination question: "How would you carry out a surprise attack on Pearl Harbor?"

On September 30, 1931, Japanese soldiers planted explosives on the tracks of the Japanese-owned railroad in Manchuria, a large province in northeastern China separated from Korea by the Yalu River. The plot to provoke a war with China failed when an express train raced over the dynamite charge without being blown up.

Then the Japanese saboteurs killed several nearby Chinese soldiers, and Tokyo fabricated a story that the Chinese had tried to derail a Japanese train. Based on that fraud, General Senjuro Hayashi, a Hakko Ichiu disciple, rushed his army in Korea across the Yalu into Manchuria and seized control of the province.

U.S. Ambassador Joseph C. Grew,
murder target of Japanese militarists.
(Library of Congress)

Militarists continued to consolidate their power in Japan by the expedient of getting rid of inconvenient persons. In 1932, a clique of navy officers murdered seventy-five-year-old moderate Prime Minister Tsuyoshi Inukai. When the minister of finance refused to increase funds for the military, he was killed by army officers.

In an effort to incite the militarily weak United States into a war, a plot, ultimately unsuccessful, was hatched to murder Hollywood superstar Charlie Chaplin (then visiting in Tokyo) and U.S. Ambassador Joseph C. Grew, a Harvard graduate who devoted most of his time toward keeping Japan and the United States from an armed conflict.

All the while, the Japanese warlords had been building one of the mightiest war juggernauts that history had known.[1]

Part One

Heading Toward the Abyss

Sinister Plots in the "New Germany"

A CLEAR BLUE SKY hovered over Berlin on the afternoon of June 29, 1934, when the chief of the German General Staff, General Ludwig Beck, was escorted into the cavernous office of Adolf Hitler, a World War I corporal. Hitler had seized absolute control of the government after being appointed chancellor seventeen months earlier by aging, senile President Paul von Hindenburg.

The fifty-four-year-old Beck was highly regarded at home and abroad as the most efficient and humane German soldier of his generation. He had sought the appointment because of mounting evidence that the new German leader was planning on rearming the nation of eighty million persons to launch a war of conquest. In measured terms, Beck told Hitler that he did not intend to build an army to conquer other countries; his purpose was to create an efficient army to defend Germany.

Hitler, noted for a quick temper, replied testily: "General Beck, it is impossible to build up an army and give it a sense of worth if the object of its existence is not the preparation for battle. Armies for the preparation of peace do not exist; they exist for triumphant execution in war."

Before he departed, Beck told Hitler that another war would become a multifront conflict that Germany could not survive.

Only minutes after returning to the imposing building on the Bendlerstrasse that housed the headquarters of the General Staff, Beck received a telephone call from Admiral Wilhelm Canaris, a cagey and highly productive spy in World War I whom Hitler had appointed chief of the Abwehr, the German secret service, six months earlier, on Canaris's forty-seventh birthday.

A slight, prematurely white-haired man who spoke with a lisp, Canaris was well educated and could speak the languages of Germany's potential enemies— England, France, and the Soviet Union. He, too, feared Hitler was embarking on a war path that would eventually destroy Germany as a nation.

Speaking in guarded tones, Canaris told Beck that the dictator was preparing to launch a purge to wipe out all sources of opposition to his Nazi regime. Among the officers on the hit list were General Kurt von Schleicher, Hitler's predecessor as chancellor, and Schleicher's close friend and assistant General Kurt von Bredow, who had once held a high post in the Abwehr.

11

Canaris told Beck that Hitler was convinced that Schleicher was conspiring with the French ambassador to get rid of the Nazi regime by restoring the Hohenzollerns, descendants of the traditional royal family, to the throne of Germany. Beck knew that Hitler's suspicions were well founded, and he sent a trusted aide to warn Schleicher of the danger. Schleicher, however, seemed unconcerned.

At high noon on June 30, less than twenty-four hours after Beck had clashed with Hitler, five men in civilian clothes barged into General Schleicher's villa. They went to the study, where Schleicher was working on some papers, pulled out pistols, and shot the former chancellor. Frau von Schleicher, who had been in another room, rushed to the study. She, too, was shot and killed.

Two hours later, General von Bredow was at the Hotel Adlon in Berlin drinking tea with a French diplomat when a messenger from General Ludwig Beck brought him an envelope with a short note telling him that Schleicher had been murdered. Bredow's face flushed in anger. Turning to the Frenchman, he said with a snarl, "I wonder why the pigs haven't killed me yet!"

Bredow told his companion that Schleicher was the only man who could have saved Germany. "He was my leader. Now there is nothing for me," he declared.

Bredow took a taxi to his home, and just past five o'clock that afternoon, he answered a ring at his front door. Two men whipped out pistols and riddled the general with bullets, killing him almost instantly.

Adolf Hitler had launched one of the bloodiest purges that European history had ever known. He realized that war was the last thing most of his generals wanted, and he was convinced that they were conspiring to restore the Hohenzollerns.

Hitler had set into motion a series of sinister plots to not only eradicate suspected foes bodily, but also to besmirch their honor. That approach began promptly when the war minister, General Werner von Blomberg, ordered that Schleicher and Bredow were to be regarded as traitors and that no general or admiral was to attend their funerals.

Despite the risk to their careers—or even to their lives—General Ludwig Beck and Admiral Wilhelm Canaris ignored the strict order and dressed in full uniform, and carrying Schleicher's medals on silk cushions, they walked behind the cortege to the cemetery. At the gates they were halted by a group of black-uniformed Schutzstaffel (SS), an elite corps that served as Hitler's bodyguard and was fanatically loyal to him.

On August 2, 1934, a month after Schleicher and Bredow were branded as traitors and buried, the long-senile, eighty-seven-year-old President Paul Ludwig von Hindenburg died at his estate in East Prussia. Earlier, Hitler had obtained a political testament from the Old Warrior that named Hitler to succeed him as president.

Now Hitler moved swiftly. He had no interest in merely being president of a great nation. Only minutes after Hindenburg died, Hitler proclaimed himself führer (supreme leader) and launched a strategy to induce his admirals and generals to swear allegiance to him.

No doubt acting on the führer's orders, War Minister von Blomberg directed all of Germany's generals—some three hundred of them—to assemble at three o'clock that same afternoon at the foot of the Siegessäule, the towering Column of Victory in Berlin. Unknown to the high brass, Hitler was preparing to inflict a *coup d'état* that would give him total control of Germany and the armed forces.

The generals had been told that they were to participate in ceremonies to honor the dead President Hindenburg. Cannons were fired. A band played mournful tunes. There were two minutes of silence. Then General von Blomberg stepped forward to take the Fahneneid—the blood oath of the Teutonic knights. The army commander, General Werner von Fritsch, and General Ludwig Beck followed. Each held the flag of Germany in one hand and the Bible in the other while reciting:

I swear by God this holy oath, that I will render to Adolf Hitler, Führer of the German nation and people, supreme commander of the armed forces, unconditional obedience, and I am ready as a brave soldier to risk my life at any time for this oath.

All over Germany at the same time the rank and file of the armed forces recited the same blood oath.

Walking with General Fritsch back to his headquarters, Beck stopped suddenly and said solemnly: "This is a fateful hour. [The oath] means physical and moral suicide."

Further along the way, Beck halted again. Both generals realized that they had been tricked into taking an oath, not to Germany or the constitution, but to Adolf Hitler.

"He took us unawares," Beck said mournfully. "I did not realize that we were swearing a completely new form of oath."

Führer Hitler in the months ahead continued to rearm Germany. But to carry out his plans for widespread conquest, he would have to rid himself of all those on the General Staff who might oppose him and replace them with those who would do his every bidding without argument or hesitation. Strangely, perhaps, one of the first targets was Werner von Blomberg, the war minister, who had been the first general to be elevated to field marshal by the führer.

Blomberg was known in the officer corps as the Rubber Lion—one willing to bend whichever way the führer desired. In December 1937 Blomberg,

Only two of these three leaders of the German armed forces survived plots against them by Adolf Hitler. From the left: General Werner von Fritsch, Admiral Erich Raeder, and General Werner von Blomberg. (National Archives)

fifty-nine years old and a widower, asked Hitler's permission to marry a twenty-six-year-old typist. The führer gave his blessing and was a witness at the wedding ceremony.

Blomberg and his new young wife departed for a honeymoon on the romantic Isle of Capri.

A longtime crony of Hitler, General Hermann Goering, immediately began to hatch a scheme to oust the war minister. Known behind his back as Fat Hermann, Goering deeply coveted Blomberg's job.

Goering turned over the exacting task of discrediting Blomberg to an expert in the field, tall, hawk-nosed Reinhard Heydrich, the young chief of the Sicherheitsdienst (SD), the security branch of the SS. Brilliant and with the instincts of a barracuda, the highly ambitious Heydrich and his underlings began poking into Blomberg's private life and found that he was quite fond of women. That was no crime in the Third Reich, but it could be a valuable blackmail weapon at some future date. Blomberg, Heydrich's agents discovered, occasionally donned civilian clothes and spent evenings in some of Berlin's more exotic nightspots.

At the same time, SD men began sifting through old reports of the Kriminalpolizei (Civil Police) and hit the jackpot. Blomberg's beautiful new wife, Erna Gruhn, had had convictions for prostitution. Her mother was also well known to Berlin police as the proprietress of a "massage parlor" that was patronized by well-heeled men, presumably in urgent need of rubdowns.

Goering was ecstatic. He rushed to see the führer and showed him the police docket. Hitler professed to be deeply distressed and immediately ordered the war minister to return to Berlin from his honeymoon.

Blomberg was promptly sacked and went into exile with his wife. He ignored suggestions from German generals he had known for many years to take a Luger and blow his brains out.

Now Hitler pondered the question about who would succeed Blomberg as head of Germany's rapidly expanding military organization. The führer was leaning toward appointing General Werner von Fritsch, whom Hindenburg had appointed commander of the army in May 1935. Aghast that he himself had not been chosen, Goering set about to "dig up dirt" on General von Fritsch.

Again Reinhard Heydrich's sleuths scanned old police vice files and came up with the name of a German officer who had been blackmailed by an ex-convict and male prostitute named Otto Schmidt. No doubt frightened to be grilled by agents of a high government official, Schmidt, known as Bavarian Joe, admitted he had committed a homosexual act with a man he identified as General von Fritsch at the Wannsee railroad station.

Hoping to gain more "proof" that Fritsch was a practicing homosexual, Heydrich's agents fanned out through Germany to interview officers in Fritsch's command. None would claim any knowledge of their boss's alleged homosexuality.

Despite a total lack of confirmation of the charges, trial papers were drawn up against Fritsch.

Learning of the trumped-up charges, Fritsch was apoplectic, and he demanded an immediate interview with the führer. Unknown to the general, Hermann Goering had arranged for Bavarian Joe to be present.

In the library of the Reichskanzlei (Chancellery), Bavarian Joe repeated his story in front of a frowning Hitler. Schmidt had been well coached. The notorious ex-convict claimed that an "elderly gentleman" wearing a monocle, a short coat with a fur collar, and carrying a silver-headed cane entered the railroad station. In the lavatory, Bavarian Joe picked up the military officer and went with him to a nearby dark lane, he claimed.

Fritsch protested that he had not been in the Wannsee railroad station for many years and that he had never owned a silver-headed cane. A soft-spoken man innocent of political throat-cutting, Fritsch played right into Goering's hands by not reacting violently to Bavarian Joe's story, the only "evidence" against him. Consequently, Hitler immediately sacked the high-ranking general.

When it was later discovered that Bavarian Joe's true client had been an obscure cavalry officer with a similar last name, Achim von Frisch, the führer refused to restore the disgraced general to his former rank.

Meanwhile, Hitler vastly reorganized the armed forces to make certain that when he was ready to go to war, the General Staff would have to comply to orders without argument. The führer created the Oberkommando der

Wehrmacht (OKW), the supreme command of the armed forces. All unit staffs would be subordinate to the OKW. Hitler took the title of supreme commander. His two top aides were both *führertreu*—totally loyal to him. They were General Wilhelm Keitel, who would be Hitler's chief of staff, and General Alfred Jodl, who was designated to be Hitler's chief of operations.

On February 4, 1938, Radio Berlin, which, like every institution in Germany, was controlled by the führer, broadcast a long statement from the Oberkommando der Wehrmacht. Field Marshal von Blomberg and General von Fritsch had retired for "health reasons," it was stated. Then the names of thirty-five other illustrious generals, who may not have been considered führertreu by Hitler or Hermann Goering, were read by the announcer. They, too, had gone into early retirement because of "health reasons."

Word of the "failing-health epidemic" that had riddled the ranks of Germany's generals was flashed throughout the world by the news wire services. In the capitals of Europe it was clear: through a series of crafty schemes and ruthless maneuvers, the Führer had gained total control of eighty million people and the now powerful army, navy, and Luftwaffe.[1]

"Burglars" Call
on a Japanese Spymaster

LIEUTENANT COMMANDER Ellis M. Zacharias, who was assigned to the Office of Naval Intelligence (ONI) in Washington, D.C., had become convinced that Imperial Navy Captain Tamon Yamaguchi was the Japanese espionage leader in the United States. Yamaguchi, the Japanese military attaché, was suave and charismatic. He spoke English fluently and seemed to enjoy the social life in Washington.

Because of his suspicions, Zacharias made it a point to have personal contact with Yamaguchi as often as possible. On one of these occasions, in January 1936, Zacharias and his wife were guests at a gala party given by Yamaguchi in the Chinese Room of the ornate Mayflower Hotel.

Sipping casually on a cocktail, the forty-four-year-old Zacharias, one of the few Jewish Naval Academy graduates of his generation, noticed that two German military attachés, Vice Admiral Robert Witthoft-Emden and Lieutenant General Friedrich von Boetticher, had become quite friendly with Yamaguchi. This development surprised the ONI sleuth. Previously, the relationship between the two Nazis and Yamaguchi had been quite frigid, reflecting the views of their respective governments.

When the party was drawing to a close, Zacharias told his wife that the couple must remain as long as possible to see what would happen between the two Germans and the Japanese host. In social events given by Yamaguchi in the past, the two Germans had always departed after only a few minutes.

Now the Nazis had stayed for nearly three hours. Zacharias felt that the party was held to provide an opportunity for the two Germans and Yamaguchi to discuss some important matters without attracting undue attention.

Across the spacious room, now thinning of guests, General Boetticher and Admiral Witthoft-Emden were still clinging to Yamaguchi. The Germans cast periodic glances toward Zacharias. Plainly, they were irritated that he had not left the party.

Nodding toward the two Germans and the Japanese, Zacharias told his wife, "Something's afoot!"

The situation evolved into a cat-and-mouse game. Who would outwait whom?

Finally, after the waiters had cleared all the dishes, Zacharias and his wife hurried to Yamaguchi's side to make certain that he, the two Nazis, and the Zachariases all left at the same time, thereby depriving the Germans of a chance to conclude their business with their host.

Early the next morning, Zacharias discussed with his boss, Captain William D. Puleston, the puzzling German-Japanese lovefest at the Mayflower. Because the principal mission of military attachés at embassies is to be espionage agents, the ONI officers agreed that the German and Japanese intelligence agencies were now working in close alliance.

Although the two ONI sleuths had no way of knowing the precise developments, their educated hunch was accurate. German Colonel Walter Nicolai, who had been in charge of Kaiser Wilhelm's far-flung intelligence apparatus in the Great War, had held secret meetings with his Japanese counterparts in Tokyo only two weeks earlier. Nicolai had suggested that the two nations pool their espionage resources.

Nicolai stressed that only Caucasians could be effective spies in the United States because Oriental agents could be more easily detected. The Japanese bought the proposal. They would spy for the Germans in the Pacific regions, where Caucasian agents would be conspicuous. In turn, the Germans would pass along intelligence gleaned from the United States and the Panama Canal Zone.

Adolf Hitler was enthusiastic over the arrangement, and he appointed Eugen Ott to be ambassador to Japan and to coordinate the two nations' intelligence exchanges.

Now, within forty-eight hours of the Mayflower Hotel party, the ONI began a surveillance of the Alban Towers, an imposing apartment building at the intersection of Wisconsin and Massachusetts Avenues in Washington. In a high-level suite, Captain Yamaguchi maintained his living quarters. Captain Zacharias believed that the suite also served as a command post for Japanese espionage activities in the United States.

On the first night of the surveillance, ONI technicians, huddled in an enclosed truck parked near the Alban Towers and using electronic devices,

Navy Captain Tamon Yamaguchi, Japanese spymaster in the United States. (U.S. Navy)

picked up mysterious noises somewhere in the building. Zacharias concluded that these sounds were being generated by a machine that encoded messages to be sent to Tokyo by sacrosanct diplomatic courier pouch or by radio transmittal.

Consequently, an elaborate scheme was hatched to gain what intelligence agencies call a "surreptitious entry" to Yamaguchi's suite, inspect the encoding machine, and "requisition" any codes or other materials customarily used in espionage work.

A major concern was that Yamaguchi might be home and catch the ONI "cat burglars" in the act, thereby igniting a major hullabaloo between the governments of Japan and the United States. Zacharias came up with the perfect answer: he and Mrs. Zacharias would invite their good friend Yamaguchi to have dinner at their home in suburban Washington on the night scheduled for the caper.

When Yamaguchi, smiling and courteous as always, arrived at the Zacharias residence, the ONI officer excused himself, went into another room, and telephoned his headquarters. He recited one code word that meant the Japanese had arrived and the "burglars" could go to work.

Meanwhile, earlier in the evening, Navy Lieutenant Jack S. Holtwick, a cryptanalyst (one who breaks codes), and a Navy radio expert named McGregor donned civilian electricians' outfits. Then they drove to the Alban Towers in a van with the name of a phony firm painted in large letters on the side. Explaining to the doorman that they had been called by a tenant, the two men took an elevator to Yamaguchi's floor, tiptoed down the corridor to his suite, and listened for any sound that might indicate there were armed guards inside.

Working swiftly and with ears tuned to any noise that might mean the approach of someone, the two intruders used a special instrument to open the door without leaving a telltale mark. They conducted a thorough search, being careful not to betray their presence by moving objects. No electronic encoding device was found.

After pocketing numerous documents from Yamaguchi's desk (hopefully he would believe he had only misplaced them), the "electricians" took the elevator to the lobby, walked past the bored doorman, and drove off in their van.

The source of the ominous clicking noises in the building continued to mystify Zacharias. He thought it was possible that some unidentified American had leased another suite in the building for Yamaguchi to use as his communications center to keep in clandestine contact with intelligence sources in Tokyo.

ONI continued its surveillance of the Alban Towers, and it became clear that Yamaguchi's suite was now the command post for the combined Japanese-German espionage alliance in the United States. Several months later, on November 25, 1936, the cozy relationship between Adolf Hitler's Nazi Germany and Emperor Hirohito's Japanese Empire became publicly known. In an elaborate ceremony in Berlin, Japanese and German diplomats signed what was called the Anti-Comintern Pact, binding both nations to counter what was described as subversive activity all over the world.

Two years later, Tamon Yamaguchi was called back to Tokyo, promoted to rear admiral, and assigned to the Navy Ministry as a principal aide to Admiral Isoroku Yamamoto, chief of the combined Imperial Fleet. In that capacity Yamaguchi played a key role in developing a top-secret project: a sneak attack on the U.S. Pacific Fleet at Pearl Harbor, Hawaii.[2]

Ten Moles in Hitler's High Command

SWITZERLAND, a small country high in the snowcapped Alps and with a population of some five million, is a land of beautiful scenery. The calm, hardworking people produce the world's finest watches and raise the choicest cows. But their most precious asset is their neutrality: the constitution of the Swiss Federation dictates absolute impartiality in case of any war in which their own country is not invaded.

Because Switzerland had for decades been an island of peace and is located in the cockpit of continental Europe adjoining the Great Powers—Germany, France, and Italy—it became a mecca for spies for many nations beginning in the late 1930s. Two German espionage services, the Abwehr and the Sicherheitsdienst (SD), had a higher concentration of secret agents in the tiny country than in any other nation.

Leaders of these two competing German spy agencies had, quite correctly, presumed in advance that any internal opposition to Adolf Hitler and his regime would center in Switzerland. Therefore, these organizations established branches in Stuttgart, eighty miles north of the Swiss border, to deal specifically with matters in Switzerland.

The secret offices in Stuttgart had twenty thousand files on Swiss citizens who might be "of use" to the Third Reich. Each year emissaries from Stuttgart slipped into Switzerland and recruited agents, who were trained in the Reich and then sent back to their own country to enlist accomplices.

At the same time that the Nazi espionage agencies were beefing up their operations in Switzerland, Alexander Radolfi, a respected Hungarian geographer, arrived in Geneva with his wife, Helene. He told neighbors that he was seeking a new challenge, and the couple opened a map publishing business, GeoPress. Actually, the company was a cover. Radolfi was a colonel in the Soviet Army, and he had been sent to Geneva with instructions to build a large espionage network in Switzerland to report on rapidly rearming Germany.

Born in Hungary but trained at Sekhjodnya, a school operated by the Soviet intelligence service just outside Moscow, Rado (as he was known to friends) had spent the past few years working for the Comintern (the Soviet Communist Party leadership), fomenting revolutions in Hungary, Poland, Czechoslovakia, and Germany.

Rado's primary source of intelligence during his early months in Switzerland in 1937 was a keen-witted spy, Otto Pünter (code-named Pakbo), who had set up his own small espionage net, *Rot*, in southern Germany with natives hostile to the Nazi regime.

A former Swiss journalist, Pünter had been a staunch Communist secret agent since July 10, 1930, when he had taken part in an airplane flight over Milan, Italy. Thousands of printed pieces denouncing the new dictator there, Benito Mussolini, had been scattered over the city.

A couple of years after Rado settled in Geneva, another Soviet agent, Alexander A. "Jim" Foote, came to the city. Thirty-three years of age, he was a big man, six feet three, handsome, and charming. An offspring of a comfortable British middle-class family, he had been a failure in several business enterprises and blamed everyone but himself.

In 1936, when the Spanish Civil War had erupted, pitting the Loyalist army of the existing regime against the rebel, Nationalist forces of Generalissimo Francisco Franco, who was provided arms, funds, intelligence, and "volunteer" German combat units by Adolf Hitler, Foote had finally found a cause worth fighting for. Within weeks he was near Madrid as a member of the British battalion of the Communist International Brigade on the side of the current government.

With the Spanish regime collapsing in September 1938, Foote returned to London and was invited to the Communist Party headquarters on King Street. There he received a surprise. Douglas Springhall, who had been the political commissar of the International Brigade in Spain, had strongly recommended him for a special post: working as a spy for the Soviet Union in Switzerland, with Germany as his main target.

Foote had wanted to be a secret agent since boyhood, so he eagerly accepted the offer and was given instructions.

He was to be outside the general post office in the Rue du Mont-Blanc in Geneva on October 10, 1938. He was to wear a white scarf around his neck and hold a leather belt in his right hand. At noon a woman would approach and ask him the time of day. In one hand would be an orange, and in her other, a green parcel.

Foote's contact turned out to be the alluring Ursula Schultz (code-named Sonia), a German-born Jewish woman who had been directing her own small Soviet cell operating from Switzerland against Germany since 1936. A tall, shapely, attractive woman of thirty-five, she resided with her two children and a housekeeper in a large villa at Caux, an upscale resort overlooking Lake Geneva, in the western tip of Switzerland.

Sonia lived in comfort on her monthly salary of a thousand Swiss francs (the equivalent to about thirty-five hundred dollars in 1999), paid by Soviet intelligence. Concealed from random eyes, a long aerial of her transmitter-receiver was set up in the garden, and the set was concealed in a bread box in her dining room. She broadcast to Moscow at regular intervals every two weeks, and received information from a handful of her agents in Germany.

Sonia gave Foote the hefty sum of two thousand Swiss francs, then ordered him to travel to Munich, in southern Germany, search out useful military information, and return to Geneva in three months. On January 10, 1939, they rendezvoused, this time in front of the post office in Lausanne. The Englishman was bursting with excitement. He had discovered that when Adolf Hitler was in Munich, the birthplace of the Nazi Party, he often dined at Osteria Bavaria, a chic restaurant near Karlsplatz. Why not have someone set a time bomb and blow up the führer?

Sonia was shocked. Hitler was always so closely guarded that the perpetrators most certainly would be detected, probably resulting in the Soviet spy network in Switzerland being unmasked and its agents in Germany caught and shot.

After cooling his assassination scheme, Sonia told Foote to go back to Munich. She said that one of her agents would contact him in April and give him more funds.

At the designated place, Foote was surprised to see that his contact was an old friend, William Philips, also an Englishman. The two had served together during the Spanish Civil War in the International Brigade. Three months later, in August 1939, Sonia ordered her two British spies to return to Switzerland. Rumors were rampant that Germany was preparing to go to war soon.

Meanwhile, two middle-aged men in civilian clothes got off a train in Lucerne, Switzerland, and went to the home of an old friend, Rudolf Roessler.

The visitors were German generals who, along with eight other high-ranking officers in the Oberkommando der Wehrmacht (High Command) in Berlin, were engaged in a conspiracy to prevent Adolf Hitler from carrying out his plans for widespread conquest in Europe.

Roessler, a soft-spoken, slightly built man whose horn-rimmed glasses gave him an owlish facial appearance, had fought as a teenager in the German Army in the Great War and been honorably discharged as a corporal. During his military service, he had made friends with ten young men who later were accepted into the peacetime Reichswehr (army). Five of them, including the two who were now visiting Roessler in Lucerne, had risen to the rank of general in the German Army, while the others had become colonels and majors.

Unlike his friends, Roessler had chosen not to be a career officer because he abhorred violence. Instead, he became a pacifist, and viewed with deep concern the rise of the Brown Shirts, as the early Nazis were called, under the firebrand former army corporal Adolf Hitler.

Roessler decided he would do all he could to awaken the *Herrenvolk* (German people) about the danger of Nazism, so he took a job as a reporter with the *Augsburg Post Zeitung* and wrote scathing articles about the Brown Shirts. Soon he became a marked man. All the while, he was meeting with his ten old army friends and discovered that they, too, were deeply alarmed about the rise of Nazism.

In the summer of 1934, eighteen months after Hitler became chancellor of Germany and began cracking down on his enemies, thirty-six-year-old Rudolf Roessler and his wife, Olga, a pretty woman much younger, had fled to Switzerland. In Lucerne he established a book publishing firm, Vita Nova (New Life).

Now the two German generals in disguise got right to the point. One of them told Rudolph Roessler, "War will break out in a matter of weeks."

They urged their old friend to play a key role in the conspiracy to keep Nazism from spreading throughout Europe by force of arms.

The generals explained that the ten conspirators could readily obtain in advance the führer's strategies because they were among the officers whose job it was to draw up his plans. One of the men in Roessler's home was the top aide of General Erich F. Fellgiebel, who was the Wehrmacht's chief of communications, so the aide had ongoing access to the huge broadcast center of the Oberkommando der Wehrmacht in Berlin, where there was almost incessant noise from the nearly one hundred transmitter-receivers. The wireless operators simply sent thousands of coded messages and likewise jotted down, with no knowledge of their meaning, the deluge of dots and dashes they received.

One general explained to Roessler that the Berlin moles wanted to radio him top-secret information. The conspirators would always do the encoding, so the wireless operators would never suspect anything. "Give the information away or sell it, as you see fit," one visitor said. "But preferably to the staunchest enemies of Hitler and Nazism."

Roessler pondered the proposal for several moments, then solemnly agreed to it.

At great personal risk, the two generals had brought with them to Lucerne a small trunk containing the newest-design shortwave radio. The transmitter-receiver was in many parts, as each component had been sneaked out of the Wehrmacht communications center in Berlin.

Did Roessler have a friend in Switzerland whom he could trust to assemble the pieces and who knew Morse code well enough to be his operator? Roessler knew just the man: a German national, Christian Schneider, who was passionately anti-Nazi.

"Das ist gut!" one general said. Before leaving, the visitors turned over codes and procedures for regular communications between the ten moles in the German High Command and Roessler in Lucerne.

Now Roessler was confronted by the most momentous decision of his life: To whom should be given the mass of secret intelligence that would soon be pouring over the radio into his home? Should he discreetly make the rounds of Allied embassies, his wares in a briefcase? No diplomat would take him seriously. He finally decided that his priceless intelligence would be offered to his adopted country—Switzerland. If Swiss intelligence so desired, it could distribute the information to other friendly nations.

A few days after the German generals had returned to Berlin, Roessler arranged a meeting with Xavier Schnieper, a young Swiss who had become a close friend. Schnieper, Roessler knew, had been serving part-time as a member of the Swiss secret service, and he had often sneaked across the border into the Third Reich wearing the uniform of a German corporal.

While being scrupulously careful not to disclose the entire truth, Roessler told his friend that he had secret contacts in Berlin who would provide him with accurate and continuing intelligence, which he wanted to communicate to the Swiss. Schnieper agreed to speak about the proposal to higher-ups.

Soon word reached Roessler that Brigadier Colonel Roger Masson, the keen-witted, seventy-year-old chief of Swiss intelligence, had agreed to allow Roessler's espionage activities on the condition that all information radioed from Berlin would also be passed along to him.

Masson had been confronted with a serious bout with his conscience for accepting intelligence from a secret agent operating on Swiss soil. Yet he knew that Adolf Hitler was on the brink of launching a widespread war of conquest in Europe, and his sympathy for the Allies caused him to search for a way to warn them of German military plans without directly involving Switzerland.

Masson's top aide, Major Hans Hausamann, a bitter foe of Nazi Germany, came up with a solution. An acquaintance known as "Uncle Tom," a Czech national, agreed to act as a go-between with the British secret service. Actually, he was Colonel Thomas Sedlacek, who would continue in that undercover role for more than five years.

Meanwhile, Rudolf Roessler had second thoughts about the trustworthiness of Christian Schneider, so he had Schneider assemble the radio left by the two German generals in Roessler's home, and teach him how to operate it. He himself would send messages to and receive them from the coconspirators in Berlin.

Unbeknownst to Roessler, Schneider (code-named Taylor) was a key agent in a Soviet spy ring headed by Rachel Duebendorfer (code-named Sissi), which operated in Geneva from the International Labor office where she worked. She lived with her young daughter Tamara and her boyfriend, Paul Boetcher, a former clergyman in his native Germany.

Early in May 1940, the conspirators in Berlin radioed Roessler that Hitler was about ready to launch Case Yellow, a massive invasion of France, Belgium, and the Netherlands. "Uncle Tom" rushed to inform the British, Dutch, and Belgian embassies, but when the Wehrmacht struck at dawn on May 10, the defenders were taken by total surprise. Roessler's warning had been ignored.

In only six weeks the powerful German juggernaut conquered much of western Europe and was poised to leap the British Channel and invade nearly defenseless Great Britain. At this point Moscow ordered Jim Foote to become the radio operator for Rado, the chief Soviet spymaster, who lived in Geneva. For security reasons Foote would operate in Lausanne, some forty miles northeast of Geneva.

Renting an apartment on the top floor of a large building, he reflected that this was an ideal location for his clandestine broadcasting. Any intruders would have to pass through two heavy, tightly locked doors, so he would have ample time while the second door was being forced to sabotage his radio and destroy his message files and secret codes.

Foote located a technician who would install an extra-large antenna on the roof without informing the police of this unusual activity by a foreigner. The oversized aerial was crucial for him to contact Moscow. Foote achieved his goal by convincing the installer that he was an eccentric British millionaire trapped in Switzerland by the outbreak of war who wanted to pick up the news broadcasts on BBC radio from London.

There was another reason why Foote needed the large aerial: to ensure that his messages could reach London. While masquerading as a staunch Communist, he actually was a double agent employed by the British secret service to penetrate the Soviet espionage networks in Switzerland and to radio London with information about Nazi Germany.

Back in 1938, after returning to London from fighting in the Spanish Civil War, Foote had soured on communism, so he had contacted Claude Dansey, deputy chief of MI-6 (the British secret service responsible for overseas operations), who recruited him as a spy. When Dansey instructed him to accept the offer made by the Communist Party headquarters on King Street to ostensibly work for the Soviet Union in Switzerland, Foote had become a double agent.

In November 1940 Foote's boss in the Soviet spy ring, Sonia, told him that she had fallen in love with her other British agent, William Philips, and the two were going to London to live. Foote was stunned. He knew that the highly efficient British counterintelligence service painstakingly screened anyone entering the country. So he drew a startling conclusion: Sonia and Philips had also been working for the British as double agents. Three days before Christmas, the couple left for England by way of Lisbon.

In the meantime, at Lucerne, Rudolf Roessler had been getting a steady flow of high-grade intelligence from his Berlin friends. A few days after Christmas 1940, he received a blockbuster message spread out over a period of forty-eight hours. It took him twelve hours more to decipher it. When his work was done, he had a complete copy of Operation Barbarossa, Hitler's planned invasion of the Soviet Union. The attack was to kick off in the spring of 1941.

Roessler was thunderstruck. He tried desperately to find a third party to warn the Soviets. Finally he contacted Christian Schneider, the man who had assembled his radio and who was thought to have Communist leanings.

Roessler minced no words. "The Germans intend to invade Russia in the spring," he told Schneider. "Do you know how I can talk to Soviet agents?" Roessler reminded Schneider of the radio and assured him that he had high-placed contacts in Berlin.

A month later, Schneider informed Roessler that "my people" have been in touch with the Ministry of State Security—known as "the Center" to Soviet spies—in Moscow and that they had agreed to put the German émigré on the payroll. Thus Roessler, a Protestant from a respectable, conservative, upper-middle-class background, became, out of hatred for Nazism, a Soviet spy.

Brigadier Colonel Masson had given his blessing to the arrangement on the condition that Roessler (whom the Center had code-named Lucy) continue to furnish the Swiss with intelligence from Berlin that would be useful to the British.

A system was worked out whereby Rachel Duebendorfer (Sissi) and Christian Schneider (Taylor) passed the information from Berlin each day from Rudolf Roessler to Jim Foote, who had recently replaced Rado as head of the Soviet spy apparatus in Switzerland.

Rado had learned that BUPO—the Swiss intelligence—was about to arrest him, so he had rapidly given Foote's address and telephone number to members of the network. Then Rado; his wife, Helene; and their two sons fled the country.

Now Jim Foote, the double agent, found himself in an incredible position. He was being inundated by intelligence from both Berlin and the entire Soviet espionage network in Switzerland. Most of his days and many nights were consumed in radioing this voluminous amount of information to Moscow and to London.

All the while, Moscow Center repeatedly demanded to know the source of Roessler's intelligence. Just as steadfastly, he refused to unmask his Berlin coconspirators. So when the German émigré warned the Soviets that Adolf Hitler was going to invade Russia along a thousand-mile front at dawn on June 22, 1941, this intelligence was ignored. Adolf Hitler's war machine gained total surprise and plunged deep into the Soviet Union.

For more than two months, Moscow Center had stubbornly refused to listen to Roessler's shouts of alarm. Now, twenty-four hours after the Wehrmacht struck, he had gained instant credibility, and the Center offered him more money than it had ever paid a secret agent—a monthly salary of seven thousand Swiss francs (about sixteen thousand U.S. dollars in 1999).

During most of the remainder of the war, Roessler, through his superbly placed contacts, supplied the intelligence that permitted Josef Stalin's army to stay one crucial jump ahead of the Wehrmacht.

Jim Foote, the double agent who had radioed Moscow Center thousands of pages of high-grade information, was notified early in 1943 that a grateful Soviet Union had made him a major in the Red Army.[3]

A Scheme to Declare Hitler Insane

SHADOWS WERE LENGTHENING over Berlin late on the afternoon of November 5, 1937, when an elite gathering of top generals and admirals in the Wehrmacht settled into plush chairs in the Little Cabinet Room at the Reichskanzelei on the Wilhelmstrasse. These leaders had been summoned by Adolf Hitler, dictator of the Third Reich, as he now called Germany.

Then forty-eight years old and slightly stooped with the beginning of kyphosis of the spine, the führer was of medium height and build, and his straight, jet-black hair draped over his forehead. His most dominating facial feature was a brush mustache, which he had worn during his entire manhood.

During the Great War, Hitler had served as an infantry corporal in the muddy front-line trenches of France for nearly four years, and he had been gassed and decorated with the Iron Cross, First Class, for valor, the latter event a unique distinction for an enlisted man.

Now as the führer strode into the Little Cabinet Room, his generals and admirals leaped to their feet and stood at attention. After he had motioned for them to be seated, Hitler swore his military leaders to secrecy. Then he shocked them with a startling announcement: he was going to immediately launch a policy of acquiring *Lebensraum* (living space) for the German people.

As the high brass listened silently in amazement, the führer, a spellbinding orator, spoke for four hours on the reason for his decision and his plans for implementing it. Even if general war were to erupt, he was determined to annex, either by diplomacy, subterfuge, or a combination of these categories, Austria, Czechoslovakia, and Poland. Then, when the Wehrmacht had become sufficiently powerful, he planned to invade the Soviet Union.

No doubt anticipating the commanders' qualms, Hitler asserted that France, which was thought to have the world's best and strongest army, and Great Britain would only launch a war of words and not interfere as the Lebensraum campaign unfolded.

In closing his marathon dissertation, the führer declared that he would accept only total obedience from his generals and admirals, and he gave them a timetable for conquest: operations were to be launched in 1938 and completed by 1943.

A hush fell over the room, as Hitler's plans had an enormous impact on the audience. However, he brushed off ensuing arguments, claiming that Great Britain and France were too timid to oppose him.

Now it was clear: Hitler was getting ready for a widespread war of conquest. There also remained no doubt about his utter contempt for his General Staff. Later he told one of his few confidants: "This presumptuous *Junker* caste is in reality nothing more than a collection of muddleheads, vacillators, and stuffed shirts."

Convinced that Hitler was going to take Germany hell-bent down the road to eventual destruction, a group of high-ranking officers, civilian leaders, and government officials created a conspiratorial group the Gestapo would later brand the Schwarze Kapelle (Black Orchestra).

Heading the covert clan was General Ludwig Beck, a curious mixture of intellectualism and military genius, who, as chief of the German General Staff, had directed the army's enormous expansion during the previous three years. He was regarded by other German generals and by foreign leaders as a man of high honor and integrity.

A positive plan to get rid of Hitler by a *coup d'état* was drawn up by the conspirators. The führer was to be arrested in Berlin, but not killed. Rather, he would be put on trial before the German people, with procedures worked out by legal experts involved with the Schwarze Kapelle.

The conspirators had managed to obtain Corporal Adolf Hitler's medical history for his service in the Great War. It seemed to indicate that Hitler had "gone mad" from being gassed. Consequently, the Schwarze Kapelle set up a secret panel of psychiatrists to issue a report on his mental fitness.

The keen military minds of the conspirators had created a plan in minute detail. At the proper time, General Erich Fellgiebel, chief Wehrmacht signals officer, would cut all communications throughout Germany, thereby isolating Hitler in Berlin. At the same time, General Erwin von Witzleben, the commander of the Berlin military district, would rush reinforcements into the capital and issue orders for them to arrest Hitler and two top aides, General Hermann Goering and Heinrich Himmler, chief of the Gestapo and the Schutzstaffel (SS), the führer's elite bodyguard.

Himmler, a lapsed Catholic and former chicken farmer, was a rare mixture of crackpot and organizational genius. As commander of Hitler's SS bodyguard and the Gestapo, he would have to be "neutralized" if the conspirators' plot were to succeed.

Hitler, Himmler, Goering, and other Nazi leaders were to be rushed southward to Bavaria by a heavily armed contingent of General Witzleben's soldiers and locked up securely in the dungeon of an ancient castle near Munich.

At his trial, according to the established scenario, Hitler was to be exposed as criminally insane and unfit to hold the office of führer. His madness had prompted him to create grandiose plans for world conquest that would destroy Germany forever as a nation. Once the trial judges ruled that Hitler was insane, he would be safely ensconced, with heavily armed guards around the clock, in a mental institution. Then a civilian of prominence and respectability not yet selected was to form a new German government along democratic lines.

Now the leaders of the Schwarze Kapelle were confronted by a knotty problem: when to strike. Although German generals and admirals were almost unanimous in their contempt for the one-time army corporal, they were confronted by the fact that Hitler had the undeniable love and trust of most of the *Herrenvolk* and the support of the rank and file of the *Heer* (army) and *Kriegsmarine* (navy). Titans of industry also were firmly in the führer's corner: his huge military buildup was making arms manufacturers extremely wealthy men of enormous influence.

Reluctantly, the Schwarze Kapelle decided to bide its time, waiting for Hitler to perpetrate some sort of disaster that would turn many of the German people against him.[4]

The Blond Beast's Ruse Backfires

SEATED AT HIS DESK in Berlin in March 1937, Reinhard Heydrich, at age thirty-three a general in the elite Schutzstaffel (SS) and one of the Third Reich's most powerful figures, was poring over a report he had just received from Nikolai Skoblin, a former general in the Russian White Army who was now an agent in Paris for the Sicherheitsdienst (SD). Brilliant and ruthless, Heydrich was chief of the SD, the intelligence branch of the black-uniformed SS, Adolf Hitler's private army.

Skoblin said in his report that a Soviet group, led by Mikhail Tukhachevsky, the Red Army's youngest marshal, was conspiring to assassinate dictator Josef Stalin. Heydrich mulled over the startling disclosure, then hatched a plot to convert the scheme into a highly favorable scenario for the führer, Adolf Hitler.

Documents would be skillfully concocted to make it appear that the Soviet generals were conniving with German generals to murder Stalin. The "evidence" would then be planted in the Kremlin. Then the führer and the other top Nazi officials could watch gleefully from afar as Stalin wreaked bloody revenge on the "conspirators."

Moving with typical alacrity, General Heydrich gave the task to a trusted aide, Alfred Naujocks, who had been assigned to many of Heydrich's most brutal missions, including kidnapping and murder.

Naujocks rapidly collected a group of skilled forgers, several of whom had served prison terms for practicing their trade. Near Berlin, Naujocks located an engraver who could precisely reproduce signatures—in this case, those of Soviet officials. From musty archives, team members obtained copies of correspondence from the past fifteen years when the Soviet and German armies had secretly collaborated to reach rearmament goals.

Within a few weeks, Naujocks and his task force had produced a thick file of damning "evidence"—all fraudulent. There were typed documents containing signatures of top Soviet military leaders and government officials; notes scribbled in longhand in the margins of the reports; and secret stamps and seals to inject bureaucratic authenticity.

Meanwhile, SD agents planted hints about the plot to murder Stalin with sources that would assure that the information reached the ears of the leaders of the NKVD, the Soviet intelligence agency.

Reinhard Heydrich's devious scheme worked to perfection. When sources friendly to Moscow disclosed that the dossier could be had by the NKVD—for a heavy price—Stalin's secret service operatives sneaked into Berlin and paid for the phony dossier.

Heydrich, whose ruthlessness had earned him the nickname of the Blond Beast among German officers, soon learned that his endeavor had achieved its purpose far beyond his wildest expectations. Stalin ordered the execution of not only young Marshal Mikhail Tukhachevsky but also of seven other generals. Later, seven of the nine judges who had presided at the "trial" of the doomed officers were also murdered. But these actions were only the beginning. Before the wave of executions of Red Army military men had concluded, the death toll reached thirty thousand—including three of every five marshals.

The highly ambitious Reinhard Heydrich regularly kept Adolf Hitler informed about the ongoing bloodbath that Stalin was inflicting. Because the führer's plans called for the eventual invasion and conquest of the Soviet Union to "wipe out the menace of communism," the leader of ninety million Germans showered his disciple with praise for the clever machination that greatly weakened the Red Army.

Neither Hitler nor Heydrich would live to learn that it had not been Stalin, but the Blond Beast who had been victimized by the Soviets' own crafty ruse. After the war, evidence would be uncovered disclosing that Stalin had been planning to launch the bloodbath against the Red Army leaders many weeks before Naujocks' forged dossier reached the Kremlin. Moreover, Nikolai Skoblin, the former White Russian Army general who had triggered Heydrich's scheme, was actually a double agent for the NKVD.[5]

Did His Generals Sabotage the Führer?

ON MARCH 11, 1938, Hitler announced the *Anschluss*, the union of the Third Reich and Austria, whose eight million people were largely ethnic Germans. General Ludwig Beck, the Schwarze Kapelle leader, issued orders for the invasion of Austria to army and SS troops assembled at the locale where the Danube and Inn Rivers join. Hitler's plan was for the invading force to fan out over Austria to "establish constitutional conditions." At 9:00 A.M. on March 12, armored spearheads began flowing across the frontier.

A day later, with a lieutenant colonel named Erwin Rommel in command of his army escort, the führer made a triumphant entry into Vienna and received a tumultuous welcome from Austrian citizens. They peppered him and his troops with a cascade of floral tributes in what came to be known as the Battle of the Flowers.

His return as a conquering hero was an emotionally supercharged event for Hitler, who had been born in Austria and had begun his political life in Vienna, where he stayed from 1909 until 1913. There he had been an impoverished vagrant, sleeping in flophouses, doing odd jobs, and often eating at charity soup kitchens. Now he was the absolute master of the city that, he felt, had once consigned him to the gutter.

When the hoopla and pomp and circumstance died and Hitler returned to the Reichskanzelei in Berlin, he began to analyze the efficiency with which his peaceful occupation of Vienna had been carried out. He was flabbergasted— and furious.

Although the German officers who had drawn up the tactical plan were highly skilled in their profession, the operation had, in fact, been botched. The main road leading from Salzburg to Vienna had been littered with tanks and trucks that had broken down en route, and there had been confusion at times in the armored spearheads.

Had the weak and outgunned Austrian Army resisted, the führer might well have suffered an embarrassing setback that would have opened the door for the Schwarze Kapelle to launch its scheme to get rid of him. The entire invasion indicated sabotage. Only the barrage of flowers from wildly enthusiastic Austrians instead of shells and bullets may have saved the day for the führer, who now was a greater idol than ever in Germany.[6]

Adolf Hitler's triumphant entry into Vienna. Did his generals try to sabotage the operation? (National Archives)

Her Serene Highness Plots
with Goering

A TEUTONIC FALSTAFF tipping the scales at 290 pounds, General Hermann Goering was known behind his back as *Der Dicke* (Fatty). He had been führertreu (extremely loyal to Hitler) since hearing the future leader of Germany speak in 1922 in a Munich beer hall. However, he was secretly aghast over his leader's plans for conquest.

On February 4, 1938, Adolf Hitler announced that he was taking over as commander of Germany's armed forces. His jawbreaker title would be: der Führer und Oberste Befehlshaber der Wehrmacht des Grossdeutschen Reichs. At the same time, he rewarded his faithful right-hand man Goering with the rank of field marshal.

Through ruthless manipulations, Der Dicke had become one of the Third Reich's wealthiest men. No one, of course, dared complain about his sharp financial practices—and Hitler was too busy to notice. With the shameless use of government funds, Goering converted a former imperial hunting lodge on one hundred thousand acres, twenty-five miles north of Berlin, as his personal residence and playground. He called his estate Karinhall.

In June 1938 Goering invited to Karinhall a clever, scheming social climber whose original name had been Stefanie Richter—Steffi to her friends. Daughter of a Viennese lawyer, red-haired, statuesque Steffi had married Prince Friedrich François Augustin Marie Hohenlohe-Waldenburg. The couple was divorced in 1920 (she charged adultery). Steffi retained her royal title and encouraged everyone to continue to address her as Your Serene Highness.

Over the years, Steffi had been a familiar figure flitting about the capitals of Europe, entertaining lavishly with funds provided by an elderly British admirer, and living the high life. Her Nazi sympathies had become well known, and she had been enthralled on being introduced to Adolf Hitler, a bachelor with a gift for mesmerizing many women with his charm.

During a lengthy conversation at Karinhall, Goering told Princess Stefanie of his pet scheme for easing mounting tensions in Europe: he personally would work secretly to gain British concessions advantageous to the Third Reich and thereby avoid a bloody war.

As Her Serene Highness listened avidly and in awe, Goering outlined his plot. He would sneak covertly into London and confer with Edward F. L. W. Halifax, the British foreign secretary. Goering had known Lord Halifax personally since the twilight of 1937, when the Briton had been invited to visit Berlin and spend a few days shooting foxes in Saxony. Halifax, the Germans knew, had been an avid huntsman since boyhood.

Despite his misgivings, the tall, reedy Halifax had accepted the invitation because his superior had thought some undefined good toward maintaining peace in Europe might accrue. Actually, the invitation apparently had been offered to give German leaders an insight into current thinking of the British government, especially toward rearming England.

While in Berlin, Halifax had been given the red-carpet treatment. He was wined, dined, and feted. Meetings were held with Adolf Hitler; Propaganda Minister Josef Goebbels; and Goering, who threw a lavish party for his British guest at Karinhall.

Goering's proposed incognito trek to London would have to be arranged with a great deal of finesse so as not to step on the toes of Foreign Minister Ulrich Friedrich Willy Joachim von Ribbentrop, who was an enemy of Der Dicke but highly regarded by Adolf Hitler. Ribbentrop must not learn that Goering was going to inject himself into the realm of foreign policy.

What was vitally needed, Goering explained to Princess Stefanie, was someone to make discreet contact with Lord Halifax and arrange for the field marshal's visit. Numerous names were discussed before the two schemers hit upon the ideal candidate—forty-five-year-old Fritz Wiedemann. Debonair and articulate, Wiedemann was widely known and respected in the Third Reich and in embassies of the world. He had been commander of an infantry com-

General Hermann Goering (left) plotted behind the back of Adolf Hitler (right) to gain concessions from the British without going to war. (National Archives)

pany with which Corporal Adolf Hitler had been awarded the Iron Cross for valor in the muddy trenches of France in the Great War.

When approached by Her Serene Highness, the tall, handsome Wiedemann was horrified. Go to London behind Ribbentrop's back—behind the führer's back? Steffi was persistent. Finally, Wiedemann agreed to take on the task, but only after obtaining Hitler's approval. Surprisingly—to Wiedemann, at least—Hitler gave him the green light.

Princess Stefanie was delighted to learn of the führer's approval. Now she was in the thick of things at the highest levels. She promptly hopped the English Channel and, through her elite social connections, rapidly arranged to meet with Lord Halifax, who agreed to confer secretly with Goering's emissary, Fritz Wiedemann.

A few days later, Halifax and Wiedemann held a long discussion. Princess Stefanie was not present, but Hitler's onetime infantry commander told her later that the conference was "quite successful." Then the scheme began to fall apart. Before Hermann Goering could sneak into England to see Halifax and wring concessions from him to avoid war in Europe, all hell broke loose in Berlin.

A furious Joachim von Ribbentrop had gotten wind of Goering's plot behind his back, and he rushed to the Reichskanzlei and talked the führer into squashing any future negotiations with Lord Halifax by Wiedemann.[7]

A Bizarre Kidnapping Scheme

KAPITAEN-LEUTNANT ERICH PFEIFFER, chief of the Abwehr *Nebenstellen* (nest) in Wilhelmshaven, Germany, and directly responsible for espionage in North America, began putting the heat on his spies abroad to obtain more military secrets. Adolf Hitler had repudiated the restrictions imposed by the Versailles Treaty, the symbol of Germany's crushing defeat in the Great War, and was rapidly building up the Wehrmacht armed forces and preparing for war. It was December 1937.

One of Pfeiffer's slickest and most productive spies in the United States was slightly built, mild-mannered Günther Gustav Rumrich, who had been born twenty-six years earlier in Chicago, where his father, Alphonse, was secretary of the Austro-Hungarian consulate. When Günther was two years old, his father was transferred to Bremen, Germany. Learning that he was a U.S. citizen because of his birth there, he returned alone to Chicago at age eighteen to seek his fortune.

Rumrich was a curious mixture of shiftlessness, arrogance, and cunning. He joined the U.S. Army in 1930, and later was booted out of the service when caught stealing money from the Fort Missoula, Montana, hospital fund. Broke and jobless, Rumrich managed to make contact with the Abwehr in Wilhelmshaven, volunteered his services as an undercover agent, and after his background was carefully scrutinized by two Gestapo men in the United States, was accepted and given the code name Crown.

Six months after he had first made contact with the Abwehr, Rumrich was handed his first "job"—to identify the units (and their strengths) guarding the Panama Canal, together with the names of the commanding officers. Within two weeks this "secret" information was on Pfeiffer's desk in Wilhelmshaven. Pfeiffer was astonished and amazed at the speed. Rumrich had not told him that he had known most of the data through memory—he had served in the Panama Canal Zone on army duty.

In the months ahead, Crown shuttled a bonanza of military intelligence to Wilhelmshaven. Then, in January 1938, Pfeiffer handed Crown an incredible mission—to steal secret plans for the defense of the Eastern Seaboard of the United States.

Undaunted by the seemingly impossible assignment, Rumrich set about devising a bizarre scheme. His target was Colonel Henry W. T. Eglin, commander of the 62nd Coast Artillery, an antiaircraft outfit, at Fort Totten in New York City. A former corporal in the U.S. Army who was familiar with military terminology agreed—for a hefty fee—to write bogus orders over the signature of Major General Malin Craig, the army's chief of staff in Washington. The phony orders would direct Colonel Eglin to gather all the Eastern Seaboard defense information and bring it to a secret meeting at the McAlpin Hotel at Broadway and Thirty-fourth Street in midtown Manhattan. Another Crown contact with a military background would then telephone Craig's "orders" directly to Eglin at Fort Totten.

*Ace Nazi spy Günther Rumrich
concocted a scheme to obtain secret
U.S. plans for East Coast defenses.
(FBI)*

Eglin would be instructed not to divulge the nature of the secret conference to anyone, to arrive alone at 12:20 P.M. on a specified day, and to wear
civilian clothes. On arrival at the McAlpin, the colonel was to take a seat in the
main lobby and await being paged by Thomas W. Conway, after which he
would identify himself by that name to a bogus army officer (a Crown associ-
ate) in civilian clothes. This "officer" would lead Eglin into a trap, a guest room
where two of Crown's men posing as window washers would overpower the
colonel and flee with his secret papers.

As an added touch to convince New York City police that the mugging—
or murder—had been pulled off by Communist agents, the strong-arm men
would leave the window washers' garb behind together with a copy of the *Daily
Worker*, the Communist newspaper published in New York.

Meanwhile, across the Atlantic, MI-5, Great Britain's highly efficient
counterintelligence service, acted on a tip from a suspicious postal carrier and
began intercepting mail sent to Mrs. Jennie Jordan, a fifty-one-year-old hair-
dresser at No. 1 Kinloch, Dundee, Scotland. Surveillance disclosed that the correspondence bore the signature Crown and was postmarked in New York City.

Mrs. Jordan removed sealed envelopes inside Crown's letters, which were
written to an N. Spielman, and, using her own return address, mailed them to a
post-office box in Germany, from where the letters were shuttled to N. Spielman.
At the time MI-5 knew that N. Spielman was obviously a Nazi master spy but was
unaware that N. Spielman was one of the numerous aliases used by Dr. Erich
Pfeiffer, the chief at the Wilhelmshaven Abwehr nest.

After intercepting Mrs. Jordan's mail, the British sleuths steamed open the
N. Spielman envelopes, made copies of Crown's letters, then carefully resealed

the covering and allowed the mail to continue to Germany routinely through the mail system.

Captain Guy Liddell of MI-5 flew copies of the incriminating series of letters to Washington and turned them over to the Federal Bureau of Investigation. Deciphering experts concluded that Crown, whoever he was, planned to kidnap Colonel Eglin, the antiaircraft commander at Fort Totten.

When informed of the Nazi plot by the FBI, Eglin laughed it off, insisting that he would never have been taken in by the phony orders from General Craig in Washington. But he agreed to play the key role of "pigeon" in a countertrap that the FBI, working with army intelligence, planned to spring to capture Crown and his unidentified cohorts.

Eglin was to follow the bogus orders from Craig, go to the McAlpin in civilian clothes, carry a bulging briefcase stuffed with newspapers, and identify himself as Thomas W. Conway to Crown's confederate in the lobby. At that point FBI agents, disguised as hotel employees and as guests idling in the lobby, would pounce on and apprehend the Nazi agents.

All was in readiness for the FBI counterplot, which would be triggered when Colonel Eglin received the telephone call from "General Craig." But the bogus call never came. Rumrich's comrades in the kidnapping had gotten nervous over the brazen plot, to be perpetrated in broad daylight in the center of bustling Manhattan.

Rumrich was depressed by the cancellation of the scheme. The badly needed thousand-dollar bonus he was to have received from Adolf Hitler's cash register for delivering plans for the defense of the Eastern Seaboard had slipped through his fingers.

About six weeks later, on February 17, 1938, the *New York Times* carried a brief story stating that Günther Gustav Rumrich, aged twenty-seven, of the Bronx, had been arrested by two New York Alien Squad detectives. He was charged with trying to fraudulently obtain fifty passport blanks at the U.S. State Department's Passport Division at Wall and Pine Streets.

Driving downtown with their prisoners, the detectives thought they had nabbed a low-level con artist. Only after Rumrich had been interrogated by FBI agents did he confess that he was indeed the mysterious Crown. N. Spielman had promised to pay five hundred dollars for the genuine passports, to be used for slipping more Nazi spies into the United States.[8]

The French Consul's Janitor

FRENCH AMBASSADOR ANDRÉ FRANÇOIS-PONCET, who was regarded in global diplomatic circles as being highly knowledgeable about the Third Reich, arrived at his country's consulate in Hamburg, Germany's second-largest city. A port inland from the North Sea, Hamburg in certain years handled a volume of shipping that was exceeded only by that of London and New York City. It was late summer of 1938, and war clouds were starting to gather over Europe.

As François-Poncet strolled through the consulate, he passed and spoke to a wiry blond man in his early thirties who had been a janitor there for the past two years. Mild-mannered and well liked, Hans Sorenson was a German, and he had applied for the job at the behest of Navy Captain Joachim Burghardt, who was chief of the Abwehr outpost in Hamburg.

Captain Burghardt had been quite successful in creating a widespread spy ring in the British Isles. But in early 1938 he found himself caught up in an internal Abwehr power struggle, and he was bounced from his post. His replacement was Navy Captain Herbert Wichmann, a clever operative who possessed a key ingredient for success as a spymaster: an intense passion for anonymity.

Now at the French consulate in Hamburg, Ambassador François-Poncet held a long discussion with the consul-general in his private office. Reaching into his briefcase, the ambassador pulled out a thick sheaf of papers and handed them to the consul, who placed them in his safe. Neither Frenchman knew that the soft-spoken Hans Sorenson had been filching secret papers from the safe and having them photocopied for more than a year.

One of the reasons that Captain Burghardt had chosen Sorenson for the French consulate mission was because the new recruit had intricate skills in opening safes that were supposed to be burglarproof. Sorenson had managed to get the job because of collusion between the Abwehr and the German labor exchange in Hamburg.

After only a few weeks, Sorenson discovered that the consul had a strictly regimented lifestyle. Each Sunday morning at precisely the same minute, he left to attend Mass. When he had departed, the janitor stole upstairs to the consul's office and, within minutes, opened the safe. He rapidly sifted through the documents, removing any that seemed to have a high security classification and others that appeared significant. On a pocket-size pad he carefully wrote down the location of each document.

On a few previous Sundays, the spy had cautiously trailed the consul to church, and he noted that Mass always ended at almost the same time. Then the consul habitually drove back to the consulate, coming through the front door at 11:00 A.M.

After removing the documents, Sorenson would climb on his motorcycle, specially provided by the Abwehr for the task, and race through the quiet Hamburg streets to the Abwehr office on Sophien Terrace. There the photography experts were always on duty. They took the documents, disappeared into their darkroom, and photographed all the papers. Then Sorenson sped back to the consulate in plenty of time to return the documents to their proper place in the safe.

For many months Sorenson had been supplying the Abwehr and the Oberkommando der Wehrmacht with a choice selection of French secret documents. Now he sensed, with the arrival of Ambassador François-Poncet, that there would be the most secret papers yet in the "burglarproof" safe.

A new factor entered the equation. With the ambassador in the consulate, the consul's customarily punctual lifestyle was altered. That night, the ambassador and the consul left to attend a social function, and Sorenson hurried to the safe. He extracted what looked like new documents that the ambassador must have brought with him.

Once again the Abwehr spy went through the routine of getting the papers photographed. He was in the process of returning them to the safe when a chill raced through him—there was the unexpected sound of an automobile outside. Moments later, the two French officials, chattering loudly, came inside the building.

Hastily the spy closed the safe door, then stole downstairs to his bedroom. He was deeply worried, convinced that he had not replaced the documents in the same places they had been when he had extracted them. If the consul examined the safe, he most certainly would know that someone had been inside. All that night the Abwehr agent tossed and turned in his bed, expecting French security police to barge in at any moment.

Sorenson convinced himself that the consul had been in the safe. But in the morning, the two French officials said nothing to him. Were they playing some sort of cat-and-mouse game to trick him into confessing that he was a German spy?

Finally, he decided that he would have to create a cover story for having been in the safe. As soon as he had the chance, he slipped into the consul's office, opened the safe, and took from it the ten thousand marks he had noticed the previous night. Clever man that he was, the spy left clues that would point to him as the *money* thief. Stealing funds could result in only a short jail term; being pegged as a German spy could have serious consequences.

Before he closed the safe, Sorenson turned the contents topsy-turvy, so the theft was discovered before nightfall. Curiously, the consul, instead of using his own security force, summoned the German Kriminalpolizei, who quickly tracked down the thief, not knowing that Sorenson was an Abwehr agent. The janitor was hauled off to jail to await trial. Within two weeks, he appeared in court on a charge of theft and was found guilty and sentenced to a year in prison.

Meanwhile, Captain Herbert Wichmann at the Hamburg Abwehr branch had been in contact with German police. When Sorenson was being returned to jail to serve his sentence, he somehow managed to slip away—while the two police escorts happened to be looking in the opposite direction.

Sorenson was told to report immediately to Admiral Wilhelm Canaris at the Abwehr headquarters in Berlin. There the spy received a hero's welcome. One of the French ambassador's documents he had photographed turned out to be an intelligence bonanza—a top-secret list of the names of all the French spies operating in the Third Reich.

Canaris, a cagey operative long schooled in the nuances of intelligence operations, merely filed the list. He gave orders that the telephones of all the French spies were to be bugged and their conversations recorded.

A year later, when Adolf Hitler was ready to begin the war in Europe by invading Poland, Canaris leaped into action. Abwehr agents began fanning out across Germany in a mammoth roundup of French spies. When the highly potent Wehrmacht was preparing to plunge into France in May 1940, French commanders had no "eyes" in Germany and their armies were taken by total surprise.[9]

A German General
Spies on Himself

EARLY IN 1939 it was widely known throughout Europe that Adolf Hitler was preparing for war and that he no doubt would be joined by his crony Benito Mussolini, dictator of Italy. In London, forty-one-year-old Frederick W. Winterbotham, chief of the Air Section of the British Secret Intelligence Service (SIS), was especially concerned because there had been a sharp clampdown on information leaving the Third Reich. The few British agents planted there were terrified of discovery and rapid execution.

Even before the Nazis came to power in 1933, Winterbotham, a clever spymaster, spent much time in Germany with the mission of befriending the German leaders under the guise of being pro-Nazi to learn as much as possible about their plans.

In the years ahead, Winterbotham played his role so well that the Nazis accepted him as a true friend. He met with Hitler, Hermann Goering, Josef Goebbels, and numerous field marshals and generals. Many of them boastfully provided detailed information about the mighty war machine that was being built, mostly under a veil of secrecy.

Through his top-level connections, the British spymaster even learned which high French leaders were on the Nazi payroll, and he spent many nights entertaining Luftwaffe pilots and plying them with alcoholic drinks so he could subtly extract secret information from them.

Toward the end of 1938 the Nazis made it known that Winterbotham was no longer welcome in Germany. No doubt they had begun to suspect his true motives in ingratiating himself with so many prominent German government and military leaders.

Although Winterbotham and his handful of agents had obtained much intelligence on the size and composition of the German Air Force during the past four years, much crucial data from within the Third Reich were still needed. This included any expansion of aircraft factories and the sites and capacity of new airfields and other military installations.

Winterbotham decided that this intelligence blackout would have to be penetrated by clandestine aerial photography, a field that the British had virtually ignored since the pioneer experiments in the Great War twenty years earlier. So he launched an intricate scheme to achieve that goal.

First, he prevailed on the Air Ministry to approve of his covertly acquiring a two-engined Lockheed executive-type airplane that was built in the United States. The craft had a heated cabin and could hold five persons, along with a pilot and a copilot. By European standards for civilian aircraft the Lockheed was far advanced.

It was arranged for the civilian British Imperial Airways to purchase and take delivery of the aircraft. Then the Air Ministry reimbursed the buyer. Winterbotham used his contacts with high British officials to "borrow" the latest cameras and equipment from a reluctant Royal Air Force.

After these photographic accoutrements were installed in the Lockheed, Winterbotham launched a search for a capable civilian pilot, one who would be patient enough to carry out experiments in high-altitude photography and sufficiently bold enough to fly over Germany to take pictures. He found just the man he wanted: Sydney Cotton, who had earned a reputation as an adventurous type.

Cotton had considerable knowledge of photography. Moreover, he already had cover. As an executive with a firm engaged in the development of color photography in England and Germany, he would be able to fly into the Third Reich without raising suspicion.

Although cameras had been greatly improved during the previous two decades, photos still had to be taken from only eight thousand feet, making it impossible to leisurely fly over Germany at this height in peacetime without being shot down by antiaircraft guns or Luftwaffe pilots.

Winterbotham and Cotton tried out the Lockheed at a height of twenty-two thousand feet, and after countless experiments, developed a procedure for taking clear photographs at that altitude. Ironically, Leica cameras purchased in Germany were used.

Before flying over the Third Reich, Winterbotham decided to make a lengthy test in the Mediterranean region, where Benito Mussolini was building defenses and military facilities. It was decided that a young Canadian would go along with Cotton as copilot.

Forged documents were made for Cotton in which he was portrayed as a wealthy movie tycoon making a survey of locations for a film. His copilot's papers identified him as a movie director.

Cotton left England in April 1939 and, flying at twenty-two thousand feet, he photographed every Italian air facility and naval base on the North African coast and did the same thing along the northern Mediterranean Sea. It had been an intelligence bonanza.

General (later Field Marshal)
Albrecht Kesselring unknowingly
spied on himself for the British.
(U.S. Army)

Now Winterbotham was ready for the main event—penetrating the tightly guarded Third Reich. Cotton made several flying trips to Berlin—without the camera equipment. Ostensibly he had come to talk with the executives on the German side of his color photography development firm. On the ground, German security men inspected the Lockheed cabin, but soon they became used to the Briton's arrival and paid no attention to his plane.

Then the sophisticated cameras—German-built cameras—were installed in the aircraft. Cotton now varied his route to Berlin, refueling at Frankfurt, Hamburg, Aachen, or other airfields, a procedure that gave his cameras a shot at new landing fields or factories turning out war materials. As the Germans believed that aerial photos could not be taken above eight thousand feet, they apparently never suspected that Cotton was snapping hundreds of pictures.

To reinforce his phony image as a wealthy tycoon gallivanting around Europe in his own expensive private aircraft, Sydney Cotton flew to the annual summer Frankfurt Air Show in Germany. He left the cameras in place, knowing that the Germans did not believe photos could be taken above eight thousand feet.

The Lockheed executive aircraft gained much attention, including that of General Albrecht Kesselring, who commanded the Luftwaffe's Air Fleet I, which was already earmarked to pace Adolf Hitler's looming invasion of Poland a few weeks in the future.

Perhaps hoping to obtain a similar executive aircraft, Kesselring asked Cotton if he could take a ride in the Lockheed. Cotton agreed. Soon the plane was winging along above the Rhine River when the general accepted Cotton's invitation to take over the controls.

Knowing that there were several important airports and other facilities along the Rhine, the Briton flipped on the camera. Green lights began flashing in the cockpit, indicating that photographs were being taken. Mildly curious, Kesselring asked the meaning of the green lights. Cotton replied nonchalantly that they merely indicated that the fuel was running evenly to the engine.

It was a peculiar episode. One of the three top commanders in the Luftwaffe was piloting a British spy plane in which German-built cameras were furiously snapping photographs of secret German facilities. In essence, Kesselring was spying on himself.[10]

A Baseball Player's Foresight

MORRIS "MOE" BERG was an extraordinary individual by any yardstick. Tall and ruggedly handsome, Berg graduated Phi Beta Kappa from Princeton and spoke German, French, Italian, Russian, and Japanese. In an era when hardly any of his compatriots had even attended college, he was a catcher on the Boston Red Sox major league baseball team.

Noted mainly for his defensive ability behind home plate, Berg, the son of a Newark, New Jersey, pharmacist, was once kidded by a teammate, "Moe, all them college dee-grees ain't goin' to help ya hit a curveball!"

Berg was also a patriot, believing that he owed a debt to the country that had been so kind to his immigrant Jewish parents. So, in the late 1930s, with war clouds gathering around the globe, he apparently agreed to act as an undercover agent for the U.S. government when leaving for a short-time assignment as a lecturer at the University of Tokyo in February 1939.

For more than ten years the generals and admirals who had an iron grip on the Japanese government held that an armed conflict with the United States was inevitable. So the warlords had drawn up a secret plan called the Tanaka Memorial. It was a blueprint for military conquests of vast expanses of the western Pacific and for war with America.

President Franklin Roosevelt suspected that the Japanese were preparing for an armed clash with the United States, but he had virtually no specifics. Incredibly, the United States was the only industrialized country that did not have a global intelligence service. Roosevelt, therefore, was "flying blind," having to make crucial decisions with regard to Japan without knowing what that nation was doing behind its bamboo curtain.

After reaching the Japanese capital, Berg's nimble brain and scientific approach to problems resulted in his going to a large civilian hospital, ostensibly to see the U.S. consul's wife, who had undergone surgery. Once inside the hospital, Moe, carrying a suitcase, located the stairs and climbed to the roof.

There he paused briefly, looked around to see that he was not being followed, and removed a 16mm Bell & Howell movie camera. With it he took hundreds of feet of panoramic views of sprawling Tokyo, which could be seen for many miles in all directions.

A little more than three years later, while outmanned, outgunned, and inadequately trained U.S. forces were being kicked around the Pacific by the powerful Japanese war machine, Lieutenant Colonel James H. "Jimmy" Doolittle had been handed a crucial but seemingly impossible mission. On April 18, 1942, Doolittle's flight of sixteen B-25 bombers lifted off from the carrier *Hornet* and set a course for Tokyo, eight hundred miles away. Six hours later, the first American bombs exploded on the Japanese capital.

Doolittle's bold raid was but a pinprick in the overall war effort. But its primary purpose was to lift the hearts and spirits of the home front and to cause the Japanese warlords to "lose face." They had boasted that no American bomb would ever be dropped on the Japanese homeland.

Jimmy Doolittle was one of the few insiders who knew that one of the reasons for the astonishing success of the Tokyo spectacular was that the planners had used the panoramic film footage taken from the hospital roof by the major league baseball player turned secret agent, Moe Berg, several years earlier.[11]

Tailing a Soviet Spy in England

LATE IN JUNE 1939, the British embassy in Washington sent an alarming warning to London. The Soviet dictator, Josef Stalin, was receiving military secrets obtained somewhere in England. So agents of MI-5, the security service handling counterintelligence within Great Britain, began surveillance of all known Soviet citizens, including A. A. Doschenko, an official of the Soviet trade delegation in London.

In early August, Doschenko boarded a train and got off at the sleepy hamlet of Leighton Buzzard, thirty-five miles north of London. The two MI-5 men tailing him were puzzled about what kind of legitimate business a high Soviet trade official could have in a tiny town like Leighton Buzzard.

After leaving the train, Doschenko began walking casually along Grand Union Canal, unaware that he was being followed. A short time later the Soviet was joined by another man, whom the MI-5 agents did not recognize. The stranger was seen slipping some papers to Doschenko, and the two men parted, walking away in opposite directions.

One British agent followed Doschenko, who was going to the Leighton Buzzard railroad station for the return trip, and the other MI-5 man tailed the stranger back to Bletchley Park, a serene village a few miles away.

Subsequent investigation disclosed that the man who had rendezvoused with Doschenko was a British citizen employed at the Foreign Office's Communications Department and its top-secret Government Code and Cipher School (GC&CS) at Bletchley Park. His job was handling Foreign Office coded messages, giving him access to secrets being sent to British embassies around the world. Because of his sensitive position, he had more information at his fingertips about the Foreign Office's plans and views than did most high-ranking officials in London.

A rash of nervous tics erupted among the handful of British government and military leaders who were privy to one of the nation's most jealously guarded secrets. Leading British scientists, mathematicians, and cryptanalysts had been laboring in an old Victorian mansion at Bletchley Park to develop an apparatus that would intercept and decode German wireless messages sent on a machine called Enigma. Previous to the arrival of the machine cipher system, enciphering had been done slowly by human hand. Now Enigma could produce an almost infinite number of different cipher alphabets merely by changing the keying procedure. Even if the British were to crack the Enigma code, the German messages would be safe because a new key was used each day. That meant that the odds were perhaps a billion to one that a snooper could decode Enigma signals.

Because Enigma was considered to be impenetrable, it had been adopted for use throughout the army, navy, Luftwaffe, and was used to encipher Hitler's communications and those of the Oberkommando der Wehrmacht. U-boats and even small ships liable to capture were equipped with the machine, for the seizure of an Enigma by an enemy would not be sufficient to enable him to read encoded messages, the Germans were convinced.

As the months passed and Europe drifted closer to armed conflict, the brainy Britons struggling with the seemingly hopeless task at Bletchley Park began to despair. But they persevered. In August 1939, while Adolf Hitler was massing his mighty legions on the Polish border ready to launch Case White, the invasion of that neighboring nation, the efforts of the British specialists were crowned with success.

The astonishing revolutionary development was nicknamed The Bomb by its creators. It was able to match the electrical circuits of Enigma, permitting The Bomb to imitate each daily change in keying procedure by the Germans.

The Bomb would prove to be an intelligence bonanza of unprecedented magnitude. Coded German messages intercepted and decoded by it would be called Ultra. From this point onward, the British (and later the Americans) had a pipeline into German headquarters at all levels. Often British commanders and government leaders would learn of German plans before the orders reached the Wehrmacht generals and admirals.

Meanwhile, after the espionage rendezvous at Leighton Buzzard, MI-5 sleuths knew that A. A. Doschenko's position as a Soviet trade delegation official was a cover for his true mission: obtaining information about the Foreign Office's communications activities at Bletchley Park.

That conclusion deeply worried the high British leaders who knew about the Ultra development. Had Doschenko been able to obtain information about The Bomb? If that were the case, Hitler would soon know about it, because he and Josef Stalin had signed a pact on August 23, 1939, in which the two countries agreed not to go to war with one another. If the führer, as a result of an intelligence coup by Doschenko, was aware of Ultra, the German signal corps would junk Enigma, thereby depriving the Western Allies of foreknowledge of German actions.

On September 27, 1939, about three weeks after Great Britain declared war on Germany following the Wehrmacht invasion of Poland, MI-5 agents arrested the British citizen who was working for the Foreign Office at Bletchley Park. Claiming to be a blackmail victim, the man confessed that he had been slipping Doschenko secret information for many months. Some of this material, it would be learned, had enabled the Soviet secret service to read coded British diplomatic messages.

The Briton was tried in court and sentenced to ten years at hard labor. He had escaped being executed for treason because his actions had taken place at a time when Britain was not at war. Apparently he had cooperated with British security officials who were seeking to determine if Ultra had been compromised. It was concluded that the spy had not had access to Ultra secrets—but MI-5 did not know that fact for certain. Only time would prove the conclusion accurate.

Meanwhile, A. A. Doschenko, a slick operative, was quietly expelled from Britain, the customary procedure for getting rid of an uncovered spy of a country that was officially neutral. Soon Doschenko's post was filled by another Soviet, who resumed espionage activities in England.[12]

Part Two

The Lights Go Out in Europe

A Weird Hoax to Launch a War

A DAZZLING ARRAY of German generals and admirals listened intently to each word Adolf Hitler was speaking. The führer had gathered them in his rustic retreat on the Obersalzberg, 6,208 feet above the picturesque Bavarian village of Berchtesgaden, to brief them on his plan to go to war. It was August 22, 1939.

Hitler got right to the point. "There probably will never again be a man with more authority than I have," he declared. "But I can be eliminated at any time by a criminal or a lunatic." Pausing briefly, he added: "There is no time to lose. War must come in my lifetime!"

Then the führer shocked the military leaders: he had signed a Treaty of Friendship with Germany's presumed archenemy, the Soviet Union, a Communist nation. It would be but a brief marriage of convenience. "Now we can strike at the heart of Poland," Hitler stated, "as Great Britain and France will not dare to come to Poland's rescue without the aid of Russia."

Hitler added that Poland would be invaded by 1.5 million troops and hundreds of panzers that were already massed at the frontier. Y-Day would be September 1. Zero hour: 4:30 A.M. Objective: the destruction of Poland as a sovereign nation.

Knowing that the stark aggression against Poland would be condemned by most of the world, the führer concluded his all-day presentation: "I shall give a propaganda cause for starting the war. Never mind if it is plausible or not. The victor will not be asked afterward if he told the truth."

Only much later would the German military leaders learn that Hitler was ready to spring a weird hoax code-named Operation Himmler. It would provide, at least in Hitler's mind, the "cold-blooded provocation" needed to prove to the German people (and to the world) that Poland had attacked first and that Hitler was unleashing his Wehrmacht to avenge the wrongdoing.

Hitler's machination would be orchestrated by Heinrich Himmler, the SS chief who was a proven master of chicanery. One of Himmler's trusted young SS officers, Alfred Naujocks, was designated to lead the operation.

Naujocks was typical of the strange breed often attracted to the SS—a combination intellectual and gangster. He had studied at the University of Kiel, where he had hoped to obtain an engineering degree, but instead spent much

A few hours after the phony German raid, the headline in this Berlin newspaper stated: "Bold attack on Radio Gleiwitz; Polish raiders cross the border; bloody fighting with German police."

of his time in brawls with Communist groups. Joining the new SS in 1934, Naujocks soon came to the attention of Himmler, who regarded the tough, resourceful officer as an ideal person to carry out unsavory projects.

Now Naujocks was preparing to implement the incredible hoax. For six days he had been holed up in Opeln, a small German town near the frontier of Poland. At noon on August 31 — Y-Day minus 1 — Berlin flashed word to Naujocks to launch Operation Himmler that night.

Twelve genuine German civilian criminals (code-named Canned Goods) had been taken from prison, brought to Opeln, and dressed in Polish Army uniforms. Now they were given injections by an SS doctor sworn to secrecy.

Naujocks and a few of his SS men also donned Polish uniforms. At 8:00 P.M. the party, including the drugged criminals, arrived outside a radio station at the village of Gleiwitz, only a few miles from Poland.

At a signal from Naujocks, his men carried the criminals around the premises and shot each one to death. Then Naujocks and several of his men dashed into the radio station. They fired shots into the ceiling, and an SS man who spoke flawless Polish shouted defiant slogans into the radio transmitter. Then the SS men fled.

Early the next morning, German newspaper photographers and reporters were rushed to the Gleiwitz radio station, and hours later, publications throughout the Third Reich carried gruesome pictures of the "Polish soldiers" killed by "German soldiers defending the station." The führer had the pretext he needed to invade.

At dawn, Adolf Hitler's massive "counterattack" against the Polish "aggressors" was launched. Unleashed was a mechanized juggernaut bristling with guns. Its speed and power and finesse would create a new word in the languages of many nations: *Blitzkrieg* (lightning war).[1]

Most Secret: Defuse the Magnetic Mines

WITHIN HOURS AFTER GREAT BRITAIN had declared war on Nazi Germany on September 3, 1939, Adolf Hitler ordered his Kriegsmarine to launch a maximum effort to strangle the islands by sinking ships that were bringing the British the food, ore, and supplies they needed. The offensive was masterminded by Admiral Karl Doenitz, *Befehlshaber der Untersee Boote* (commander of submarines).

During the next ten weeks in London, First Lord of the Admiralty Winston S. Churchill became steadily more concerned about the success of the German blockade. Shocking intelligence reports informed him that 114 British and neutral merchant ships had been sunk by U-boats, surface raiders, and a revolutionary type of explosive known as magnetic mines.

Dropped by parachute or laid by U-boats, the magnetic mines made it almost impossible for a ship to pass anywhere nearby without the underwater device being drawn to the metallic mass and exploding. Usually the vessel plunged rapidly to the bottom, taking her entire crew to a watery grave.

The Germans "sowed" hundreds of these fiendish devices off the coasts of England, around the entrance to British naval bases, and in the broad estuary of the Thames River, which flows into London, with its many miles of docks and bustling ship traffic. Within three months, fifty-nine merchantmen were sunk by magnetic mines.

Playing it cagey, Hitler's propaganda genius, Paul Josef Goebbels, issued communiqués boasting of the mighty feats of the U-boats, implying that their torpedoes, not a new secret weapon, were sinking ships wholesale.

On the night of November 22–23, 1939, the gods of war smiled on the British. A German bomber dropped a magnetic mine off Shoesburyness in the Thames estuary. The large, deadly missile landed on a mudflat and was discovered at low tide after dawn.

Royal Navy scientists and technicians rushed to the site. They had never seen a mine such as this one. So the cardinal question was: How can this lethal

*A British bomber fitted with a huge doral hoop to explode magnetic mines.
(Author's collection)*

device be rendered safe so that its secrets could be uncovered and countermeasures taken?

Lieutenant Commander J. G. D. Ouvry, knowing that he would be under-
taking a highly perilous task, volunteered to defuse the mine. Gingerly beginning the job, Ouvry was connected to a radio several hundred yards away
onshore by a throat microphone into which he calmly described what action
he was about to take. If he were suddenly blown into powder, the next man to
attempt to defuse a magnetic mine would have the peace of mind of knowing
what *not* to attempt.

With a final delicate turn of a small tool, Ouvry succeeded in disarming
Adolf Hitler's secret weapon. Later Ouvry was decorated with the Distinguished
Service Order for gallantry by King George VI. Had it not been for Ouvry, the
impact of the magnetic mines could have been disastrous for Britain.

As soon as the infernal device had been disarmed, it was rushed to a
British scientific laboratory to discover its secrets and create countermeasures.
All of this, including Ouvry's feat, were kept Most Secret, the highest British
security category.

Two techniques were developed for neutralizing the magnetic mine. In
one, a Wellington bomber was fitted with a huge doral hoop, almost as large as
the aircraft itself, which produced a strong magnetic field when energized.
When flying low over shipping lanes, the Wellington would detonate any magnetic mines over which it flew.

At the same time, the Britons began "degaussing" ships as a protective
measure. Degaussing involved stringing a cable around the vessel and passing
an electric current through it, which neutralized the ship's magnetic field, thus
preventing the ship from drawing up any mine over which it might pass.

By the spring of 1940, the Royal Navy had won the secret war against Hitler's magnetic-mine threat. But the carnage in the Atlantic, the English Channel, the North Sea, and the Mediterranean would continue to rage on and below the surface for another three years, with both sides suffering appalling losses in ships and men.[2]

Mystery Explosion in a Nazi Shrine

ADOLF HITLER was delivering a fire-and-brimstone speech before hundreds of the Nazi Old Guard—those zealots who had supported him during the 1923 *Putsch* (uprising), his first attempt to seize power in Germany and one that had landed him in prison. The site was the Bürgerbräukeller (Beer Cellar), a sort of Nazi shrine, in Munich. It was in this dingy basement that the future dictator and his clique had schemed to overthrow the legal government.

It was November 8, 1939, about two months since Hitler had invaded Poland and since England had declared war on Germany. The führer had arrived at the hall at 8:00 P.M., and he began speaking ten minutes later—twenty minutes ahead of time. After ranting and raving against Great Britain for nearly an hour—a much shorter speech than was his custom—he hurried out of the cellar with his bevy of aides.

Only seven minutes after the German supreme leader had departed, a time bomb planted in a pillar a few feet behind where he had been speaking exploded, killing seven and wounding sixty-three of the Nazi Old Guard, including the father of Hitler's girlfriend Eva Braun.

During the darkness of the early-morning hours in Düsseldorf in the wake of the bomb blast, SS Colonel Walther Schellenberg, a top official in the Sicherheitsdienst (SD), the intelligence branch of Reichsführer Heinrich Himmler's elite SS, was awakened from a deep sleep by the jangling of his bedside telephone. The big boss, Himmler, was on the line from Berlin.

"There's no doubt the British secret service is behind this plot," Himmler declared. "The führer says, and this is an order, when you meet the two British agents for your conference tomorrow [in Holland] you are to kidnap them and bring them to Germany. This may mean a violation of the Dutch frontier, but the führer says that is of no consequence."

Since the outbreak of war ten weeks earlier, the twenty-eight-year-old Schellenberg had slipped into neutral Holland in civilian clothes several times to meet secretly with the two British agents, Captain R. Henry Stevens and Captain S. Payne Best, who were now abduction targets. On these clandestine incursions into Dutch territory, the SD officer posed as Major Schaemmel, supposedly assigned to the German High Command. He had convinced Stevens and Best that he was the emissary of a group of German generals plotting to overthrow Hitler.

Adolf Hitler speaking in Munich's Bürgerbräukeller only minutes before a bomb exploded in the pillar behind him after he had departed earlier than scheduled. (National Archives)

Both sides hoped to gain from the cat-and-mouse game in Holland. Hitler and Himmler had been getting sketchy reports that some German generals were conspiring against the führer, and Schellenberg was hoping to unmask them. The British had been attempting also to learn the names of the presumed German conspirators to possibly assist them.

Now Hitler and Himmler had a new goal: bring the two British agents back to Berlin to stand trial for the Munich bomb-blast "murders."

In midafternoon the next day, Schellenberg was sipping wine on the terrace of a café in Venlo, Holland, a stone's throw from the German border. The two British agents, accompanied by a Dutch secret service agent named Klop, drove up in a Buick, parked the car behind the café, then were greeted by a hail of bullets fired by twelve German agents Schellenberg had brought with him.

Klop was killed instantly with a bullet through the head. Best and Stevens were overpowered before they could alight from the vehicle and were pitched, along with the dead Dutchman Klop, into a car. Moments later, the big Mercedes was racing across the German border. The entire kidnapping operation had taken but five minutes.

In Berlin, meanwhile, Josef Goebbels, the regime's propaganda genius who controlled all German newspapers, magazines, and radio stations, launched a ferocious campaign that accused the British secret service of the Munich "murders." Blaring headlines in German newspapers demanded revenge. A reward equivalent to two hundred thousand dollars (some three million dollars in 1999) was offered for information leading to the arrest of the culprits who had done the British bidding.

Because the Munich blast had been perpetrated with such stealth and professional skill, Hitler and other Nazi leaders would have been flabbergasted to know that the lone perpetrator had been a thirty-six-year-old German carpenter named Georg Elser.

Elser came from a poverty-stricken family, and his drunken father used to boast that he had "never beaten my wife with a chair or a club." The boy quit school and went to work when fourteen years of age. Over the years, he held a series of menial jobs. In 1938, after the führer sent his Wehrmacht into Czechoslovakia, the slightly built Elser pledged to himself to rid the world of Adolf Hitler.

In planning the assassination, Elser had been confronted by a major problem: Where would Hitler be certain to appear without fail and at a specific date and time? Soon he was struck by an obvious answer: the Bürgerbräukeller in Munich, where the Führer appeared each November 8 to meet with the Nazi Old Guard.

It was too late in 1938 to implement his scheme, so he targeted 1939. This would give him a year to prepare. First he would have to inspect the beer cellar and the neighborhood, because he had not been in Munich in nineteen years. So he climbed aboard a train in his hometown of Königsbroon for the eighty-mile trip to Munich.

After inspecting the Bürgerbräukeller, Elser was convinced that he had selected the ideal place for the assassination. He noticed a large pillar running from the ceiling to the floor only a few feet behind the rostrum from which Hitler would be speaking. Elser decided that he would build a time bomb and plant it in the pillar.

In early April 1939 he returned to Munich and headed for the Bürgerbräukeller for a detailed reconnaissance of the premises. He strolled as nonchalantly as possible through the front entrance, past the small dining room packed with guests, and through the swinging doors that led into the great hall where the Old Guard met to swizzle copious jugs of beer and sing the praises of Adolf Hitler.

Elser spent a week in Munich and made it a point to eat several meals in the Bürgerbräukeller to get on friendly terms with the waitresses. At his request they posed for his camera in front of the rostrum where the führer spoke each November 8. Not by happenstance, the pillar behind the young *Frauleins* would be clearly visible in the finished photograph.

Back in Königsbroon, Elser sought a job with a local quarry where large amounts of explosives, detonators, and fuses were stored in a bunker. After being hired, he returned to the site late at night on five or six occasions, pilfering small amounts of the ingredients he needed to make a time bomb.

Elser experimented with several different types of infernal devices, then settled on electricity supplied by storage batteries to provide energy to spark the detonation. A clock would be set to close the electrical circuit at the time Hitler was speaking.

On August 5, Elser again boarded a train at Königsbroon, lugging along a large, heavy-duty wooden box weighing some 150 pounds. Soon after he rented a room in Munich and concealed his box of explosives, detonators, and fuses, he received a tool kit he had mailed to himself before leaving home.

Each night he ate a leisurely supper in the beer cellar dining room. At about ten o'clock he paid his bill, picked up his knapsack holding tools, and strolled casually through the doors leading into the dark and empty festival hall where Hitler would speak. Then he would hide until the dining room closed at 11:30 P.M.

Using the dull beam of a flashlight, Elser, an expert craftsman, removed a panel from the pillar and began chipping away. After working for three or four hours, always mindful of telltale footsteps, he replaced the panel, swept up evidence of his work, then fell asleep in a chair.

Just past 8:00 A.M., when the eating facility opened, Elser strolled out the front door and returned to his rooming house.

In the nights ahead, the tedious work and the enormous tension continued. Using steel hand drills, chisels, and hammers, he laboriously chipped out a cavity from the brick, stone, and cement of the pillar. Each tap of the hammer on the chisel reverberated through the empty hall, sounding like a pistol shot. Always he carefully replaced the panel.

Nearly a month after Elser began his work, war broke out in Europe when Adolf Hitler sent his mighty Wehrmacht plunging into neighboring Poland on September 1, 1939.

While work on the pillar continued, the conspirator spent his days in his rented room working on the apparatus to trigger the explosive charge. The mechanical aspect was complicated, but he finally designed a system that would permit him to time the explosion up to 150 hours after starting the device.

By November 2, six nights before the führer would speak, Elser picked the lock on the service entrance to the dark Bürgerbräukeller, stole inside, and planted fifty pounds of explosives in the large cavity he had hacked in the pillar. Sixty pounds more were brought in and placed on the following night.

Just past midnight on November 8, Elser for the last time slipped into the deserted beer hall, and by the dim flashlight beam he inserted the clockwork mechanism inside the pillar and hooked the wires to the two detonators. Then came the crucial part of the plot. Counting on the führer to be punctual for the Old Guard rally as he had been in the past, Elser set the timer to detonate the dynamite sixty-three hours and twenty minutes later—in the middle of Hitler's speech.

Elser silently left the Bürgerbräukeller and headed for his rooming house. He had spent thirty-five nights working alone under enormous stress to complete his job.

At about 7:30 P.M. on November 9, the train on which Elser was making his getaway was nearing the border of neutral Switzerland. Back in Munich, Adolf Hitler was climbing into his specially built Mercedes-Benz sedan, with its bulletproof glass and armor-plated body, for the short drive to the speaking site. At 8:00 P.M. he strode briskly into the Bürgerbräukeller while the band blared the refrains of "Horst Wessel Lied," the Nazi theme song.

As the Old Guard thundered roars of approval, the Führer walked to the lectern and began speaking at 8:10 P.M., twenty minutes ahead of schedule. Only a few feet behind him the time mechanism in the bomb was ticking away.

At about 8:30 P.M., Georg Elser got off the train fifteen hundred yards from the Swiss border and began stealing through the darkness toward freedom. Suddenly two German frontier police emerged, pointed their weapons at Elser, and hauled him off to their guardhouse. Searching the prisoner, the police found a clock spring and a picture postcard of the interior of the Bürgerbräukeller.

When Elser could offer no plausible reason for trying to sneak across the border into Switzerland, the police took him to a nearby Gestapo headquarters. At first the interrogating Gestapo agent thought Elser was a small-fry hoodlum engaged in some illegal transaction. The prisoner remained calm and explained that he was on his way to visit a friend's home when he got lost.

The Gestapo official was about to release Elser when he was handed an urgent telegram: An attempt had just been made to assassinate Adolf Hitler, and border guards were warned to be on the alert for suspicious characters trying to escape to Switzerland.

Now the interrogator felt that he had before him one of the culprits. Under brutal questioning, Elser finally admitted that he had been responsible for the beer hall explosion. The prisoner was rushed to Gestapo headquarters in Munich.

Despite intensive grilling that included sessions with professional hypnotists and truth serum injections, Elser stuck to his story: He had acted alone. In Berlin, Reichsführer Heinrich Himmler was gripped with anger and disbelief. Clearly no one man could have conceived and implemented such a sophisticated and complicated assassination attempt. The British secret service had to have been the mastermind, and its agents must have secretly placed the explosives and timing mechanism.

Himmler promptly flew to Munich to confront Elser. When the prisoner refused to deviate from his story, that he had acted alone, the Gestapo chief kicked him in the body, had him beaten badly, then drove his boots hard into the prisoner once more.

Back in Berlin, Adolf Hitler was furious. Any idiot would have known that this simpleminded carpenter could not have acted alone. The führer demanded a public show trial of Georg Elser and the two British secret service agents, Henry Stevens and Payne Best, whom Walther Schellenberg's men had kidnapped at Venlo. But that propaganda scheme fizzled when SS intelligence and the Gestapo could not tie Stevens and Best with Elser.

Now the entire Bürgerbräukeller affair took a curious twist, one that would never be explained. Instead of having Elser executed, Heinrich Himmler ordered him to solitary confinement at the Dachau concentration camp.

Elser would never be tried for the attempted assassination of the führer and being in league with British agents. Rather, the carpenter would survive nearly five years of inhumane treatment. Then, on April 5, 1945, with Allied armies closing in on Berlin from east and west, Himmler sent orders to Dachau for Elser to be executed. For whatever reason, the Gestapo chief wanted the prisoner to die of "massive head injuries" from a bomb during the next Allied air raid in the region.

Four days later, Georg Elser was dead.[3]

Goering Hires a Rainmaker

IN THE WAKE OF ADOLF HITLER'S BREATHTAKING BLITZKRIEG, which had doomed Poland in six weeks in September 1939, the shooting war in Europe had turned into a conflict of propaganda and lame jokes. Along the Western Front some two million German troops faced an equal number of French, British, Belgian, and Dutch soldiers. Few shots were fired. The confrontation was referred to as the *Sitzkrieg* or Phony War.

The führer's primary offensive weapon during these curious days was his diminutive communications genius, Josef Goebbels. His task was to launch a propaganda campaign designed to lull the enemy to sleep. The main impact would be directed toward the French soldiers, who were ensconced inside the "impregnable" Maginot Line.

After visiting the Western Front, Goebbels correctly deduced that the average French soldier was weary, bored, miserable, and wanted only "a warm bed, a woman, a garden, and peace." Consequently, he took aim at the French state of mind, instructing German soldiers to shout friendly greetings across no-man's-land, engage the French in brotherly conversation, and suggest that both sides drop their weapons and return home. At night German loudspeakers broadcast sentimental French ballads to the homesick soldiers huddled in and along the Maginot Line.

A sidebar to the Goebbels propaganda blitz was to divide the French from the British. Before signing off, the announcer, who spoke flawless French, would say something similar to: "Good night, dear friends. We don't like England's war any more than you do. So why should we shoot each other? Let's all have a good night's sleep."

In the daytime, the French troops were showered with leaflets, one of which depicted a soldier shivering in a foxhole while his wife back home was in bed with a British soldier.

During the first few months of 1940, Adolf Hitler was waiting for a stretch of five clear days during which the Luftwaffe could spearhead a mammoth offensive. Field Marshal Hermann Goering, commander of the air force and legal heir to succeed Hitler, anxiously attended the daily weather conferences, during which the chief meteorologist, Heinz Diesing, was badgered to give forecasts longer than three days.

For the past several weeks the weather had been unpredictable, sunshiny for a day or two, then a period of cloudiness and rain. Diesing explained that he could give forecasts for three days but that it would be foolish for him to predict the weather for five days.

Goering was frustrated and irritable. In desperation, he hired one Hans Schwefler, who billed himself as a rainmaker, and paid him a hundred thousand marks. It was not known if the field marshal ordered Schwefler to produce five clear days.

Whatever may have been the case, shortly after dawn on May 10, 1940, the air over the Western Front was darkened by twenty-five hundred of Goering's warplanes, and airborne troops and ground forces poured across the border into France, Belgium, and the Netherlands. Code-named Case Yellow, the mighty offensive gained total surprise.[4]

Churchill's Amazing Gamble

IN LONDON on the morning of May 10, 1940, Prime Minister Neville Chamberlain, who for two years had been trying to appease Adolf Hitler, resigned. King George VI promptly summoned First Lord of the Admiralty Winston Churchill to Buckingham Palace.

After greeting Churchill graciously, he asked him to sit down. Then the monarch looked at the visitor searchingly for several moments and said: "I suppose you don't know why I have sent for you?"

Adopting his whimsical mood, Churchill replied, "Sir, I simply couldn't imagine why!"

Laughing, King George said, "I want to ask you to form a government [replace Chamberlain]." The offer was eagerly accepted.

For an hour, the two men discussed the bleak war picture. Then the new prime minister, in a series of bows, withdrew.

Churchill, a politician for forty years, plunged into his new duties with customary vigor. But there was nothing he could do about the Allied debacle unfolding across the Channel. In only three weeks, Hitler's legions had forced Belgium and the Netherlands to surrender and trapped much of the Allied armies around the small English Channel port of Dunkirk, France.

On June 6 Churchill was in his bombproof command post deep beneath the pavement in London. Drawing on a long, black cigar and peering through eyeglasses resting near the tip of his nose, he was scanning reports on Operation Dynamo, a rescue mission by some 850 mainly civilian vessels to evacuate to England 337,131 British and French troops from Dunkirk.

Churchill was stunned. Crossing the Channel with the soldiers were only 25 tanks, 12 artillery pieces, and a handful of machine guns. Left behind at Dunkirk were 120,000 vehicles, 2,300 artillery pieces and mortars, 8,000 Bren guns, 90,000 rifles, and 7,000 tons of ammunition and shells.

Great Britain had suffered one of the worst military disasters in her history. A few weeks later, France surrendered. Now Great Britain stood alone against the awesome might of Hitler's war juggernaut deployed along the English Channel coast in France, Belgium, and the Netherlands.

Churchill confided to an aide: "If they come, we'll have to hit them over the head with bottles! That's all we've got to fight with!"

In this hour of mortal danger for Great Britain, the prime minister ordered a plan developed to whisk the Royal Family and government leaders to Canada if the Germans invaded. The war against Hitler would be continued from there. Then Churchill called in his cabinet and briefed them on an amazing gamble he code-named Operation Fish: Seven billion dollars worth of Britain's gold and securities would be transferred clandestinely to Canada, starting immediately.

At the outbreak of the war in September 1939, British citizens had been required to register with the government treasury all their securities, both foreign and domestic. Utilizing his unique wartime powers—or what he conceived to be his powers—the prime minister now commandeered the section of the British treasury that had the list of securities.

In a finely tuned maneuver, government agents swooped down on banks in Great Britain and grabbed the citizens' securities, an action that was the only one of its kind in history. Then these tons of documents were packed into thousands of large boxes and rushed to regional collection centers.

Within only a few days, heavily guarded trains, their crews sworn to secrecy under penalty of long prison terms, raced northward with government gold and citizens' securities. At Greenock, a port on the Firth of Clyde in southwestern Scotland, the heavy cargo was unloaded at night onto the British cruiser *Emerald*.

Belowdecks away from prying eyes were 2,230 heavy boxes, each holding four gold bars. Stashed away elsewhere on the cruiser were nearly five hundred boxes of securities, with a value of $400 million (equivalent to some $4 billion in 1999).

There was no certainty that the *Emerald* would ever arrive in Canada. Admiral Karl Doenitz, the German U-boats commander, had his submarines prowling the sea lanes between Scotland and Canada, some three thousand miles to the west. In that month, fifty-seven Allied ships had been sunk in the North Atlantic.

Under cover of darkness on June 24, 1940, the *Emerald* slipped down the Clyde and into the Atlantic, where she rendezvoused with an escort of several destroyers. The convoy would be the first of several similar ones to follow.

Captain Francis C. Flynn, the *Emerald*'s skipper, scanned the latest weather report: Storm demons were shrieking over the Atlantic up ahead. A few hours later, a warning was received from the Admiralty: Two U-boats were lurking in the sea lane the *Emerald* was to take.

Had spies in England or Scotland notified Berlin of the exceptional cargo aboard the ship? Had German intelligence cracked the British naval code and learned precisely the route to be taken by the *Emerald*? Flynn kept his forebodings to himself, but no doubt he was greatly relieved when no contact was made with the U-boats.

During the next forty-eight hours the ocean was so violent that the *Emerald* and its escort of destroyers had to cut their speed. Crewmen became violently ill. On the third day, the weather cleared, the ocean calmed, and on the morning of July 1, the *Emerald* reached its destination, Halifax, Nova Scotia.

Armed sentries from the *Emerald* blocked off the dock to outsiders. Almost immediately, the unloading process began. Each box of gold and securities was checked off the *Emerald* by officials of the Bank of Canada, then rechecked as it was put into a car of the special train that had been waiting on a railroad spur beside the dock.

Only twelve hours after the *Emerald* had reached Halifax, the treasure train pulled away and headed for its first stop, Montréal. Waiting at Bonaventure Station there were Sidney J. Perkins of the Foreign Exchange Control Board and David Mansur, secretary of the Bank of Canada.

As soon as the train halted, guards sealed off that portion of Bonaventure Station. Then the cars carrying the securities were cut loose, and the train, with its fortune in gold bullion, raced on toward Ottawa, seat of the Canadian government.

Before the treasure train had arrived in Montréal, Sidney Perkins and David Mansur were confronted by a gargantuan problem: Where could the hundreds of boxes of securities be safely hidden? Mansur had the answer: in the Sun Life Assurance Company's twenty-six-story building on Montréal's Dominion Square. The structure had three subterranean levels, the lowest of which would be designated "The United Kingdom Security Deposit."

Shortly before midnight, Montréal police blocked off the streets between Bonaventure Station and the Sun Life building. The trucks began to roll, and by dawn the last box had been placed in "The United Kingdom Security Deposit."

At Ottawa, in the meantime, the train with the railroad cars crammed with gold bullion reached the station at night, so the darkness could cover the transfer of the precious cargo by trucks to the cavernous vaults of the Bank of Canada on Wellington Street.

On July 5, Operation Fish continued when five ships sailed from Scotland with the greatest combined load of treasure ever transported by land or sea. Carrying gold and securities with a total value of $1.7 billion (equivalent to some $18 billion in 1999), the converted commercial liners rendezvoused offshore with an escort of the powerful battleship *Revenge*, a cruiser, and several destroyers.

The convoy covered three-fourths of the trip uneventfully, although numerous other Allied ships had been sunk along its sea lane. Then trouble struck. The Free Poland ship *Batory*, loaded with treasure, developed engine problems and could not sail at normal speed. Not wishing to risk his other ships, the convoy commander, Admiral Ernest R. Archer, ordered the *Batory* to head for St. John's, Newfoundland, escorted by the cruiser *Bonaventure*.

Halfway to St. John's, the two ships were engulfed by thick fog, and icebergs were floating about. For nearly thirteen hours the two ships had to sit dead in the water, prime targets for any prowling U-boat. Eventually the *Batory* and the *Bonaventure* reached St. John's.

Eight days after leaving Scotland, the first three ships in Admiral Archer's convoy sailed into Halifax Harbor, where they were joined in a few days by the repaired *Batory* and the *Bonaventure*. Five trains were required to carry the gold bullion on to Ottawa. Within days, thousands of twenty-seven-pound ingots were piled to the ceiling in the sixty-by-one-hundred-foot vault in the Bank of Canada. Only at Fort Knox in the United States was there a greater amount of gold.

In the meantime, back in Montréal, a crash project had been launched at the Sun Life building to construct a huge vault, measuring sixty feet square and eleven feet high, to hold the many trainloads of securities that had arrived during Operation Fish. Sound detection devices in the vault were so sensitive that they could record a drawer being opened on any one of the nine hundred filing cabinets.

David Mansur recruited 125 Canadians—retired bankers and brokerage house and investment firm employees—and swore them to secrecy. Then they were put to work sorting and itemizing the enormous array of securities in this secret, curious stock-and-bond business.

When the unprecedented project was completed, the Admiralty determined that gold worth more than $2.5 billion had been shipped to Canada. Astoundingly, during the three months when 134 Allied and neutral ships had been sent to the bottom by German action in the North Atlantic, not one treasure-carrying vessel was sunk or even attacked.

An even more astonishing aspect of Fish, however, was that as many as 1,000 persons on both sides of the Atlantic were involved in the transfer of Great Britain's treasure—and the secret was kept from Adolf Hitler.[5]

A Covert Weather War

OFF THE SOUTHWESTERN COAST of lava-covered Iceland, about 520 miles north-west of Scotland in the Arctic climes of the North Atlantic, British Major General Robert Sturges stood on the bridge of the cruiser *Berwick* and peered intently through high-powered binoculars at Reykjavik, the large island's only major city. Searching for any sign of German military activity, Sturges detected nothing to cause concern.

Two hours later, the *Berwick* tied up at a Reykjavik dock, and a contingent of Royal Marines and crewmen of the cruiser, all heavily armed, hurried down the gangplank. Then they split into groups and fanned out in the bleak city on predesignated missions.

Within a few hours, Sturges's men had taken into custody the Nazi consul-general, rounded up two spare U-boat crews, and seized a weather-reporting station that radioed forecasts to Berlin. It was May 10, 1940.

In the week ahead, the British invaders of Iceland, which had been made an independent kingdom in personal union with Denmark during World War I, secured the island and began setting up a weather-intelligence post to send information to London. This operation had been the opening round in what would become a deadly, covert weather war that would rage unnoticed by the outside world for the next five years.

Even before the outbreak of the conflict in Europe eight months earlier, both the British and the German high commands had recognized that accurate weather forecasts would be crucial in planning strategy and day-to-day tactics in the western part of Europe. Precise weather intelligence could be the deciding factor in which adversary would win.

For the beleaguered British in particular, it was critical that the powerful German war machine be denied as much weather intelligence as possible. Between the eastern tip of northern Canada and the western coast of Scotland, most European weather originates.

Once Iceland was secure—at least for the present—the British rapidly moved against Greenland, a huge island some two hundred miles west of Iceland, captured several German weather-reporting stations, and converted them into British operations.

Deprived of land-based outposts, the Kriegsmarine tried to establish a network of weather-reporting trawlers, small vessels used for fishing. However, the trawlers were located when the British intercepted and decoded German messages, and in April 1941, three British cruisers and four destroyers were dispatched to the Iceland-Greenland region to wipe out the floating weather stations. After tracking the German trawlers *München* and *Lauenburg* by wireless intercepts, the British warships caught and sank them.

Meanwhile, under the orders of President Franklin D. Roosevelt, the United States, while officially remaining neutral, was becoming steadily more

U.S. soldier stands guard in Iceland during the covert weather war. (U.S. Army)

involved in the war in Europe. On April 9, 1941, Roosevelt announced that Greenland, most of which lies within the Arctic Circle, was to be a U.S. "protectorate." Although separated by thirteen hundred miles of ocean from Denmark, Greenland was a crown colony of that tiny nation.

Within a few days, green American soldiers, most of them draftees eager only to get out of the army and return home, landed in Greenland. They promptly began destroying German weather stations and building their own ones for eventual use in European operations.

In a secret pact with British Prime Minister Winston Churchill, President Roosevelt agreed that the United States, although not at war with Germany, would patrol the seas around Greenland to prevent the Nazis from returning to the island, which is about one-fourth the size of the United States and which today is known as Kalaallit Nunaat.

On September 13, 1941, the U.S. Coast Guard cutter *Northland* spotted the German trawler *Buskoe* off southern Greenland. Through his binoculars, Commander Edward Smith, the *Northland's* skipper, saw that the *Buskoe* was painted in swatches of ice-blue and white, camouflage to help hide the vessel when it would lay silently next to one of the giant icebergs floating in the region. Smith also saw that the trawler was equipped with an array of aerials and powerful wireless paraphernalia.

Smith had to reach a critical decision. Should he sail on, or halt the *Buskoe* and take its German crew into custody? Any hostile action on his part, he knew, could very well drag the "neutral" United States into the European conflict. His mind was made up: He ordered a shot to be fired across the trawler's bow.

Moments later, the *Buskoe* hoisted a flag indicating her captain was halting his engines. Then the *Northland* edged alongside the German vessel and a party of its crew boarded the trawler. Its members soon returned and told Smith that there were twenty-seven men and one woman in the *Buskoe's* crew and that their papers showed them to be Norwegian "trappers" and Danish "hunters."

Smith knew the papers were phony, and he ordered the *Buskoe* to sail to McKenzie Bay, where the American skipper boarded the trawler and told the crew that it was under arrest for "espionage." Smith also learned from a crew member that the *Buskoe* had put two parties, each equipped with wireless transmitters, ashore near the entrance to Franz Josef Fjord, on the northeastern coast of Greenland.

Leaving a few of the *Northland* crew to guard the trawler, Smith headed his cutter on a beeline for Franz Josef Fjord to capture the men put ashore from the *Buskoe*. A landing party, armed with rifles, tommy guns, and grenades, scoured the region. Just past midnight on September 14, the Americans discovered a shack that had antennae on the roof and smoke pouring out of a makeshift chimney. The shack was surrounded, then several muscular types burst open the door with their shoulders. Inside, huddled around a potbellied stove, were three startled Germans, who were taken into custody.

After Adolf Hitler declared war on the United States on December 11, 1941, the U.S. Coast Guard greatly increased the number of its cutters and trawlers patrolling the Greenland coasts to keep the Germans from reestablishing weather posts on the thinly populated island. Danes and Eskimos living in Greenland were recruited to search for any kind of German activity in remote regions.

So crucial was weather data to the Wehrmacht in pursuing its campaign of conquest in Europe that repeated efforts were made to set up reporting stations in Greenland. Consequently, the covert weather war in the North Atlantic was fought on the strangest of battlefields, one often lit eerily by reflected arcs of the aurora borealis, whose flickering frost-white beams and ever-changing hues seemed to move as if in a breeze.

It was bitterly cold in much of Greenland. Windchill factors as low as 60 degrees Fahrenheit below zero and icy storms with winds of 150 miles per hour made it painful for a man to inhale. When he exhaled, clusters of ice beads formed on his beard. Many lives, ships, and airplanes on both sides were lost during the savage, frigid struggle.

In mid-December 1942 the U.S. Coast Guard trawler *Natsek*, commanded by Lieutenant Thomas S. LaFarge, set sail from Greenland for Boston with a crew of twenty-seven. Soon it began to snow, and the wind reached gale force. Then black ice began to form—a strange phenomenon that had sunk many a ship in the North Atlantic. Layers of this ice soon weighed scores of tons. Desperately, the crew used picks and chisels to fight the black ice for three days and nights. Always the *Natsek* was in danger of capsizing.

Steam was tried. It was useless, the steam itself freezing after being sprayed over the ice layers. It was a hopeless battle. The *Natsek* became top-heavy, flopped over on its side and disappeared below the water. No man could survive in the water unless he were in a boat, and even then, he would live only a few hours unless rescued.

All of those aboard the ill-fated *Natsek* perished, more victims of the covert weather war.[6]

Masquerade on the High Seas

EARLY IN MAY 1940, the skipper of the British liner *Exeter* peered through high-powered binoculars at the unidentified ship approaching on the South Atlantic horizon. He was highly suspicious, as heavily armed German surface raiders were known to be roaming Great Britain's vital sea lanes in search of prey. On her deck, a woman could be seen pushing a baby carriage. Lolling about were a few crewmen, their shirttails hanging out, as was the custom of Japanese commercial sailors.

Soon the *Exeter* skipper breathed a sigh of relief. He could see the rising-sun flag of Japan fluttering on a pole, and from her contours, he identified the cargo ship *Kashii Maru*, from a neutral country. The two vessels passed without a signal.

Actually, the "*Kashii Maru*" was the disguised German surface raider *Atlantis*, skippered by an exceptionally able and compassionate officer, Captain Bernhard Rogge. The "woman" on deck had been a crewman wearing a wig and a dress, and the baby buggy had been empty. Because he had recognized that the *Exeter* was carrying a large number of civilian passengers, Rogge had decided not to sink her, which he could have done easily.

Beginning the war as the 7,800-ton cargo ship *Goldenfels*, her name had been changed to *Atlantis* and she was fitted with 6 5.9-inch guns, 10 smaller guns, torpedo tubes, tons of mines, and a seaplane for scouting. All these lethal devices were hidden from view until ready to be used on unsuspecting merchantmen.

Also concealed below were some 350 technicians and combat men. Behind a masquerade of props—plywood ventilators, canvas funnels, and flags of numerous nations—the *Atlantis* was a deadly predator. By the time the captain of an approaching ship decided that Rogge's vessel was not Soviet or Japanese or Norwegian, it was too late. German sailors belowdecks would fire torpedoes with deadly accuracy, and often a badly damaged target would be finished off with gunfire.

Bernhard Rogge, a tall, husky officer thirty-nine years of age, was a cherished figure to his men. Everyone on board was treated exactly the same. All shared equally in the luxuries taken from captured ships—candy, beer, food snacks. Rogge's grandfather had been a clergyman, so the skipper insisted that all of his officers attend church services on Sundays. Then he invited them to his cabin for a drink, which they dubbed "Bernhard's church cocktail."

Rogge's solitary maritime venture was as close to being "civilized" as a brutal, bloody conflict can be. He took aboard the *Atlantis* all the prisoners that his men could fish out of the water from sinking ships. In twenty months at sea, he provided shelter at one time or the other for more than one thousand prisoners of all ages, both sexes, and eighteen nationalities. They ate the same rations as the *Atlantis* officers and crew, and they were permitted to swim in the canvas pool. When prisoners were transferred to other ships, Rogge gave farewell parties for their skippers.

Nazi Germany's war of the disguised surface raiders was global in scope. Beginning in April 1940 and continuing for more than two years, the *Atlantis* and five raiders had sailed from German ports to remote regions of the world. Camouflaged as a Soviet cargo ship, the *Atlantis* had sneaked up the coast of Norway, turned west into the North Atlantic, then headed southward.

After crossing the equator on April 25, 1940, Captain Rogge ordered the Soviet flag taken down, a Japanese flag raised in its place, and for his technicians to go to work putting up fake funnels to impersonate the *Kashii Maru*, which would pass the *Exeter* on the high seas.

Another disguised German surface raider, *Komet*, had made the Northeast Passage with the aid of Soviet ice-breakers, skirted Siberia, and reached the Pacific, where she took a heavy toll of unwary ships. *Penguin* wrought havoc with Allied and neutral ships off the Antarctic ice pack, then captured three Norwegian whaling ships. In an amazing feat of seamanship, the skipper of the *Penguin* managed to avoid British sea patrols and bring the Norwegian vessels a few thousand miles back to Germany.

Yet another masquerading surface raider, *Thor*, was involved in an episode that could have changed the course of the war in the Pacific. In the Indian Ocean, halfway around the world from Germany, *Thor* captured the unarmed British freighter *Nankin*, which was en route from Wellington, New Zealand, to Ceylon, India.

On board the *Nankin* were top-secret Royal Navy mailbags. Without being opened, these bulging containers were transferred to *Thor's* supply ship *Regensburg*, which docked at Yokohoma, Japan, on July 18, 1942, more than seven months after America had been bombed into the war at Pearl Harbor.

At Yokohoma, the mailbags eventually were dumped at the German embassy in Tokyo. There Rear Admiral Paul Wenneker, Adolf Hitler's astute naval attaché, began sifting through the documents in the mailbags and immediately recognized their importance. Wenneker was especially interested in the weekly summaries of the Combined Operations Intelligence Center (COIC) of the New Zealand armed forces. After sending the details to Berlin, Wenneker was given permission to hand the documents over to the Japanese.

U.S. intelligence sources at Pearl Harbor had supplied COIC with a large amount of highly sensitive data. Some of it was labeled top secret and circulated to only twenty-two officers, including Admiral Chester Nimitz, the commander of the U.S. Pacific Fleet. This information was a bonanza for the Japanese. It specified the positions of all Allied warships and the estimates of the Japanese dispositions in the Pacific by Nimitz's intelligence officers at Pearl.

If the *Thor* skipper and other German officers who had handled the *Nankin's* secret mail had turned it over promptly to the Japanese instead of waiting nine months, even the most dull-witted intelligence officer would have recognized at once that the Americans had broken the Japanese naval code and that U.S. intelligence was reading Japanese messages gained from radio intercepts. In that event, Admiral Isoroku Yamamoto, commander of the Combined Fleet, would have immediately installed new operational codes, thereby depriving Admiral Nimitz of his gargantuan intelligence advantage of knowing in advance details of Japanese naval plans in the Pacific.

Meanwhile, Captain Bernhard Rogge had been marauding through the South Atlantic, then around the Cape of Good Hope and into the Indian Ocean. A few days later, the *Atlantis* radio operators intercepted a British warning that a German surface raider, disguised as a Japanese cargo ship, was roaming the Indian Ocean.

Immediately Rogge put his prop men and "set decorators" into action. They took off the *Atlantis's* kimono and she became the Netherlands ship *Abbekerk*.

Captain Rogge continued to pile up the victims, sinking numerous ships and capturing others. Messages found by *Atlantis* crewmen in the wastebasket of one vessel paid off big: The information permitted the Germans to break the British merchant naval code. Another British ship, the *Automedon*, surrendered when a shell killed everyone on her bridge. A German boarding party turned up an intelligence gold mine: mail for the British Far East High Command and a top-secret War Cabinet report.

The *Atlantis's* activities spread near-panic among Allied skippers of merchantmen. Every ship spotted on the horizon was suspect: a friend, or an enemy masquerading as a friend? British warships, badly needed elsewhere, were sent out to track down the *Atlantis*. Captains of Allied cargo vessels lost much time when they zigzagged on long routes when Rogge's marauder was hundreds of miles away. Cargo-ship crews were hard to recruit, and they demanded hazardous-duty pay.

An innocent-looking German cargo ship (above) was actually a deadly raider in disguise. Captain Bernhard Rogge (left) of the Atlantis, *which sank twenty-two ships. (National Archives)*

With time Bernhard Rogge had begun to conjecture that he was operating on borrowed time. Admiral Erich Raeder, commander of the Kriegsmarine, had sent out six masquerading raiders a year and a half earlier, and most of them had met with disaster. On May 8, 1941, off Somaliland, the *Penquin* was surprised and sunk by the British cruiser *Cornwall*. On November 19 the *Kormoran*, while prowling off the western coast of Australia, was involved in the equivalent of that rarity in the boxing ring—a double knockout. Badly crippled by shellfire from the Australian cruiser *Sydney*, the *Kormoran* loosed two torpedoes before going down, and they scored direct hits. The *Sydney* sank with most of her crew.

Three days after the double knockout off Australia, the *Atlantis* was cruising in the Atlantic midway between Brazil and Africa when her scout plane was damaged on touching down on the water. It could be a disastrous loss, because the raider was to meet a U-boat the next day to take on fuel—a potentially perilous project in which the "eyes" of the seaplane would be crucial.

Just after dawn the two vessels rendezvoused, and the fuel-pumping operation got under way. A few members of the *Atlantis* crew were in a launch alongside the U-boat, and the submarine's skipper was on board the raider, exchanging the latest information—and gossip—with Bernhard Rogge. At the same time, one *Atlantis* engine had been taken apart for repairs.

Suddenly a lookout caught sight of a ship that was bearing down on the two German vessels with throttles wide open. It was the British heavy cruiser *Devonshire*. Had the *Atlantis*'s seaplane been available and in the air, no enemy ship could have gotten close to the Germans without being detected.

The lines holding together the two German ships were quickly cast off, and the U-boat dived. Its skipper was marooned on the *Atlantis*. Rogge conjectured if the U-boat had been seen. He doubted it. So he decided to launch a cat-and-mouse game with the skipper of the *Devonshire*, hoping to gain time until the U-boat could get in position to launch its torpedoes against the cruiser.

Royal Navy Captain R. D. Oliver, a seasoned veteran of the ocean war, was cautious—and suspicious. Why was a cargo ship sitting idle in the middle of the Atlantic Ocean? Moreover, except for ventilators and a few other parts, the ship fitted the Admiralty's description of one of the masquerading German raiders that had been wreaking havoc on British and neutral ships.

Taking no chances, Oliver stayed out of torpedo range and steamed back and forth. Then he bracketed the *Atlantis* with two salvos, a signal for the ship to identify herself. Captain Rogge promptly radioed a message: His vessel was the *Polyphemus*, of Greek registry.

Oliver was still highly suspicious. He radioed the British commander in the South Atlantic, inquiring if this ship was the genuine *Polyphemus*. For nearly an hour, the *Atlantis* sat gently rolling in the swell while Rogge tried to string out the radio discussion with the *Devonshire*, hoping the U-boat could get into torpedo range. However, the senior officer on the submarine, instead of having the U-boat maneuver into position to fire his torpedoes, clung closely to the *Atlantis*.

Within an hour, Captain Oliver received an answer from the South Atlantic commander: This was not the real *Polyphemus*. Three minutes later, *Devonshire*'s eight-inch guns barked. When a few shells struck and critically damaged the disguised vessel, Captain Rogge ordered time charges to be set and the crew to abandon ship.

Twenty minutes later, as Rogge and his crew members watched from lifeboats, the *Atlantis* began to go under. Holding his Scotch terrier Ferry beside him, Rogge stood up and saluted as the ship disappeared into the deep.

In the meantime, the *Devonshire*, following strict standing orders from the Admiralty, sailed out of sight. She could not stop to pick up survivors because of the quite real risk of being torpedoed by a U-boat as she sat in the water.

Bernhard Rogge took inventory and found that 7 crewmen had been killed by the *Devonshire's* guns. The remaining 340 were in lifeboats, swimming about or clinging to pieces of wreckage. The U-boat surfaced and took below perhaps 20 wounded men, and 52 others were given life belts and blankets and huddled on the submarine's deck.

Six lifeboats crammed with 200 survivors were connected to the U-boat, which headed for Germany, some 2,000 miles away. Twice each day, a dinghy from the U-boat made a visit to the boats with a hot meal. Three days after the *Atlantis* sank, the U-boat was met by the submarine supply ship *Python*, and the survivors were taken aboard. Within forty-eight hours the *Python* was blasted from the water by the British cruiser *Dorsetshire*, and Rogge and his men were again floating around aimlessly in lifeboats.

Five weeks after the *Atlantis* met her doom, the survivors finally went ashore at St. Nazaire, France, from German and Italian submarines. Arriving in Berlin just after New Year's Day 1942, Bernhard Rogge was given a hero's reception and promoted to rear admiral.[7]

Nazi Spies in the U.S. Capitol

ALL THROUGH THE FIRST HALF OF 1940, George Sylvester Viereck had been dashing between his plush Fifth Avenue apartment in New York City and the hallowed halls of Congress in Washington, D.C. Despite the capital's notorious sweltering summers, Viereck began commuting twice weekly during June. His Abwehr contact in Washington had handed him an urgent mission: Prevent a huge weapons bill to help rearm the United States from passing Congress. Viereck was a clever Nazi spy.

In Berlin, Abwehr chief Admiral Wilhelm Canaris, who spoke with a trace of a lisp, had described the United States as being "one of our key targets" in the cloak-and-dagger agency's worldwide operations.

"The U.S.A. is a sleeping giant and must be regarded as the decisive factor if it enters the war," the spymaster declared. "The capacity of its industrial power is such as to assure victory, not merely for the U.S.A. itself, but for England and any other country with which it may be associated." Everything possible had to be done to keep the United States from building up its woefully weak military, the admiral stressed.

Each waking moment, Canaris was playing a dual role: Adolf Hitler's trusted spymaster, and a leader in the Schwarze Kapelle conspiracy to eliminate the führer.

George Viereck was born in Munich, Germany, in 1884 and came to the United States in 1901. Glib, crafty, and energetic, he may have been the world's highest-paid propagandist. Each month he was pocketing $500 (equivalent to about $5,000 in 1999) from Dr. Otto Kiep, the Nazi consul general in New

York. But that "fee" was peanuts compared to the additional $1,750 per month he was being paid by a New York "publicity firm" under contract to the German Tourist Bureau.

As U.S. correspondent for a Munich newspaper, *Munchner Nauests Nachrichten*, whose editor was Dr. Giselher Wirsing, a confidant of Nazi propaganda chief Josef Goebbels, Viereck was paid the $500 per month. Wirsing was especially interested in having his correspondent probe into U.S. plans to expand its armed forces. And the Nazi propaganda agency in the United States, which was operating under the cover name German Library Information, located at 17 Battery Place, New York City, slipped Viereck yet another $500 monthly.

Viereck's machination to sabotage the impending arms bill would be a semipublic secret mission. He set up his propaganda mill in the Capitol suite of Senator Ernest Lundeen, a devout isolationist from Minnesota. Although the lawmaker was reputed to have contacts in Nazi Germany and made speeches to German-American groups, he apparently knew Viereck only as a freelance journalist and considered him to be a consummate publicist and speechwriter.

Viereck was totally at ease working in the suite of a U.S. senator. Neither he nor Lundeen made an effort to conceal the fact that they were collaborating to keep the United States out of the war in Europe and to halt heavy congressional spending for weapons and for aiding besieged Great Britain militarily.

Viereck dictated speech drafts to Phyllis Spielman, a secretary to Lundeen, and he would break off his delivery on occasion to telephone the German embassy in Washington for needed information. A short time later, a messenger would arrive with an envelope bearing the return address of Dr. Hans Thomsen, the chargé d'affaires—and master spy—at the embassy.

Hundreds of thousands of reprints of Senator Lundeen's Senate-floor "keep out of the war" speeches, reprints of anti-Roosevelt and antiwar editorials, transcripts of keep-America-neutral radio broadcasts, newspaper and magazine clippings, and anything else with an isolationist theme were put in the mails by Viereck—all at the expense of the U.S. taxpayers. Included in the bulk mailings were articles that Viereck himself had authored under a phony name, then connived to get published.

Soon it became clear that Senator Lundeen's suite had a serious flaw: Its mailing facilities were inadequate for the millions of reprints Viereck wanted to send out. So arrangements were made for the bulk mailing to be done in Room 1424 of the House Office Building. Room 1424 was the suite of Representative Hamilton Fish, who had known Viereck for several years and, like Lundeen, was a strident isolationist.

Fish, a New York legislator, introduced Viereck to forty-five-year-old George Hill, a mild-mannered clerk in the congressman's office. A thin, nervous man with a trace of a mustache, Hill was told by his boss that Viereck wanted to send out reprints of Lundeen's speeches and for Hill to use Fish's frank (free mailing privilege) and the mailing list of the National Committee to Keep America Out of Foreign Wars—whose chairman was Hamilton Fish.

TRANSLATION

Munchner Neueste Nachrichten   Munich.
Office of the Editor-in-Chief   Sendlingerstr.80

C O N T R A C T

between the Chief Editorial Department of the
Munchner Neueste Nachrichten, Munich,

and

GEORGE SYLVESTER VIERECK,
305 Riverside Drive, New York.

the following Agreement has been concluded today:

1). Mr. Viereck assumes the representation of the Munchner
Neueste Nachrichten for the United States of North America.
He obligates himself in accordance with the General instructions of the Editor-in-Chief of the Munchner Neueste Nachrichten to furnish reports on the general situation, digests
of the press, etc. as well as material for publication at
regular intervals. Mr. Viereck will furnish at least once
a week the above mentioned digests from the press. He will
write, at least once a month, one article of a political or
economic nature, for publication in the Munchner Neueste
Nachrichten.

2). The Munchner Neueste Nachrichten compensate Mr.Viereck at
once with the sum of $2000. (read two thousand dollars) and
will attend to the transfer of this sum to New York. These
$2000. represent traveling expenses and salary for the months
of August and September, 1939. Beginning with October, 1939,
Mr. Viereck will receive a monthly compensation of $500. -
(read five hundred dollars) for the above mentioned services.

3). It is expressly understood by both contracting parties that
in case the transfer of dollars to the United States, owing
to the general condition of exchange, should not be possible,
either with beginning of October 1939, or at any later date,
this contract becomes null and void without further formality.

4). Special expenses for trips will be dealt with and regulated
in accordance with mutual agreement.

5). No more oral agreements beyond this contract exist between
the two parties and have no validity.

Munich, July 30,1939.   (signed) Dr. G. Wirsing, Editor-in-Chief
                                                  Munchner Neueste Nachrichten
(signed) George Sylvester Viereck

George Sylvester Viereck's cover for espionage activities in the United States. Translated copy of his contract with the Münchner Neueste Nachrichten *(Munich newspaper) controlled by Josef Goebbels. (Author's collection)*

Hill was apprehensive. Use taxpayers' money to send out massive amounts of what he called politically motivated propaganda? But an order was an order. The first mailing was to 125,000 names on a list to receive the keep-out-of-the-war speech that Viereck had written and Lundeen had delivered on the Senate and House of Representatives floor. Hill had to hire an extra crew of women to get the job done on time.

When the mailing task was completed, Viereck covertly slipped two rolled-up fifty-dollar bills into Hill's hand and gave the jittery clerk a sly wink. From that point, unpretentious George Hill, a hapless, confused family man, was trapped by Dame Fate in a high-stakes game of espionage poker. He would be sucked deeper and deeper into Viereck's high-powered Capitol propaganda mill.

At Viereck's instigation, Hill and Lundeen got most of the material to be mailed inserted in the *Congressional Record,* a daily compendium of every word spoken and action taken on the Senate and House of Representatives floor. This ploy permitted Hill to get hundreds of thousands of free reprints from the U.S. Government Printing Office.

Hill arranged for U.S. postal trucks to be used to haul tons of keep-America-neutral mailings to the Washington post office. Not only was Congressman Fish's franking privilege used, but also those of twenty-four other isolationist members of Congress who were allegedly collaborating in the propaganda project or who were Viereck's dupes.

Despite the vigorous efforts of George Viereck, the world's highest-paid propaganda virtuoso, his U.S.-taxpayer-sponsored campaign ended in defeat. Congress, aware that Adolf Hitler had conquered most of the western part of Europe and was now threatening to engulf militarily weak England, passed the armaments bill by a narrow margin.

Dispensing Nazi propaganda was a perfectly legal method for a U.S. citizen to make money—provided he or she told the federal government everything he was doing and who was paying him to do it. However, based on information collected by the FBI, a New York City grand jury concluded that Viereck had suffered a convenient loss of memory in failing to disclose the hefty fees he was receiving from numerous German sources. So he was indicted on five counts.

Viereck, who had gotten rich tooting a Nazi trumpet in the adopted homeland that had been so good to him, soon was occupying a cell in a federal prison. A jury had found that operating a propaganda mill for Adolf Hitler in the U.S. Capitol was not a legitimate activity for an American "author and journalist." Viereck would serve a term of two to five years.

At about the same time Viereck was being tried, a jury in another Washington courtroom returned a guilty verdict against frail, introverted George Hill, who had been doing Viereck's bidding. Hill, a pitiful figure, received a sentence of two to six years.[8]

Two Tiny Tots Escape to England

JUNE 20, 1940, was a lovely, warm day in France—and one of the blackest in that nation's long history. In a railway car in a clearing in Compiègne Forest north of Paris, German dictator Adolf Hitler and his military chiefs looked on with gloating satisfaction as French officials signed a document of surrender. It had taken the mighty Wehrmacht only six weeks to crush the vaunted French Army.

The surrender terms called for German troops to occupy more than half of France, including the entire Atlantic coastline in the West. The remaining roughly one-third of France, in the South, would have a puppet French government, headed by eighty-four-year-old Marshal Henri Philippe Pétain, a legendary symbol of French glory whose body but not whose mind had survived World War I.

Soon the seeds of isolated instances of defiance began to spring up among the French people. The acts were spontaneous. A family would hide a British, French, or Belgian soldier trying to make his way to neutral Spain and then on to England. In the crowded Paris Métro (subway), pregnant women refused seats offered by German soldiers. Nazi propaganda posters were ripped from walls almost within minutes after they were put up.

In the movie houses, the audiences applauded loudly when German newsreels showed the British perpetrating "atrocities." Under pain of arrest, the French were forbidden to boo or hiss scenes of German soldiers performing "humane tasks." And so those episodes were greeted by a sudden epidemic of loud coughing and clearing of throats to blot out the film's narrator's voice.

With each tiny success, the French people grew bolder, and a measure of self-respect was restored. An organized resistance movement began to mushroom in France. One of those growing increasingly rebellious was Jean Marc Saladin, a slight boy of thirteen who lived with his parents in Brittany, on the English Channel coast.

Despite his tender years, Jean Marc committed petty sabotage almost daily, letting the air out of the tires or soaping the windows of German vehicles. Along with other boys, he strewed nails and broken bottles on roads taken by German convoys. They especially enjoyed giving the wrong directions to convoy officers, knowing that the action would cause long delays.

Jean Marc served as a courier for messages between underground cells, and he regularly distributed defiant leaflets and pamphlets printed clandestinely in basements by the resistants. But the boy wanted to do even more to damage the hated Boches (a derogatory term for the Germans). From broadcasts over BBC Radio in London, he learned about Frenchmen escaping to England to join the Free French forces and continue the fight against the Nazis. So he and a ten-year-old friend planned to flee to London.

The tiny tots had available an eighteen-foot sailboat belonging to Jean Marc's father, who knew nothing about his son's scheme. The crossing alone could be hazardous; Channel tides are tricky, and sudden storms could churn up huge waves and swamp the small vessel. Moreover, the trek from Brittany to England would be about 150 miles, and the only navigating device the boys had was a primitive compass that could go haywire without warning.

Little by little, the conspirators stocked the boat under the noses of the Germans. Then one day when the wind, moon, and current were favorable for crossing the English Channel, Jean Marc left a note on the bed of his parents, who were out of town. It explained that at all costs he and his younger friend had to join the Free French forces in England.

Jean Marc had to be especially careful—eight German soldiers had been assigned to live in the first floor of the Saladin home. At 11:00 P.M. he climbed out an upstairs window, stole silently across the lawn, and scaled the wall adjoining the road. At the bottom of a sharp, grassy incline was the Channel, and the sailboat was hidden along the shore.

On the far side of the wall, Jean Marc made contact with his ten-year-old comrade, and they slipped back onto the Saladin grounds to steal some gasoline from the Germans. Suddenly they froze when they heard a rushing noise. It turned out to be a tarpaulin that had slid to the ground from the cans of gasoline.

Each boy grabbed a can of fuel, and as fast as possible they headed down the embankment to the boat. Just as they reached the craft, they heard heavy footsteps in the darkness. One or more of the Germans were after them, they were convinced. Holding their breaths, the boys flung themselves to the ground. Two Germans, who clearly had been heavily imbibing in town and were returning to the Saladin home, wobbled past only six feet from the prostrate boys.

Minutes later, the youngsters pulled the sailboat out from its place of concealment in thick brush, poured the stolen German gasoline into the engine's tank, and let the current carry them into the English Channel. When they were out of sound range, they started the engine and set a course for England. Five miles offshore and beyond sight on a moonless night, they hoisted sail.

Eventually the boys reached England and made contact with officers of the Free French forces. Although they were assigned to worthwhile tasks, the youngsters were disappointed that they were not handed guns and put into a combat unit.[9]

The War's Dumbest Spy

A BRIGHT SUN WAS BEAMING DOWN on Berlin, on the morning of June 22, 1940, when the Abwehr head, Rear Admiral Wilhelm Canaris, strolled into the cavernous office of General Alfred Jodl, the principal strategic adviser to Adolf Hitler. Field commanders frowned on the astute Bavarian Jodl as a desk soldier, but the führer saw no need for his top staff officers to visit the front.

Jodl handed Canaris a directive for a major intelligence operation against the British Isles and neighboring Eire to pave the way for a looming invasion by the Wehrmacht.

Canaris had been in the espionage business for most of his adult life. In World War I he had been one of Kaiser Wilhelm's most successful spies, and since being appointed by the führer to be his intelligence chief in early 1935, the white-haired admiral had built a global espionage apparatus.

Canaris had personal traits that many persons considered to be peculiar at best. No matter where the master spy traveled, at home or abroad in recent years, it had been his habit to telephone his headquarters in Berlin daily to inquire into the state of health of his two beloved dachshunds. An aide would give him a detailed briefing on the dogs' eating habits and bodily functions. When the animals were ill, the admiral plunged into depression.

At Abwehr headquarters an ambitious officer's chances for promotion would forever be squashed if Canaris even heard a rumor that he had spoken disparagingly about dogs. Consequently the building at 72–76 Tirpitz Ufer was crammed with outspoken dog-lovers.

Now General Jodl began bombarding Canaris with probing questions: "How many agents do you have in England?" The admiral began to fidget. He could not afford to disclose a shocking situation: Within hours of Great Britain's declaration of war on September 3, 1939, agents of MI-5, the counterespionage agency, and Scotland Yard men had begun fanning out over the British Isles in a mammoth roundup of German spies.

The British spybusters had been faced with a daunting task. Canaris had 256 agents in Great Britain, many of whom had been deeply under cover for several years. Nearly all, if not all, of the Abwehr spies had been rounded up, however, along with hundreds of others suspected of spying for Adolf Hitler.

Canaris, a quick thinker, immediately lied to Jodl that the Abwehr had spies planted throughout the British Isles. He told in glowing terms of the valuable work being done there by this nonexistent agent or that one.

Jodl seemed pleased. But what was needed, he explained, were several brand-new espionage networks in the British Isles to furnish the Wehrmacht with "hot" intelligence on the spot.

"Sea Lion [code name for the invasion] may take place as early as September 15," Jodl stated. "Your target date is August 15 to have your new spies at their stations. Can you do that?"

"Undoubtedly," Canaris lied.

Fuming, the Abwehr chief stomped out of the Oberkommando der Wehrmacht headquarters. Jodl's order, reflecting Hitler's wishes, had been an absurd one. Although the admiral would make an effort to comply, it would take many months, perhaps years, to establish new espionage networks. He had been given thirty days to get the job done.

Canaris gave the task of creating new espionage networks in England and neutral Eire (the ancient Gaelic name for Ireland) to his station chief at Hamburg, Captain Herbert Wichmann. Under great pressure to produce results,

Wichmann rounded up fifteen low-grade agents, none overburdened with brains, and with only cursory training infiltrated them by parachute and submarine into England. Only one could speak English. All were quickly caught.

Wichmann's effort to establish a new intelligence presence in Eire began with the infiltration of Ernst Weber-Drohl, an aging circus performer who had appeared throughout Europe for thirty-five years as "Atlas the Iron Giant" and "The World's Strongest Man."

Weber-Drohl, who had performed in Eire many times, stole ashore at night from a submarine. He had been instructed to start a chiropractic practice as a cover. In the meantime, he set out to locate his Irish "relatives"—two illegitimate children by a mistress three decades earlier. Hopefully they would help him to meld into Irish life.

While in search of his "relatives," he was arrested by Irish police as a vagrant. Fined a small amount, he was released when he promised to obey the law and get a job.

Eventually he found his two children, whom he had never seen, but they refused to have anything to do with him. Broke, fearful of being apprehended and charged with being a spy, Weber-Drohl contacted authorities at the British embassy, identified himself, and, to avoid being jailed, agreed to work against Germany as a "turned" spy.

At the same time, Hermann Goertz, a Hamburg lawyer with impeccable manners, was also preparing to be a spy in Eire. The seeming quality of Goertz reassured Canaris. Scion of a distinguished Hanseatic family of Lübeck, he was reared by an English governess of culture and influence.

After noncombat service in World War I, Goertz married an admiral's daughter and tried for several years to make a go of it as a lawyer. He was a flop. His Abwehr dossier, however, described him as a man with high agent potential. So Canaris had no way of knowing that Goertz would soon establish himself as the war's dumbest, and unluckiest, spy.

Twice He-111 bombers carrying Goertz developed engine trouble and had to turn back to their base. On the third effort, he parachuted into the blackness, landing in a remote pasture. Wearing the heavy flight overall of a Luftwaffe officer and carrying a mixed bag of forged military identity papers, his misfortunes began at once.

Goertz was unable to locate a second parachute that brought down a container with his kit, including a radio and a spade. So he could not bury his parachute as instructed because of the missing spade. He set off cross-country. After walking only a mile, he made an alarming discovery: He was not in Eire, but in Ulster (later called Northern Ireland), seventy miles from where he was supposed to be, a safe house in Dublin. Soon the batteries in his flashlight gave out, and he had to stumble across the rough terrain, taking repeated pratfalls. He could not risk walking on roads.

Goertz hiked through the countryside for four days. Although he was wearing a Luftwaffe uniform and high boots, the numerous natives he passed in the daylight did not seem to find it unusual that this stranger was traipsing across the landscape. Had any locals called the police, Goertz's true identity would be clear: Without the knowledge of his Abwehr controllers in Hamburg, he was carrying his medals from World War I.

When he came to the swift-flowing Boyne River, he found that soldiers were guarding the bridges. So he plunged into the water and began swimming. Halfway across he became convinced that he was going to drown because the weight of his uniform caused him to be nearly exhausted.

Lying on the far bank and gasping for breath, Goertz found that the swim had cost him the loss of his secret ink, which he was to use to send intelligence reports back to Hamburg. The vial holding the liquid had been sewn into the shoulder padding of his overall. The solution was washed out by the waters of the Boyne.

Hungry, tired, and fearful of discovery, Goertz took off his uniform and hid it by the road, planning to return and retrieve it. Then he put on some old clothes found in a barn and continued his trek, a black beret perched on his head.

Although Goertz was carrying a hefty sum of British and U.S. currency provided him by the Abwehr, he did not know that British money was readily accepted in Ireland. So he marched twenty hours a day and ate nothing.

Eventually, the German lawyer, his feet blistered, his body weary, his stomach pleading for sustenance, took refuge in a villa in Dublin, the home of thirty-eight-year-old Stephen Held, a wealthy factory owner. Held had been designated as Goertz's contact. There Goertz met Stephen Hayes, who was a top leader in the Irish Republican Army (IRA), a bitter foe of Great Britain.

A few days after Hayes's visit, four IRA men wearing masks bolted into the Held villa and stole all of Goertz's money at gunpoint.

Sixteen days after the spy's arrival in Ireland, the police raided Stephen Held's villa at midnight and took him into custody. Hearing the racket, Goertz scrambled out the back door and over a high garden wall, leaving behind most of what remained of his espionage paraphernalia.

Goertz submerged himself in the large city of Dublin as the Irish police searched for him. A bounty was put on his head, and posters appeared throughout the region. Somehow the German evaded capture for a year and a half, but then an informant tripped him up and he was arrested.

Apparently giving up hope that anything good would ever happen to him and fearful of his future, he used the only bit of espionage paraphernalia that he retained, biting into a cyanide capsule. Within minutes, he was dead.

This act was the only facet of Hermann Goertz's spying career that he hadn't botched.[10]

Global Celebrity a Secret Agent

Two old friends were talking. It was the summer of 1940, after France had fallen. Nöel Coward, the internationally famed British actor, playwright, and composer for the stage and motion pictures, was pleading with Prime Minister Winston Churchill to let him join an intelligence service.

"No, no," Churchill replied, jabbing the air with his lighted cigar for emphasis. "You're far too well known to be a spy."

Coward responded, "But Winston, that's the whole point. I'll be so well known nobody will think I'm doing anything special."

Churchill kept shaking his head and emphasizing that a face known around the world could never make a spy. Finally, Coward wore down the British Bulldog's resistance, and the global celebrity was launched into the murky, often lethal field of secret intelligence. He would be a real-life spy.

During the past ten years, Coward had become known for his sparkling dialogue in such sophisticated stage comedies as *Hay Fever, Private Lives, Tonight at 8:30,* and *Blithe Spirit.* His best-known songs were "I'll See You Again" and "Someday I'll Find You." His exceptional skills in acting and singing were limited mainly to the leading roles in his own stage plays.

Coward traveled around the world, in South America (a hotbed of Nazi spies), Asia, and what was left of unoccupied Europe. He sang his songs and charmed his hosts. His disguise, he would say, was his reputation as a bit of an idiot.

When it was suggested that Coward send back reports by invisible ink, he quickly shot down that scheme: "I can't even read my own writing when it's visible!"

Global celebrity Nöel Coward was a British spy. (Author's collection)

Just as Coward had insisted to Churchill, his show business celebrity status did indeed provide him with remarkable cover and direct contact with influential figures in neutral countries, few of which were truly neutral. He shrewdly reported back to his British controllers the opinions of these top foreign leaders and the political climate among the people of their countries, and deftly planted fake rumors as part of a global mosaic of misinformation.[11]

A POW's Wife Unlocks a Code

WHILE ADOLF HITLER and his generals were rapidly rearming Germany and drawing up plans for widespread conquest in Europe, they had anticipated a need for a special camp, known as a *Sonderlager*, to hold highly important prisoners and those who habitually tried to escape from regular places of incarceration. Subsequently, four-hundred-year-old Colditz Castle, perched on a steep hill overlooking the Mulde River in east-central Germany, was selected.

Designated *Oflag IVC*, an abbreviation of *Offizierlager* (officers' place of detention), Colditz was a towering structure, six stories high, beautiful, majestic, and yet forbidding. The outside walls were seven feet thick. The massive castle was a maze of concealed staircases and intercommunicating doors, of hidden passageways and hundreds of rooms, nooks, and crannies. Major redesign work was rushed through to make the castle escapeproof.

In mid-1940, after Hitler's Blitzkrieg had conquered much of western Europe, prisoners started arriving at Colditz. They were told by the *Kommandant*: "You cannot escape. *Sie beissen hier auf Granit!*" (Here you will bite into granite!)

Intended to hold two hundred POWs, the inmate population—Britons, Poles, Dutch, Belgian, and French—soon far exceeded that number. Early on, many became restless and began hatching schemes to escape the brooding castle, although once outside the walls it would be four hundred miles in any direction to reach the frontiers of the Third Reich.

Two of the leaders in the British contingent, Captain P. R. Reid and Captain Rupert Barry, concluded that no significant number of escapes could be successful without clandestine help from the War Office (the nerve center of the British armed forces) in London.

Pooling their ideas, Reid and Barry concocted a simple code that could be used in a seemingly innocent letter from a prisoner to a loved one in England. Rupert sent a coded letter to his wife, Dodo, a highly intelligent young woman who could solve the complicated *Times of London* crossword puzzle while sipping her morning tea.

Dodo's first reaction was that her husband had taken leave of his senses from being locked up in Colditz. He wrote about their having been at places she never heard of and asked her to say hello to cherished relatives who were unknown to her.

On second thought, maybe he was trying to communicate with her by means of a code woven into his letter. So before the day was over, she had deciphered the message he was trying to put across. Dodo was told: "Go to the War Office, ask them to send forged Swedish diplomatic papers for Reid, Howe, Allan, Lockwood, Elliott, Wardle, Milne, and self."

Early the next morning, Dodo rushed to the War Office and told an officer seated at a desk at the main door that she had an important message for someone in military intelligence. She was presented with a form to fill out in which she was asked a long series of questions, including what topic she wanted to discuss.

Dodo pitched the paper back on the desk, declaring angrily that what she had to talk about was highly secret. A strident argument erupted when it became obvious that she was not going to be allowed into the building. While the shouting was taking place, another officer happened to walk past and she explained her situation to him. Could he help?

This officer happened to be in military intelligence, and he escorted her to his office. After perusing the letter from Captain Barry and hearing her decipher the message, the officer gave her instructions. She was to write back to her husband in plain language (knowing that the German officers would inspect the letter) and tell him that she had met Rupert's elderly aunt, Christine Silverman, who had not seen him in years. Aunt Christine was deeply saddened to learn that her nephew was a POW in Germany and she would write soon, Dodo was told to state.

Two weeks later, Captain Barry received a letter from "Aunt Christine," and he and P. R. Reid were able to unscramble its simple code. They were crushed by the message: "The War Office considered the use of Swedish diplomatic papers to be too dangerous."

Undaunted, Barry fired back another coded letter to his wife, who took it to her contact in military intelligence. "We will consider the danger and not the War Office," her husband declared. "Would you please expedite request?"

Barry and Reid found that they were butting their heads against an immovable object: the bureaucracy in the War Office. The Swedish diplomatic papers were never sent, but communication had been established between Colditz and the War Office, thanks to Dodo's astuteness.

In a few days, a coded letter from Dodo (written under the direction of the War Office) informed her husband that she was sending him some parcels (through the Red Cross network). The innocent-looking packages arrived in two weeks. Along with a few items of clothing, one parcel contained six handkerchiefs, each with a different-colored border. A coded message told the POW captain to place the one with a green border in a bucket of hot water, stir for several minutes, take out, read the message that appeared in secret ink, then destroy.

Ancient, towering, "escapeproof" Colditz Castle. (Author's collection)

The handkerchief gave instructions for the use of two complicated codes. These were to replace Barry's primitive code, which, the War Office was convinced, the Germans would eventually detect.

These new codes were considered by the War Office to be unbreakable, so the Colditz POWs could ask for anything they wished. Soon items for escape kits were flowing into the castle, concealed in private parcels. The entire scenario was being orchestrated by ingenious minds in MI-9, the escape and evasion service in London.

MI-9 also sent Colditz detailed information about German activities on frontiers, sentry positions, railroad timetables, Gestapo tactics, and food-ration stamps. MI-9 obtained a detailed architect's blueprint of Colditz Castle, floor by floor, and this crucial intelligence was sent via the magic-handkerchief technique.

Relentlessly, cat-and-mouse games were played at Colditz. The intransigent POWs pitted their courage and ingenuity against the alertness of the German guards. In attempts to gain freedom, the prisoners sewed fake German uniforms, memorized train routes to Switzerland, scrambled over high walls, dug through yards of rock, scaled battlements, communicated with London by secret code and hidden radios, and forged tools.

Efforts to escape ranged from simple bluffs to sophisticated disguises. Because of the efficiency of MI-9 in London, almost every officer at Colditz had a compass, detailed maps, and a quantity of genuine German money. Many were equipped with fake but realistic identity papers and other documents that would be required once an escapee got outside the castle walls.

These crucial documents were created in a top-secret counterfeiting operation conducted by MI-9 in London. It may well have been the world's largest and most sophisticated specialty print shop, with a skilled staff of engravers, artists, retouchers, and offset cameramen.

Producing documentation that would pass sharp-eyed Gestapo agents and German police required painstaking research. To obtain current information from within the Third Reich, MI-9 operatives closely questioned German prisoners of war, especially those who had just returned to the front after a leave at home. Who issued a certain document? When and where was it likely to be checked? What did each rubber-stamped entry mean?

Fake documents required seemingly piddling nuances. A finished document could be too perfect, so it had to have trifling mistakes. Photographs on identity cards had to be "aged." Genuine German money could not be new, so thousands of Reichmarks were poured on the floor of a room in the print shop and the technicians walked back and forth on the currency for many days until the paper was realistically worn.

Meanwhile, at Colditz Castle, Hauptmann (Captain) Reinhold Eggers, the security officer, was showing symptoms of tattered nerves. He wrote in his diary:

> The prisoners, the British and French in particular, are doing all they can to get me out of camp by making life unbearable for me. They have reason enough—I discovered the church tunnel and their attempts to get out under the stage. I discovered one of their radios.

Over a period of five years, 130 prisoners managed to escape from Colditz. But of those, only 32 hit home runs, as the POWs called evading death or recapture to cross the frontiers of the Third Reich to a safe haven and eventual return to their homelands. Among those hitting home runs was Captain P. R. Reid, who, along with Captain Rupert Barry, had concocted the simple code that had triggered the mass of escapes.[12]

Canada's Covert "Luxury Fleet"

EARLY IN JULY 1941, British intelligence learned, probably through Ultra intercepts, that the Germans were preparing to make a bold move. They would land troops and establish bases on two islands off the coast of Canada and in the Gulf of St. Lawrence. The huge gulf becomes a river that carries large ships hundreds of miles inland through the cities of Québec and Montréal and on to Lake Ontario.

If the Nazis succeeded in this scheme, more than three thousand miles from their closest naval bases in western France, they might succeed in blow-

*Canada's secret "luxury fleet" guarded the Gulf of
St. Lawrence from German U-boats and surface raiders.*

ing up key facilities along the St. Lawrence that would block passage for long
periods of time or create other mischief damaging to the Canadian war effort.

Already hard-pressed, the Royal Canadian Navy did not have the ships to
patrol the Gulf of St. Lawrence and its approaches, as German intelligence
knew. However, U-boat commanders were perplexed by the sudden expansion
in the number of Canadian vessels patrolling around the strategic gulf. Even
when a U-boat torpedoed and sank the *Raccoon*, a Canadian navy vessel guarding the gulf, German intelligence did not realize that it had the key to the secret
in its hands.

Actually, the *Raccoon* was a converted American luxury yacht, one of the
fourteen similar oceangoing vessels that had suddenly become part of Canada's
coastal defense system.

A few weeks earlier, in Washington, President Franklin D. Roosevelt had
been briefed on the German threat to the Gulf of St. Lawrence region. Because
the United States was still technically neutral, Roosevelt turned a blind eye to
a machination hatched to strengthen Canada's navy.

The fourteen yachts had been "requisitioned" from their American owners, then turned over to Canadian civilians, who, in turn, "sold" them to the government. In this way, the United States had not provided direct aid to a belligerent.

On reaching Canada, the yachts were denuded of their luxury trappings, which were replaced by communications equipment and submarine-detection gear. This restructuring permitted the "luxury fleet" to summon genuine warships whenever a U-boat or German surface raider was discovered.

Throughout the war, the Canadian luxury fleet continued to expand. Canadian Navy officers, dressed in civilian clothes and masquerading as wealthy businessmen, visited marinas in the United States to pick out suitable ocean-going yachts to augment their fleet.

No more was heard about German plans for installing bases in the Gulf of St. Lawrence region.[13]

One Airplane Infuriates the Führer

BY MID-1940 ADOLF HITLER, through the skillful and ruthless employment of his mighty war machine, had in less than a year planted the swastika across an enormous swath of western Europe. German territory stretched all the way from the northern tip of Norway southward to the Pyrenees Mountains on the Spanish-French frontier.

Despite his colossal conquests, one tiny airplane infuriated the führer. Twice each week, this aircraft operated between Leuchars in Scotland and Stockholm in neutral Sweden. The plane carried not only secret documents in a diplomatic bag for the British embassy in the Swedish capital, but also British propaganda materials—films, magazines, and newspapers—for use against the Third Reich in Sweden.

What enraged Hitler was the insolence of this lone British aircraft crisscrossing the skies above *his* Norway on the direct route between Scotland and Sweden. In response to the führer's demands, the Luftwaffe scrambled planes in an effort to intercept and shoot down the pesky aircraft. But its efforts were in vain, much to the embarrassment of the Luftwaffe's pompous leader, Field Marshal Hermann Goering.

After the Luftwaffe failure, Admiral Wilhelm Canaris, the Abwehr chief, received orders to destroy the courier plane. Canaris and his top aides were not enthused. The aircraft, along with the other materials, was bringing British newspapers to Sweden, where they were purchased by German undercover agents and rushed to Berlin. These publications were a prime source of information for the Abwehr.

Canaris knew that the aircraft was carrying German newspapers back to Britain on each trip, but he felt the exchange was more beneficial to Germany than it was to England. So when Hitler kept demanding action, Canaris, to appease him, ordered the Abwehr's top agent in Stockholm to sabotage the plane when it was parked at the airport just outside the city.

This official order had been sent through routine command channels, and a copy of it was sent to the führer's headquarters. At the same time, Canaris rushed a trusted aide to Stockholm with instructions that the official order to sabotage the British plane not be carried out.

"The Abwehr, unlike [Reinhard] Heydrich's Sicherheitsdienst [the SS intelligence service], is not a murder organization," the admiral declared. He stressed that he was against the murder of innocent passengers if a bomb were concealed in the aircraft.

Canaris's sabotage of the sabotage did not last long. Soon Hitler's anger at the British plane evolved into an obsession, so Major General Erwin von Lahousen, head of the Abwehr's Abteilung II, the sabotage division, was forced to prepare a plan of action.

Lahousen selected an Abwehr agent (code-named Citadel) to travel from Germany to Stockholm to blow up the airplane. A twenty-two-year-old Brazilian-born agent was assigned as an assistant. The operational plan, worked out in a Hamburg dockside pub, the Medropole Bodega, called for the two saboteurs to be issued fake Dutch passports, in which they were described as seamen.

Then Citadel and the Brazilian contacted two Finns—a sea captain and his first mate. Although natives of a neutral nation, both were Nazi sympathizers. The Finns agreed to hide explosives on their coaster, and the pair of saboteurs signed on as crewmen.

The small ship edged through the Kiel Canal in northern Germany and sailed into the Baltic Sea. As soon as the coaster docked in Stockholm, its skipper told Swedish port authorities that the ship had engine trouble and that he estimated it would take ten days to fix it. Citadel had felt that would be sufficient time to sabotage the British plane.

While repair work was feigned, Citadel was told by a local Abwehr agent that the targeted aircraft had arrived. That night, Citadel and the Brazilian reconnoitered the airport and saw the plane sitting on the tarmac behind a heavy barbed-wire fence.

On the following night, the two young men, wearing dark clothing and with faces blackened, were driven to the vicinity of the airport. They carried pistols, wire cutters, and a time bomb. They decided to approach the field from behind a hangar, knowing that the British plane was parked on the other side.

Stealthily they skirted the hangar, then lay down and began slithering ahead. One agent poked his head around the corner of the hangar and saw the plane with its British markings only fifty yards away. Six floodlights bathed it in iridescence, and a squad of Swedish soldiers armed with automatic weapons stood guard.

Quietly, the two saboteurs retreated from the airfield and returned to the Finnish coaster. Clearly, blowing up the tightly guarded British aircraft would require far more than two men. The engines of the coaster underwent an astonishingly rapid repair, and the next day the ship sailed for Hamburg.

Adolf Hitler soon was involved with directing what had turned into a global war, and the pesky British plane no longer was an obsession with him. The courier aircraft would continue its flights over German-occupied Norway without hindrance for the remainder of the conflict.

In his eagerness to destroy a lone British plane, the führer apparently had not realized that if the sabotage had been successful, Britain would merely have replaced it with another plane and continued the trips between Scotland and Stockholm.[14]

Part Three

Thrusts and Counterthrusts

A Cunning Forgery Pays Off

ALTHOUGH THE UNITED STATES PUBLIC was eager to keep out of the war raging in Europe, when British Prime Minister Winston Churchill suggested that Great Britain be permitted to establish in the United States a center for clandestine operations throughout the Western Hemisphere, President Roosevelt agreed. The whole affair was kept so hush-hush that not even the U.S. State Department was let in on the secret.

Adopting the innocuous title British Security Coordination (BSC), the agency's head, William Stephenson, quickly set up his command post at a most unlikely place: the thirty-fifth and thirty-sixth floors of the International Building in Rockefeller Center in New York City in mid-1940.

Stephenson, a wealthy Canadian industrialist, possessed a stout heart, enormous drive, and a keen and devious mind. His organization mushroomed rapidly to major proportions, and the headquarters staff alone would eventually number more than one thousand persons.

A year after Stephenson launched the covert operation, both U.S. and British intelligence agencies became increasingly concerned about widespread German infiltration of Brazil, where the government had become dangerously generous in helping Nazi operations against the United States. Stephenson and his key aides decided that the best solution to the problem would be to plant fake documents to cause the president of Brazil to withdraw from his cozy relationship with Adolf Hitler.

The fraudulent letter would have to be a flawless masterpiece, both in its written words, the typewriter involved, and the paper stock. Brazilian experts could be counted on to inspect the document with a microscope — literally — to assess its authenticity.

Stephenson flashed a coded message to the British secret intelligence chief in Brazil:

> We propose to convey to the Brazilian government a letter purporting to be written by someone in authority in Italy to an executive in Brazil. Purpose is to compromise the Italian transatlantic air services

which provide safe passage for enemy agents, intelligence documents and strategic materials. We would welcome details and specimen Head Office letter of the LATI airline.

Now the BSC secret agents sprang into action. In Italy, a letter was stolen from Aurelio Liotta, president of the airline. It provided a specimen of his handwriting. Twenty-four hours later, a courier delivered the precious item to Stephenson in New York.

A follow-up radio message from Rio de Janeiro suggested to Stephenson that the forged letter should be addressed to Commandante Vicenzo Coppola, the airline's regional manager in Brazil (and also a top agent for the Italian secret service).

Within a few weeks, the fake letter was in production. The paper stock was that normally found only in Europe (stolen there by BSC operatives). The engraved letterhead of the Linea Aereo Transcontineali Italiane (LATI airline) was reproduced by the BSC's expert counterfeiters. An Italian typewriter with type imperfections that precisely duplicated the old one used in Rome by the head of LATI had been painstakingly constructed.

The fraudulent letter to Coppola was "signed" by LATI's president. It said, in part:

Thank you for your letter and the report enclosed. . . . I discussed your report immediately with our friends. . . . It made me feel proud. . . . There can be no doubt the "little fat man" is falling into the pocket of the Americans, and that only violent action on the part of the "green gentlemen" can save [Brazil]. I understand such action has been arranged for by our respected collaborators in Berlin.

The clever forgery conveyed the impression that an Italian and German plot was under way against Brazilian President Getúlio Vargas, the "little fat man." The "green gentlemen" referred to a notorious gang that had been trying to oust the Vargas regime.

A final insult was cunningly created in the last line of the fake letter:

The Brazilians may be, as you said, a "nation of monkeys," but they are monkeys who will dance for anyone who can pull a string!

Microfilm copies of the letter were smuggled into Rio and blowups leaked to members of Vargas's clique. The president was furious. He promptly canceled LATI's landing rights and ordered the arrest of Commandante Vicenzo Coppola, who was caught on his way to Argentina with the equivalent of a million dollars that he had just embezzled from LATI bank accounts.

Bill Stephenson's machination had paid off handsomely. President Vargas was so enraged at the Italians (and their partners the Germans) that Brazil moved silently into the Allied camp.[1]

Shopping for U.S. Secrets

IN FRANCE, ENGLAND, AND ELSEWHERE in the late 1930s and early 1940s, Nazi spies often had to risk their lives or freedom and pay thousands of dollars to acquire specifications of new military airplanes for a Germany preparing for war. But most data of this type could be acquired in the United States for the expenditure of a few cents, merely by buying a newspaper or a trade magazine.

There also was convenient over-the-counter espionage in the United States. A trip to the U.S. Government Printing Office in Washington could yield confidential information at a cost of less than a dollar. Many of the U.S. Army's and Navy's training, equipment, and weapons manuals were offered for sale—no questions asked.

Often a Nazi spy in America did not even have to leave his home or office. For the cost of a three-cent postage stamp, he could usually obtain highly important technical information. One Nazi agent who relied on the U.S. postal system to generate a flow of classified American industrial data was Edmund Carl Heine, a thirty-thousand-dollar-per year (a hefty sum at the time) executive with the Ford Motor Company.

Highly educated, well bred, and a flashy dresser, Heine had been an executive with Ford since 1920, in Spain, South America, and Germany. At the latter job, he became friends with Dr. Ferdinand Porsche, an automotive designer who had developed the Volkswagen (People's Car) and who was a freelance agent for the Abwehr, Germany's secret service.

Porsche and Heine became good friends, and they held numerous conversations at plush cocktail lounges in Berlin. The German, appealing to Heine's "patriotism" (he had been born in Germany), convinced the Ford executive that he should find an excuse to return to the United States, arrange to be given a post in Detroit, and collect information "not normally available" about the American automobile and aviation industries.

Soon Heine was taking training at Klopstock Pension, the Abwehr's secret espionage school in a multistory building near police headquarters in Hamburg. He had no way of knowing that the führer always called this facility the Academy, or that the German dictator checked regularly on the number of spies and saboteurs produced there.

Indeed, it was operated much like an academy. The place to which Heine was sent to learn the tricks of the spy business was much like a college classroom. The instructors, who used aliases, sat at a desk on a raised platform, and there were blackboards behind them.

Heine glanced around and saw that there were about thirty recruits in his class, mainly males over thirty years of age, with a sprinkling of women. He and the other students were taught the use of the Leica camera and how to make microfilm, a piece of celluloid about half the size of a postage stamp and used in a camera equipped with a special lens.

When a sheet of ordinary paper measuring eight by ten inches was photographed on microfilm, the tiny piece of film could easily be concealed, even under the tongue. In emergencies the film could even be swallowed and, with luck, retrieved several hours later. At its destination, enlargement equipment could restore the document to its original size. Microfilm was an incredible technological advancement for that era.

Heine and his classmates were taught the time-honored use of invisible inks for sending reports to Germany and to other spies. The most common of these secret liquids was made by dissolving a headache remedy called Pyramidon in alcohol. Each ingredient could be purchased routinely over the counter at drugstores almost anywhere in the developed world.

The academy students learned how to use codes (simple ones, in most cases), and sophisticated techniques for using explosives and deadly poisons. Instructors explained how to operate a special radio transmitter-receiver, the Agenten-Funk (Afu, for short). Compact and lightweight (thirty pounds), the Afu fitted easily in a small suitcase, and spies could readily carry it about without arousing suspicion.

Heine breezed through the espionage course and was told that he was to receive a captain's commission in the Luftwaffe Reserve. Returning to the United States in early 1940, he was unable to coerce Ford management to assign him to Detroit, so he resigned, accepted a high-paying job with Chrysler, and launched his career as a spy.

Although Heine had absorbed the clever techniques of a modern-day spy in Hamburg, he chose to do his work without leaving his upscale Detroit home at 4447 Baldwin Avenue. For ten cents he purchased a copy of *Popular Aviation* magazine and spotted an advertisement of the Consolidated Aircraft Corporation in San Diego. A huge defense contractor, Consolidated boasted in its ad that it had taken only nine months to conceive and fly a new airplane. It did not identify the aircraft, presumably because such information was kept secret by the U.S. military.

Searching his fertile mind, Heine concocted a scheme to obtain the missing ingredient—the type of airplane involved. On July 22, 1940, he wrote a letter to Consolidated, using the official letterhead and envelope of Chrysler Corporation. He gave his home address for a reply. His letter said:

> In order to settle a few disputes among a number of friends, would
> you kindly answer the following question: Was it the B-24 [a four-

engine bomber] that was conceived and made its first flight in only nine months?

In San Diego, it was clear that Norman Davidson, the public relations chief at Consolidated, and other executives were quite proud of their company's exceptional achievement. Davidson fired back a reply to the inquisitive Chrysler executive: Yes, indeed, it was the B-24.

Like most other defense contractors in the United States, Consolidated's security was virtually nonexistent. Although a war was raging in Europe and the United States was steadily being sucked into the conflict, most federal government leaders, army and navy generals and admirals, and executives running huge defense plants virtually ignored the quite real possibility that scores of German and Japanese spies were roaming about the nation unmolested, as indeed was the case.

Airplane plants, mostly on the West Coast, were especially vulnerable to enemy espionage. To test the security of Consolidated Aircraft, in San Diego, a captain in U.S. Naval Intelligence dressed two of his German-speaking officers

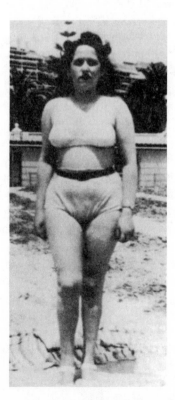

Lilly Stein. Her Manhattan apartment served as a letter drop for Nazi spies to send reports to Germany.

in civilian clothes and sent them to Consolidated. Much to their surprise, the two sleuths got inside easily by merely strolling past a bored watchman.

For nearly three hours, the two navy officers wandered around the plant without being stopped or questioned. From time to time, they would halt, point to a new-design warplane being assembled or to a crucial piece of sophisticated machinery, and confer animatedly—in German.

Hearing of his disguised sleuths' adventure, their boss, the navy captain, went personally to call on Ruben Fleet, head of Consolidated Aircraft, urging him to beef up his guard force and issue identification tags with facial photographs to everyone in the plant—including Fleet.

Fleet was unimpressed. "But Captain, we have no spy problem at Consolidated," he declared. At the time, Fleet had no inkling that the Abwehr, a year earlier, had planted two agents in the factory, and that the firm's secrets had been flowing to Hamburg and Berlin almost weekly.

In the meantime, back in Detroit, Edmund Heine was euphoric to receive the highly confidential letter from Norman Davidson, the PR man at Consolidated. Within days, the information on the new U.S. Army bomber (which would be a mainstay workhorse in the coming war) was in the hands of Lilly Stein, a dark-haired young woman who described herself as a "model."

Stein, an Austrian by birth, also had "graduated" from the Abwehr academy at Hamburg, and she was sent to New York City in the spring of 1939. In her pocketbook were a few hundred dollars, a secret code designed just for her, and a microfilm of instructions concealed in the bottom of a box of face powder.

Lilly was awed by New York, its hustle and bustle, towering buildings, and innate hostility. As instructed in Hamburg, she rented an apartment at 232 East 79th Street, which served as a letter drop for Nazi spies. When she received secret information, such as that from Edmund Heine in Detroit, Lilly mailed it to an innocent-sounding address in Hamburg, one that had been provided to her by Abwehr controllers.

Meanwhile, Heine was still digging out data that would be of value to his mentors in the Third Reich. Again, his business was conducted from his home. He placed an advertisement in *Popular Aviation*, stating that he was an airplane enthusiast and would pay twenty dollars for information on the latest developments in the industry.

Perhaps Heine himself was surprised by the results. A flood of replies poured in, some of them providing significant data from knowledgeable sources. The Nazi agent spent another three cents to thank the contributors by mail and to send each a twenty-dollar bill.

Abwehr officers in Hamburg were delighted with the results of their Detroit agent's espionage efforts. Clearly he must be dashing relentlessly around the United States, at considerable risk, to collect such a wealth of intelligence.[2]

A Scientist on a Covert Mission

AT THE SAME TIME as the Battle of Britain was raging and the outcome remained in doubt, Henry Tizard, scientific adviser to the British chief of air staff, slipped quietly into Washington. Known as Tizard the Wizard in the Royal Air Force, he had been sent to the United States on a secret mission by Prime Minister Winston Churchill after the British had learned through Ultra of Hitler's plan to invade England.

On August 10, 1940, the Wizard checked into the Shoreham Hotel, and bellhops made several trips to lug upstairs his many suitcases, cardboard boxes, crates, and a black metal box. Inside these containers were many of Britain's most secret scientific documents, including countless papers created by the British Uranium Committee while developing a theory for a revolutionary device that would be known as an atomic bomb.

There were research documents, blueprints, and models of amazing new accoutrements of war that either had been developed by the British or that were being researched: radar, jet engines, chemical weapons. The "magic black box" was a cavity magnetron, which generated shortwave-length electronic beams that made possible the cenimetric radar that was small enough to fit into destroyers and airplanes. The device was eventually manufactured in the United States in large numbers and was instrumental in turning the tide in the U-boat war in the Atlantic.

Soon after the Wizard had settled into his Shoreham suite, he telephoned William Stephenson, the multimillionaire Canadian World War I fighter-pilot ace, former amateur boxing champion, and now the "director of British security coordination in the United States." His job was to coordinate antisubversive efforts with FBI Director J. Edgar Hoover.

Stephenson hurried to the Shoreham and was flabbergasted by the huge amounts of assorted containers, piled to the ceiling. He was shocked to hear the Wizard remark in an offhand tone, "An officer of the FBI has just telephoned and said he wants to see me to make arrangements to place my cargo in secure hands."

The Wizard, a brilliant scientist, was a novice in the world of espionage. Stephenson suspected immediately that the caller was a fake, probably an Abwehr agent working under a fictitious diplomatic title out of the German embassy, a hotbed of intrigue.

Stephenson promptly telephoned J. Edgar Hoover, who said he knew nothing about any call to the Wizard, adding that he would drive to the Shoreham immediately. From the hotel suite, Hoover placed a series of telephone calls to FBI officials, and none knew about the situation.

As a security measure, Stephenson obtained a number of men of the Royal Canadian Mounted Police to protect the Wizard and his priceless cargo.

Back in his office in the Department of Justice Building the next morning, Hoover had his technicians check the tapes of the routinely monitored telephone calls going out of the German embassy. As the sleuth suspected, the call to the Wizard had been made by someone in the embassy who spoke with a decided American accent.[3]

"Black Propaganda" Warriors

IN THEIR BARRACKS, COMMAND POSTS, AND BUILDINGS in northern France, men of the triumphant Wehrmacht, waiting for the signal to cross the English Channel and invade Great Britain, idled away the time by tuning their radio dials to London's BBC to hear a German-speaking voice broadcast the latest war news. Unbeknownst to the *Feldgrau* (field gray, the average German soldier), the voice was that of thirty-five-year-old Sefton Delmer, who had spent several years in Germany, where his Australian father had lectured at the University of Berlin.

Delmer also played popular German ballads, including "Lili Marlene," and threw in tidbits of gossip and the latest rumors from the Third Reich. Portraying himself as a German who had become disillusioned with the Nazi regime, he sought to taunt and subvert the Feldgrau, to weaken their morale.

Delmer's broadcasts were a component of the "black propaganda" campaign conceived and orchestrated by Britain's Political Warfare Executive (PWE), a clandestine group that operated out of Bush House in London and at Woburn Abbey in the English countryside. PWE's mission was to "approach the German mind . . . and throw it off guard by appealing to the selfish motives in the [soldier and civilian]."

Sefton Delmer's scripts were carefully created to make certain that the subtle mix of true events, fiction, and rumor was credible to the German listeners.

Before the war, Delmer had been head of the Berlin bureau of the *London Daily Express*, and he had interviewed such Nazi giants as Hitler, Goering, Himmler, and Goebbels.

Speaking as fluently as any Berliner, his chats on BBC were designed to make the German soldiers fearful of taking part in the looming invasion of England. "The barbaric British have developed a fiendish apparatus with which they are going to set the English Channel ablaze as soon as your assault boats near the beaches," Delmer said.

To a degree, that disclosure was true. British scientists had created an anti-invasion defense whereby oil would be piped to large containers offshore. When ignited, a thick barrier of fire and smoke would rise from the water. However, this ingenious apparatus would not halt an all-out amphibious assault, because it was installed on only a few potential landing beaches.

A closely guarded secret. If Germans tried to invade England in 1940, the British would unleash a wall of flame just offshore. Above is a postwar demonstration. (National Archives)

Then Delmer informed the Germans in France that he would teach them a few useful English phrases.

"For your first lesson," he said, "We will take *Kanalüberfahrt*—the Chan-nel cross-ing . . . the Chan-nel cross-ing.

"Now, repeat after me: *Das Boot sinkt* . . . *Das Boot sinkt* . . . the boat is sink-ing . . . the boat is sink-ing.

"*Das Wasser ist sehr kalt* . . . the wat-er is ver-y cold.

"Here is a verb that will be most useful. Please repeat after me: *Ich brenne* . . . I burn . . . *Du brennst* . . . you burn . . . *wir brennen* . . . we burn.

"And now I suggest that you learn another important phrase: *Der SS Sturmführer brennst auch ganz schoen* . . . the SS cap-tain is al-so burn-ing quite nice-ly."

The theme of the Germans burning to a crisp on the English Channel was tied in with information planted by British deception services, using turned spies and whispers in neutral embassies in London, Madrid, Stockholm, and Geneva.[4]

A Trojan Horse Hoax

REICHSMARSCHALL HERMANN GOERING, the most pompous of the Nazi bigwigs, anticipated with great relish the crucial task handed to him by Adolf Hitler: Wipe out the Royal Air Force Fighter Command before German armies deployed along the English Channel invaded Great Britain in a massive operation code-named Sea Lion.

Goering had long planned for this mission. His own intelligence service, Abteilung, had collected a mountain of photographs and detailed data on nearly every city and major target in the British Isles. This information was obtained covertly during the previous three years, 1937 to 1939, when German "civilian" planes had crisscrossed Britain, purportedly gaining weather reports for the Third Reich's civilian airline, Lufthansa. Actually, the scout planes had been on photographic missions for the Target Data Unit Information Department of the Air Ministry in Berlin.

August 13, 1940, was Adler Tag (Eagle Day). At dawn, thousands of airmen began climbing into Junkers, Dorniers, Heinkels, Stukas, and Messerschmitts—3,358 warplanes in all—at scores of airfields in France, Belgium, Denmark, the Netherlands, and Norway. Soon the craft were speeding down runways and heading for designated targets on the far side of the Channel.

All across southern England, RAF pilots leaped into their Spitfires and Hurricanes and soared skyward to meet the challenge against heavy odds. These fighter pilots were a breed apart—brash, scrappy, courageous—the elite. The stakes were heavy: survival of the British Empire.

By mid-September the Battle of Britain (as Winston Churchill labeled it) had been raging for a month. Ultra had provided the Royal Air Force Fighter Command headquarters in Middlesex with the Luftwaffe targets, permitting tactical officers to gather their fighter squadrons at the right places, at the right times, and at the right altitudes.

Despite this colossal tactical advantage, the RAF lost 461 fighter planes, 103 pilots were killed, and 128 were seriously wounded. In one ten-night period, the Luftwaffe lost 214 fighters and 138 bombers, but could more easily absorb those losses, being much larger than the RAF.

The scales had turned against the RAF Fighter Command, whose remaining pilots were near exhaustion from a seemingly endless series of fierce, murderous clashes that raged over southern England and the Channel ports. There was deep anxiety in official British circles. A few more weeks of this carnage in the sky and Goering might make good on his boast of bringing Britain to her knees with airpower alone.

In this hour of peril, the British turned to a ploy as old as warfare: decoy targets. The task of rapidly creating dummy facilities to draw off at least a portion of the bombs was handed to Colonel John F. Turner, an officer of exceptional ingenuity.

Turner first focused on RAF airfields that were being bombed at night. He had two rows of parallel flares set in open country about two miles from each airfield. The flares were to simulate emergency airstrips. German airmen, it was hoped, would conclude that the British planes were using these improved fields because their regular bases nearby had been knocked out by heavy bombings.

It was a desperation measure. Would it work? Few in the RAF held out much hope. But German night bombers were attracted to the flames of the flares as moths to candles. As ground antiaircraft shells exploded around them, the Heinkels and Dorniers plastered the fake strips with bombs.

In the days and nights ahead, while countless dogfights were raging in the sky, Colonel Turner and his men raced about southern England, expanding their Trojan horse hoax. The flares on dummy emergency landing strips were replaced by dim electric bulbs called Q lights.

Near major airfields, the decoy strips were provided with taxi aprons and phony recognition beacons. At night, when the Luftwaffe was overhead, salvaged automobile headlights mounted on wheels were dragged up and down the fake airfields, conveying the impression that RAF planes had turned on their lights to land.

Within a few weeks there were scores of these dummy airfields scattered throughout southern England, causing Luftwaffe bombardiers to drop thousands of bombs on open fields, explosives that otherwise could have wreaked havoc on genuine RAF bases.

The camouflage, or *ruse de guerre*, was expected to be unmasked eventually. But the important thing was to cause delay, confusion, and a waste of German bombs.

A camouflage-in-reverse project was successful on occasion. Dim lights were placed on a fake strip, and the nearby real airfield was lighted to where its glow could be seen for many miles. The Germans took the bait—and plastered the dummy field with bombs.

A novel creation of British camoufleurs and royal engineers was fake bomb damage on genuine airports. This scheme was intended to discourage a second Luftwaffe attack. The day after a night bombing, the Germans sent reconnaissance planes to take photographs. When the photos were developed, they disclosed that large numbers of bombs had hit the runways and hangars.

Actually, in many instances, the RAF fields had suffered little or no damage. So as soon as the night raiders had departed, camouflage crews began distributing around the targeted field large piles of debris that had been collected for that purpose. On occasion, old rubber tires were placed about the airfield and set on fire the morning after the raid. German reconnaissance pilots would report that the airfield was still burning from the night's bombing.

Adding to the "carnage" that greeted the eyes of Luftwaffe photo interpreters were the blackened skeletons of Spitfire and Hurricane fighter planes, ones that had crashed in southern England, were beyond repair, and had been collected by camouflage teams. After an airfield had been attacked at night, the hulks were rushed to the site and placed about the runways.

If a British airfield had suffered the heavy damage camoufleurs wished to convey to the Germans, it would have bomb craters. So artists and designers, many from Britain's movie colony, painted crater likenesses on hundreds of large pieces of canvas. After the Luftwaffe had paid a night visit to a real RAF field, a number of these painted craters would be fastened to runways. From the air and in photos, they looked so realistic that on occasion a passing British pilot would report to his base intelligence that a certain field had been bombed so heavily that it was useless.

In a few days, German recon photos would show that the craters had been repaired—meaning the camoufleurs had removed the pieces of canvas.

Goering failed in his all-out effort to crush the RAF, forcing Hitler to cancel Operation Sea Lion, the invasion of England.[5]

The *Bulldog* Bites the German Navy

IN THE AUTUMN OF 1940, Great Britain alone stood between the United States and Adolf Hitler's seemingly invincible war juggernaut, the mightiest that history had known. Highly alarmed, President Franklin D. Roosevelt ordered the army and the navy to beef up their forces, and he declared America to be the "arsenal of democracy."

Using heavy arm-twisting, the president ramrodded through Congress a program known as Lend-Lease—a technique for providing the accoutrements of war to Great Britain for only token payment. The United States was now "neutral" against Nazi Germany.

In March 1941, airplanes, tanks, trucks, small arms, and munitions began flowing in large ship convoys across the North Atlantic to Great Britain, an action that deeply concerned Adolf Hitler and his advisers in Berlin. The führer was furious. He ordered the Kriegsmarine to launch a massive submarine offensive in the Atlantic to cut off Great Britain from her main source of supply.

Soon the U-boats were taking a colossal toll on British and neutral-country ships. Prime Minister Winston Churchill recognized this ominous threat to Britain's survival. To focus attention on the death struggle, he proclaimed to the world that "the Battle of the Atlantic has begun."

Ever since Great Britain had gone to war against Germany on September 3, 1939, the lords of the Admiralty had been hoping to capture intact a U-boat and collect its supersecret Enigma, an encoding machine twenty-four inches square and eighteen inches high, enclosed in a wooden box. It had been adopted for use throughout the Wehrmacht, even on U-boats and small ships.

The führer was not concerned about an Enigma falling into British hands because it could produce an almost infinite number of ciphers merely by changing the keying procedure. So the possession of an Enigma would not permit an enemy to read encoded wireless traffic — or so the Nazi High Command thought.

Unknown to German intelligence, the British had created an ingenious device (code-named Ultra) that intercepted and decoded Enigma messages. However, for some mysterious reason, Ultra failed to function adequately against the German Navy's Enigma.

On May 7, 1941, Kapitänleutnant Fritz Lemp, skipper of the *U-110*, picked up the signals of a British convoy of thirty-eight vessels carrying a wide variety of goods to the United States. Like a shark smelling blood, the *U-110*, one of the newest and most technologically advanced submarines, attacked the convoy and claimed two sinkings.

Lemp, a bold skipper, continued to stalk the convoy. Two days later, off the coast of the large island of Greenland, *U-110* torpedoes scored two more hits.

Lemp's curiosity would be his undoing. Instead of diving and racing out of harm's way, he kept the submarine at periscope depth to watch the two British ships go down. His scope was sighted by lookouts on the warship *Escort*, which launched a pattern of ten depth charges into the area.

In less than a minute the *U-110* rose to the surface, and destroyers and corvettes began raking it with shellfire. Aboard his destroyer *Bulldog*, Commander John Baker-Cresswell was preparing to ram the U-boat when he was startled by the sight that greeted his eyes: the German crew began leaping into the ocean.

Thunderstruck by the potential for striking a damaging blow against the deadly U-boat campaign, Baker-Cresswell sent a party to board the *U-110*, whose officers and crewmen were being fished out of the water by other ships. The boarders were amazed to find that Lemp had made no effort to destroy the Enigma, nor its operating instructions, manuals, keying tables, and a large stack of messages that had been sent and received.

Using the Royal Navy's highest-grade code, Commander Baker-Cresswell informed the Admiralty that the *Bulldog* had pulled off a seemingly impossible task — capturing a U-boat intact. He was ordered to take the submarine in tow and head for Iceland, the large, bleak island some two hundred miles east of Greenland.

Three days after its capture, the *U-110* began taking on water fast, and it became clear to Baker-Cresswell that it would not make an Icelandic port. A few hours later, at dusk, the sleek vessel, pride of the Kriegsmarine, reared its bow high into the air, slipped the towline, and sank.

The *Bulldog*'s crew were dejected: their prize was resting on the bottom of the Atlantic. However, Baker-Cresswell, with the knowledge of only a handful of trusted officers pledged to secrecy, had safely hidden on the *Bulldog* the Enigma and its secret papers.

The Enigma machine. The Germans thought its code was unbreakable. (Author's collection)

A deception plan was hatched to keep Adolf Hitler and his commanders from knowing about the Enigma seizure. When the *Bulldog* returned to her base at Scapa Flow, the vast anchorage of the Home Fleet in the Orkney Islands of northeastern Scotland, her battle pennant was flying to trumpet the fact that she had sunk—not *captured*—a U-boat. Code experts and intelligence officers were on hand to take charge of the priceless booty—the Enigma and its papers.

John Baker-Cresswell and several of his officers and crew received decorations for their ship's *sinking* a German submarine. But tight security kept word of the capture from leaking out. It would be twenty-six years before the British government allowed the public to learn of the *Bulldog's* feat.

Enormous operational advantages for the Royal Navy began to accrue almost immediately. Because of the Enigma and secret papers seized in the *U-110*, when combined with intelligence gained earlier from other sources by Ultra, the Admiralty was able to locate the cruising areas of nearly all sea elements of the Etappendienst. A supersecret organization, the Etappendienst had a number of large, fast, and modern supply ships to sustain the warships, surface raiders, and submarines that were marauding the oceans in search of merchantmen carrying materials to Britain.

Armed with the crucial intelligence, Royal Navy cruisers and destroyers were dispatched to the designated locales and gained dramatic results. Between June 4 and 23, 1941, British warships sank, captured, or caused the crews to scuttle ten Etappendienst supply vessels.

Although the Battle of the Atlantic was far from over, the destruction of the Etappendienst fleet was a major turning point in the ocean war.[6]

Keeno, King of the Robots

AL D. BLAKE was hardly Hollywood's version of an espionage agent. Prior to World War I, he had spent four years in the U.S. Navy, and on his release, he obtained a tiny role in Charlie Chaplin's movie *Shoulder Arms*. While engaged with the production of the film, Blake became friends with Chaplin's chauffeur, Toraichi Kono.

When the filming was concluded, Blake and Kono went their separate ways. Blake became a vaudeville performer with a unique act. Known as Keeno, King of the Robots, he had been credited with setting a world record by standing motionless for one hour and twenty-seven minutes. Curiously, perhaps, people paid money to see the act involving absolutely nothing.

Early in 1941, the King of the Robots was out of work, flat broke, desperate, and in Los Angeles. By chance, he met up with his old friend from twenty-one years earlier, Toraichi Kono, who introduced Blake to his boss, a man in his early thirties named Yamato.

Yamato operated a string of whorehouses in southern California and presumably had a hefty bank account. So, trying to impress the entrepreneur, Blake boasted that he had a good friend in the U.S. Navy who could provide him with secret information.

Yamato was impressed. Much to Blake's surprise, Yamato offered Blake the fabulous sum (at the time) of five thousand dollars if he could obtain secret information on the U.S. Navy at the Los Angeles and San Diego bases.

Actually, Yamato was an alias. He was Lieutenant Commander Itaru Tachibana, and the brothel chain was a front for his true mission: spying for Japanese intelligence in Tokyo.

Blake soon realized that his boasting about his connections in the U.S. Navy had triggered Tachibana's cash offer, which would be larger than the combined income of the King of the Robots during the previous three years. However, Tachibana demanded a sample of the type of intelligence that Blake could provide before handing over the five thousand dollars.

Knowing that he had plunged into deep water, Blake went to the Federal Bureau of Investigation office in Los Angeles and told of "Yamato's" heavy cash offer. Moreover, he admitted that he had no friend in the navy, and he agreed to cooperate in any investigation of Tachibana. The FBI then notified the Los Angeles office of naval intelligence, which cabled the headquarters of Admiral Husband E. Kimmel, commander in chief in the Pacific, at Pearl Harbor, Hawaii.

Promoted to his present post ahead of thirty-two admirals in February 1941, Kimmel was deeply concerned about the Hawaii command setup, and he so informed the chief of naval operations, Admiral Harold R. Stark, in Washington. A divided command in which the army was responsible for defense of the island of Oahu and the navy with the defense of the Pearl Harbor naval base could lead to a disaster, Kimmel declared.

On learning of the "Yamato" incident, Lieutenant Commander Edwin T. Layton, Kimmel's chief intelligence officer, urged the admiral to permit him to launch a widespread undercover operation to trap "Yamato" and other spies and, at the same time, to mislead the Japanese high command. Kimmel was enthused and gave Layton the go sign.

Ed Layton had a broad background in intelligence work, spoke Japanese fluently, and had been the officer in charge of the Japanese translation section of the cryptoanalytic unit of navy communications, the secret group charged with cracking Japanese codes.

Plunging into the new challenge with typical alacrity, Layton created a ruse that featured Al Blake as the centerpiece. It was arranged for Blake to write a nonexistent "pal," who was given the phony name of "Paul Mitchell" and who was supposed to be stationed on the battleship *Pennsylvania.*

"We can make a heap of dough if you cooperate," Blake stated in his contrived letter, mailed from Los Angeles.

In Honolulu, one of Layton's operatives posed as "Mitchell," and he wrote back on *Pennsylvania* stationery, telling how fed up he was with the navy. Moreover, "Mitchell" complained, he was desperately in need of money, adding that he was eager to see his old pal Al and hear the details about how he could make "a heap of dough."

Back in Los Angeles, Blake rushed to see Commander Tachibana, who was so impressed with the "Mitchell" letter that he gave the American a good-sized amount of cash and booked passage for him on the *President Garfield,* which sailed for Honolulu on April 25, 1941.

In the meantime, Commander Layton and his intelligence officers prepared for Blake's arrival. When Blake strolled down the gangplank and hailed a taxi, it was driven by a naval agent. The driver went to the Alexander Young Hotel, where the clerk seemed to be assigning a guest room at random. Actually, the room had been reserved and the premises bugged.

Layton also had a cover for Blake and a cover for the cover. If Japanese agents tailed him, U.S. naval intelligence would have a tail on the tail. Knowing that the Japanese would be watching Blake's every move, he and his phony pal "Paul Mitchell" (a navy agent) made the rounds of Honolulu nightclubs and scenic locales for ten days; then the onetime "motionless man" climbed aboard another liner and headed back to the United States. In his possession was a large batch of secret documents on the Pacific Fleet, all conceived in the fertile mind of Willard A. "Bill" Kitts Jr., the staff gunnery officer. The data and drawings were close enough to the truth to seem to be accurate, but they would be useless to Japanese intelligence.

Within hours after Blake reached the mainland, he turned over the "purloined" documents to Commander Tachibana, who was delighted. Within twenty-four hours he boarded a train and carried the precious data to the Japanese embassy in Washington. There the military attaché was so happy with the documents that he ordered Tachibana to send Blake back to Hawaii on a second secret mission.

Meanwhile, Bill Kitts and others doctored more bait for Blake. Twenty-four hours after Blake's arrival in Honolulu, Layton received a telephone call from the Office of Naval Intelligence (ONI) informing Layton that Blake had blown his cover. By happenstance, he had met an old girlfriend from his vaudeville days, and after wining and dining her, the couple went to his room.

Between amorous sessions, Blake bragged about being a spy for the United States. Bugs recorded the entire episode.

Ed Layton was furious. He sent an aide into Honolulu to bring Blake to the naval base at once. There Layton scolded him with every choice word in his vocabulary, informing Blake that his Hawaiian vacation was finished and that he was going to be sent back home immediately. The intelligence chief made it quite clear that if Blake caused any further difficulties, Layton was going to have the woman's husband notified.

At the same time, one of Layton's officers called on her at her home outside of Honolulu. If she didn't remain stone silent about what Blake had told her in the hotel, her husband would be given a recording of the activities in the bedroom.

Despite his indiscretions and blabbing to his old girlfriend, Blake was given a second bundle of doctored documents, which he took back to Los Angeles and handed over to Itaru Tachibana, who had just added another whorehouse to his chain. Tachibana presumably gave the phony papers to his immediate boss, Commander Hideki Nagasawa, the Los Angeles representative of the naval attaché at the Japanese embassy in Washington.

Within hours, FBI agents, who had long been surveilling Tachibana, swooped down and arrested him and seized all his belongings, including thousands of documents. Three of the navy's crack Japanese translators were rushed to Los Angeles to study the papers.

Tachibana's arrest apparently created an enormous flap within the Japanese espionage network scattered throughout the United States. That fact came to light when code breakers in Washington intercepted an urgent message from the Japanese consul in Los Angeles, asking for the princely sum (at that time) of twenty-five thousand dollars to "subsidize" (i.e., bribe) Al Blake "in view of the fact that he might give evidence unsatisfactory to Tachibana."

Presumably the Japanese spymasters had not deduced that Blake had been a double agent.

Among Tachibana's effects was a bulging suitcase that was the property of another Japanese spy working on the West Coast, Lieutenant Commander Sadatomo Okada, whom U.S. naval intelligence and the FBI had long suspected was engaged in espionage activities.

Okada's suitcase held a gold mine of data relating to national defense in the Pacific Northwest, including antiaircraft batteries, production at the huge Boeing airplane plant in Seattle, extensive information on ships being built and others to be constructed, timetables for the arrival and departure of warships, identity and size of troop units, and aerial views of army and navy bases.

The FBI and U.S. naval intelligence had scored a coup. The abundant espionage data would have been of such enormous value to the Japanese war machine that Secretary of the Navy Frank Knox insisted that Tachibana, Okada, and a third Japanese agent, named Yamada, be charged with conspiracy to violate U.S. espionage laws.

Incredibly, diplomats in the State Department in Washington got into the act, and they succeeded in having the serious charges against the three master spies reduced to the equivalent of misdemeanors. Smiling and affable, Itaru Tachibana left the United States in style: a squad of FBI agents escorted him to the gangplank of the liner *Nitta Maru*, which was bound for Tokyo.

Arriving in Tokyo on or about July 1, 1941, Tachibana was promptly assigned to the Third Section (intelligence), where his experience and unique talents supervised and analyzed the flood of information pouring in from spies in the Pearl Harbor region. When the Japanese sneak attack wiped out much of the U.S. Pacific Fleet five months later, Commander Itaru Tachibana had played an important role in pinpointing targets.[7]

A German POW Makes History

THE WEATHER WAS BITTERLY COLD on the morning of January 24, 1941, when a train carrying several hundred German prisoners of war was chugging through Ontario to a camp on the Canadian shore of Lake Superior. Suddenly, a Luftwaffe fighter pilot, Oberleutnant Franz von Werra, leaped out a window he had managed to open, struck the ground hard, but was able to reach a nearby wood.

After watching the train disappear around a bend, Baron von Werra worked his way southward for twenty-five miles to the broad, icy St. Lawrence

River, where he found a rowboat along the bank and paddled across to Ogdensburg, New York.

Werra felt a flash of exultation. No doubt the government of the neutral United States would provide him with passage back to Germany. Instead, the U.S. Immigration and Naturalization Service arrested him, charging illegal entry. Werra was handed over to the Ogdensburg police, who pitched him into a cold jail cell.

Undaunted by his predicament, the extroverted Luftwaffe pilot called in American reporters and news photographers and held a unique press conference from his cell. He regaled the journalists with fanciful tales of his exploits in the air war in Europe. As one cynical reporter would write: "He gave the impression that he had single-handedly shot down the entire British Air Force—twice."

Werra's boastful recitations achieved the desired results: the fact that he was behind bars in Ogdensburg was plastered on front pages across the United States. A day later, a member of the German consulate in New York City came running, put up a five-thousand-dollar cash bond, and spirited away the escapee.

In New York City, Baron von Werra became an instant celebrity: a dashing Luftwaffe ace, an aristocrat with a title, and the perpetrator of an amazing escape. Reporters sought interviews. He was wined and dined royally by the society elite at such plush nightclubs as Sardi's, El Morocco, and the Diamond Horseshoe.

Later, in March, Werra's celebrity bubble burst. The German consul advised him that the U.S. government was going to hand him over to Canadian authorities on a criminal charge—stealing the twenty-five-dollar rowboat in which he had crossed the St. Lawrence River. Werra was outraged, claiming he did not steal the boat. He had merely borrowed it and left it on the far side.

Moving rapidly, the Luftwaffe pilot, wearing civilian clothes, sneaked aboard a train at New York's Grand Central Station and rode it all the way to the Mexican border at El Paso, Texas. No one had even been suspicious of him. Disguising himself as a Mexican laborer, the pilot slipped across the border and reached Mexico City, where the German embassy arranged transportation for him back to the Third Reich.

In Berlin, the beaming Oberleutnant received a conquering hero's welcome. Adolf Hitler awarded him the Knight's Cross, and Reichsmarschall Hermann Goering, chief of the Luftwaffe, promoted him to *Hauptmann* (captain) and gave him command of a crack fighter squadron.

Franz von Werra had made history of sorts. During the war, some 480,000 German and Italian prisoners would be brought to the United States. Almost every day, one or more of them would manage to flee their camps, but all were recaptured. Only Werra was able to escape and make his way back to Germany.[8]

A Kamikaze Plan Against Pearl Harbor

SEATED AT A DESK in his cabin aboard the battleship *Nagato* anchored in Hiroshima Bay in late January 1941, Admiral Isoroku Yamamoto took pen in hand and began outlining a plan to destroy the U.S. Pacific Fleet at Pearl Harbor. As the commander of Japan's Combined Fleet, he was convinced that a surprise attack on Pearl Harbor would be but the first step in defeating America. Powerful Japanese forces would have to invade California, push across the deserts, mountains, and plains, fighting every foot of the way, and finally capture Washington, D.C., after a bloody battle.

Admiral Yamamoto was the most Westernized of Japanese military leaders. In the early 1920s, as a promising young officer, he was sent to Harvard University, where he learned to speak English fluently, became a poker addict, and amused his American friends with his impromptu acrobatics, such as standing on his head on a chair for nearly a half hour.

After his Harvard graduation, Commander Yamamoto was assigned to Washington as naval attaché (sort of a "legal spy"), and he studied U.S. defenses and ship-building programs. Back in Tokyo in 1934, Yamamoto was promoted to vice admiral, and soon he was recognized as Japan's most brilliant and visionary naval officer.

Now on the *Nagato* in early 1941, Yamamoto envisioned an assault on the U.S. warships with only torpedo planes. However, he was informed by Commander Kosei Maeda, an expert on aerial torpedo warfare, that "unless a technical miracle can be achieved, this type of attack would be altogether impractical."

Maeda explained that the water where the ships would be anchored at Pearl Harbor would be too shallow. A solution might be to fasten parachutes to the torpedoes to keep them from sinking too deeply into the water and lodging in the soft mud below.

Yamamoto frowned. Who ever heard of an aerial torpedo attack by parachute?

Then Yamamoto's concept turned to the more conventional design: attacking Pearl Harbor with carrier-based aircraft. Because he felt that wiping out the U.S. fleet in one fell swoop was crucial to an invasion of California, the admiral toyed with the idea of knowingly sacrificing perhaps 350 of Japan's best pilots to assure success of the surprise attack. This concept was called *katamichi kogeki* (one-way attack).

Yamamoto's idea was to launch the planes off their carrier decks some six hundred miles from Pearl Harbor. Such a long distance from the target would permit the carriers to immediately head for home and be out of harm's way before the Americans could recuperate from the bombing raid.

In the meantime, the Japanese warplanes would knock out the U.S. fleet, then turn back to sea in the direction of the carriers. But the aircraft would run out of fuel and have to crash into the ocean. Theoretically, destroyers and submarines would fish the pilots out of the water; but Japan did not have the huge number of these vessels that would be required—if indeed they could even locate a downed pilot in the immense Pacific.

What Yamamoto was proposing would later in the war be known as a *kamikaze* attack, in which the pilots voluntarily went to their deaths for the greater glory of the Japanese emperor. The admiral would be willing to wipe out the cream of the Imperial Navy pilots in the first few hours of a war with the United States to achieve his goal of eventually capturing Washington, D.C.

Other Japanese Navy officers managed to scuttle Yamamoto's kamikaze plan by pointing out that the carriers must get as close as possible to Pearl Harbor and recover their planes to allow for a follow-up onslaught if necessary to wipe out the remainder of the U.S. Pacific Fleet.[9]

Hijacking Mussolini's Money

FOR MANY YEARS, Richard Eichenlaub and his wife had placidly drawn beer and served wiener schnitzel to customers at the Little Casino Bar at 206 East 85th Street in New York City. This bar had long been the hangout for members of the largest Nazi spy ring in the United States—and in the past year, it had been a haunt for Federal Bureau of Investigation agents in disguise.

Suddenly, on the morning of Saturday, June 29, 1941, Eichenlaub and his wife vanished. Elsewhere in the teeming city and its suburbs, other men and women, most of whom had been Eichenlaub's customers, also disappeared. Seventy-two hours later, J. Edgar Hoover, the dynamic director of the FBI, who could barely conceal his deep satisfaction, told the world that thirty-three Nazi spies had been swept up in a dragnet.

The coordinated sweep by the FBI had been the "greatest spy roundup in U.S. history," Hoover declared. "This is one of the most active and vicious gangs we have ever had to deal with."

All of those arrested—mostly German nationals, some homegrown—were charged with conspiracy to violate U.S. espionage laws. In one fell swoop, Hoover and his G-men had virtually wiped out Adolf Hitler's spy apparatus in the United States.

Hard on the heels of the FBI's massive roundup, President Franklin D. Roosevelt struck another telling blow against Nazi skulduggery in the United States. He ordered German consulates (which had been little more than Abwehr branches) to be closed and their staffs to board the first ship for the

Third Reich. Roosevelt declared: "The [Nazi] consuls general have been engaging in activities wholly outside the scope of their legitimate duties."

In Berlin, the FBI demolition of the Nazi spy network, built up over many years, created an enormous flap. Soon, however, Abwehr Chief Wilhelm Canaris got over his initial shock and began making arrangements to create a vast espionage network in Mexico, from where secret shortwave radio stations could send and receive messages from the United States and Germany.

With bribery of Mexicans, Canaris was able to rapidly build a Nazi undercover operation centering on a major *Aussenstelle* (outpost) in Mexico City.

Using a middle-level diplomatic job in the German legation as a cover, an energetic young German, Joachim A. Hertslet, with a forged passport and identity papers, roamed far and wide to smuggle thousands of tons of fuel out of Mexico on Italian and Japanese ships for the thirsty German war machine.

Hertslet and his vivacious wife gained a wide circle of influential friends by throwing lavish parties in their home in suburban Mexico City. These key contacts were most beneficial in helping Hertslet to establish a string of secret bases in remote regions along the Gulf of Mexico and in the Caribbean at which long-range U-boats could refuel and rearm for attacks on U.S. shipping.

Another high-powered German operative, Heinrich Norte, laid the groundwork for what would become the widespread "Bolivar network" of clandestine shortwave transmitters relaying from Mexico to Germany such perishable intelligence (most obtained from the United States) as convoy routings. This crucial information permitted U-boat wolf packs to ambush convoys.

Presiding over the formidable array of Nazi spies, saboteurs, and couriers in Mexico was Colonel Friedrich Karl von Schleebruegge, an able soldier but a novice in the cloak-and-dagger trade. He had been sent to the significant Mexico City post because he was a relative of Franz von Papen, the German ambassador to Turkey, whose goodwill Wilhelm Canaris cultivated.

Schleebruegge soon established himself as a first-class bungler, but his key agents performed brilliantly because they knew their business and ignored their boss's ideas and instructions.

The outpost in Mexico City was among the costliest the Abwehr operated. Schleebruegge needed much money to pay hundreds of agents in the United States and in Central and South America. When it appeared that the entire Mexican-based apparatus would go out of business because of bankruptcy, Berlin finally moved to help.

Wilhelm Canaris knew that Italian dictator Benito Mussolini had established a slush fund of nearly $4 million (equivalent to some $40 million in 1999) in U.S. banks under the names of fake corporations to finance espionage and propaganda in the nation. Because the Italian secret service had done virtually nothing in the United States, Canaris rushed to Rome and coerced Mussolini into "lending" the money to the Abwehr to fund covert operations in Mexico.

A scheme was hatched to get the money to the Aussenstelle in Mexico City. Two Italian consuls and an embassy secretary withdrew the funds and put the currency in sacrosanct diplomatic pouches. Two of the Italians would carry about $2.5 million to Rio de Janeiro, from where it would be smuggled into Mexico. The remaining $1.5 million would be taken by train directly to Mexico City.

Unbeknownst to the three Italians, suspicious bank executives, noting the large lump sum that had been withdrawn, reported the episode to J. Edgar Hoover, the FBI chief. He was powerless to interfere legally because Italy and the United States had a "correct" relationship.

Any action Hoover took, such as putting a tail on the Italian diplomats who had picked up the money, would have to be done "unofficially," on the grounds that the funds might be used for subversive activities.

President Roosevelt was advised of the Italians' actions, and he turned a blind eye to whatever countermeasures might be taken. However, his legal adviser informed Hoover that if the Italians moved the funds physically into Mexico, they could be confiscated once they crossed the border.

Consequently, the FBI boss contacted William Stephenson, head of British Security Coordination (BSC), the New York City post whose mission was collecting information on German activities in the Western Hemisphere and taking appropriate countermeasures. Stephenson promptly got in touch with one of his top agents in Mexico who had a close relationship with an important Mexican police official. A reception was arranged for the Italian courier as soon as he reached Mexican soil with the money.

Tailed by two FBI agents, the three Italians took a train to Brownsville, Texas. There they separated. The two consuls headed for New Orleans to board a ship for Brazil. The embassy secretary continued on into Mexico, where he was approached by a stranger.

Flashing a badge, the man identified himself as an agent of the Mexican secret service. He grabbed the diplomatic pouch, then spun on his heel and disappeared, leaving the young secretary badly shaken.

The furious German ambassador in Mexico City rushed to protest the "hijacking" to the foreign minister, who was sympathetic and apologized profusely. He explained that it had been "the inexcusable act of an inexperienced clerk who was trying to make a name for himself."

The Mexican foreign minister assured the German that he would try to locate the money. But neither the Nazis nor the Italians would ever see it again. Reportedly, Mexican officials placed the funds in a secret bank account under a fictitious name.

One-third of the Mussolini funds earmarked for German espionage activities against the United States thus vanished. The Nazi network based in Mexico City soon collapsed.

Meanwhile, Bill Stephenson's operatives in Rio de Janeiro drew from the Brazilian foreign minister a pledge that the $2.5 million the two Italian consuls were bringing into the country would be given "special protection"—that is, confiscated by Brazilian authorities.

At the same time, two BSC agents went to the port of Pernambuco (Recife) in Brazil, where the ship carrying the Italian consuls was to dock. The BSC men planned to sneak aboard the vessel, steal the diplomatic pouch with the funds, and race away.

The scheme was thwarted. In a poor country where a police chief could be "bought" for a couple of hundred dollars, the Brazilian foreign minister pulled a double cross. He arranged to have the ship's route altered, so that it docked at Rio, not at Pernambuco. An armed squad met the vessel and escorted the two consuls and their money to the Italian embassy.

Although $2.5 million had slipped through the fingers of the BSC, the money never reached Mexico City. Rather, it was sent to Rome.[10]

Hitler's Doom Seen in the Stars

LOUIS DE WOHL had been touring U.S. cities as "the famous Hungarian astrologer," and an ever-growing audience was becoming convinced that he had supernatural powers. He had been built up in the press through stories of his amazingly accurate predictions on the course of the war in Europe.

A pudgy, middle-aged man with a high forehead, de Wohl was actually a captain in the British Army, and he had been brought to the United States in August 1941 as the centerpiece of an elaborate scheme by British Security Coordination (BSC) to help demolish the widespread public viewpoint that Adolf Hitler was invincible.

In New York, de Wohl's reputation as a prognosticator of events that were to happen in the European war drew a large crowd of reporters. Actually, the BSC had been feeding him enough accurate secret war information in advance so that his predictions were validated.

A consummate actor, de Wohl told the New York journalists that Adolf Hitler's horoscope showed the planet Neptune in a house of death and that the führer was involved.

A month later, the Associated Press flashed a story around the world about the annual convention in Cleveland, Ohio, of the American Federation of Scientific Astrologers. Its headliner was the "distinguished Hungarian astro-philosopher Louis de Wohl." The astrologers agreed that Hitler's days were numbered, the AP report stated. If they had said anything else, it would have been strange indeed: the federation was a BSC brainchild.

In an interview with a Cleveland newspaper, de Wohl complained that astrology had "too many quacks."

De Wohl was ensconced in a modest Manhattan hotel. On a certain night of the week, a BSC agent would sneak up the fire escape and hand de Wohl his salary in untraceable dollars through an open back window. At the same time, the emissary would hand over any anti-Hitler information that de Wohl could use in his now widely read newspaper column, "Stars Foretell."

Before creating each column, the Briton had to scrounge astrology information from textbooks to make certain he knew what he was talking about. Then the doomsday predictions about Adolf Hitler obtained from the BSC agent were woven into the narrative.

Meanwhile, British propaganda warfare experts were generating prophecies that would confirm Louis de Wohl's seemingly matchless superiority. A few days after the phony Cleveland astrology conference, a "friendly" Cairo, Egypt, newspaper carried a fascinating article that quoted a highly regarded soothsayer, Sheikh Youssef Afifi: "Four months hence a red planet will appear in the eastern sky. A dangerous evildoer who has drenched the world in blood will die." BSC saw to it that the prediction gained global circulation.

A Nigerian priest conveniently saw a vision: "A group of three men on a rock. One with black hair [Hitler], one fat little breadfruit [Goering], and third monkey-faced and lame [Goebbels]." Newspaper readers everywhere easily recognized the unnamed Nazi bigwigs. The priest predicted a sudden plunge from the rock of the one with the black hair.

Such planted stories were echoed around the world—in Malaya, in Sweden, in China, in Spain, in Hong Kong. BSC milked the ploy for all it was worth.[11]

Abwehr Dupe: Vice President Wallace

WAR CLOUDS WERE DRIFTING from Europe across the Atlantic Ocean toward the United States. Although Franklin Roosevelt had taken to the airwaves in his trademark "fireside chats" to assure the American people that their sons would never get involved in a "foreign war," the president knew that the nation was most likely going to be drawn into the conflict.

Roosevelt decided it was time to meet and confer with British prime minister Winston Churchill. Each leader sailed to Argentia Bay, Newfoundland, where they exchanged visits aboard the cruisers USS *Augusta* and HMS *Prince of Wales*. It was August 9 to 12, 1941.

The conferences were remarkable, as they produced a joint statement by the leader of a belligerent nation, Churchill, and the head of a nonbelligerent country, Roosevelt, outlining the reasons why the war was being fought. The statement would be known as the Atlantic Charter.

Five days after his return to Washington, Roosevelt called in his cabinet and gave its members a detailed briefing on what had transpired at the Argentia Bay talks. Only a few hours later, Admiral Canaris, the Nazi spymaster in Berlin, was seated in his office in the five-story gray-stone building at 72–76 Tirpitz Ufer that was the Abwehr headquarters and reading an account of the

Nazi dupe: U.S. Vice President Henry A. Wallace. (National Archives)

historic conference between Churchill and Roosevelt that had produced the Atlantic Charter.

Canaris had obtained this high-grade intelligence from an agent (code-named Habakuk) whom the Abwehr chief had planted a year earlier in the Swiss Foreign Ministry in Bern. Habakuk had pilfered a copy of a top-secret telegram that the Swiss consul in Washington, Charles Bruggmann, had sent to his home office.

In a letter to Canaris accompanying the stolen telegram, the military attaché in the German embassy in Switzerland stressed that the information was "precise and reliable" because Bruggmann had obtained the details "in strictest confidence from Vice President [Henry A.] Wallace."

Bruggmann was a fifty-two-year-old career diplomat who had met Mary, the sister of Henry Wallace, when Bruggmann had been assigned to Washington in the 1920s. The couple was married the next year in Paris.

Bruggmann had established a close family bond with Wallace long before the Swiss's second assignment in Washington, in 1940. Because of their geographic proximity, Wallace and his brother-in-law met in person often and talked on the telephone almost daily. A native of Iowa, where he had once been editor of the family's magazine *Wallace's Farmer*, the vice president trusted his Swiss brother-in-law to be discreet about the confidential, even secret, information Wallace had confided in him.

An almost daily flow of intelligence from the cagey Habakuk in Bern reached Berlin. No doubt his most important theft was a copy of a telegram sent by Bruggmann to Bern three days after the Japanese sneak attack on Pearl Harbor, Hawaii, that plunged the United States into the global conflict.

Bruggmann's telegram described in detail two conferences President Roosevelt had held in his office early in the afternoon of December 7, 1941, a few hours after much of the U.S. Pacific Fleet had become a twisted, smoking mass. The first solemn session was with his cabinet and the other was held to brief congressional leaders.

Roosevelt pulled no punches, the telegram disclosed. He told his audiences that the United States had suffered an almost mortal blow at Pearl Harbor, giving precise details of the colossal destruction and loss of American lives. There had been only one person other than Roosevelt who had been present at both White House meetings—Vice President Wallace.[12]

The Nazis' Most Unlikely Secret Agent

DARKNESS HAD GATHERED over German-occupied Athens, Greece, on October 10, 1941, as the sleek Mercedes sedan carrying two passengers in the backseat sped toward the municipal airport. One of the men was Hans Müller, an Abwehr officer, and the other was Paul Ernst Fackenheim, who had received several decorations for valor as a German Army officer in World War I and who later became a prosperous hardware dealer in Berlin.

At the Athens airport, Fackenheim boarded a black-bodied German transport plane, which took off and set a course for a pasture outside Haifa, one of the chief ports of Palestine (later Israel). Soon the former businessman bailed out of the aircraft and floated toward the ground in a parachute. He was the Nazis' most unlikely secret agent of the war: a Jew.

Fackenheim's weird odyssey into the murky world of espionage had begun a few weeks earlier, when Field Marshal Erwin Rommel's vaunted Afrika Korps had been stalled by British forces in the Germans' drive to reach Egypt. In Berlin, Admiral Wilhelm Canaris, the chief of the Abwehr, had been given the task of recruiting an agent to report on the strength of British reinforcements being collected in the Middle East for a counteroffensive against Rommel.

Canaris's aides concluded that the spy would have to be Jewish so he would be warmly received by Zionists when he arrived in Palestine. So an Abwehr officer went to the Dachau concentration camp and interviewed Paul Fackenheim, an inmate. The Jew was flabbergasted to be taken off a rigorous work detail, escorted to a room in the administration building, and interviewed by a courteous Abwehr officer. His amazement increased when the Abwehr agent called him *Herr* (Mister), a courtesy never accorded to Jews in Germany.

Soon the interviewer was convinced that Fackenheim was the ideal man for the espionage job. He was highly intelligent, had been known for his great energy, and spoke several languages fluently, including Hebrew. In fewer than twenty-four hours, Fackenheim was given a haircut, and his tattered prisoner garb was replaced by a new civilian suit, shirt, tie, and shoes.

The espionage recruit was escorted to Berlin, then flown to Athens, where he was given a brief course in spying techniques, operating a suitcase-size radio set, writing with secret ink, and identifying British tanks, airplanes, and unit insignias. Then he took a practice parachute jump and was assigned the code name Paul Koch.

As he rode through the night toward the Athens airport, Fackenheim had no way of knowing that he would be a pawn in the lethal rivalry between the Abwehr and the Sicherheitsdienst (SD), the intelligence arm of the elite Schutzstaffel (SS), the black-uniformed private army led by Reichsführer Heinrich Himmler. An SD agent tipped off the British to the time and place of Fackenheim's arrival outside Haifa. However, the British were told that the parachutist would be a prominent SS general, Obergruppenführer Erich Koch.

The purpose of the SD machination was to discredit Admiral Wilhelm Canaris in the eyes of Adolf Hitler by arranging for the secret espionage mission to be botched. Then, the SD leader Reinhard Heydrich hoped, the Abwehr would be absorbed into the SD and he would become chief of a single German intelligence agency. As such, Heydrich would become the Reich's second most powerful figure after Hitler.

Above the dark countryside outside Haifa a green light flashed on in the German transport plane, and Paul Fackenheim bailed out. Hardly had he parachuted to earth than he became aware of the headlights of numerous vehicles parked on an adjacent road. He could discern dim figures dashing about, and hear orders being shouted in English.

As envisioned by Heydrich, the British had concluded that a high-ranking SS general would be parachuting secretly into Palestine to orchestrate a huge sabotage operation or to instigate a massive Arab uprising. Consequently, the British High Command in the Middle East was eager to capture this dangerous German general.

Fackenheim managed to slip out of the British trap. At dawn, he lined up with residents at a bus stop, then took the conveyance into Haifa, where he melted into the crowds. Soon he became aware that British military police were posted at almost every corner, checking identity papers in an effort to nab the presumed SS general.

Finally, Fackenheim entered a British headquarters and told the officer in charge that he was a Jewish refugee from Germany who had landed in a boat on a Haifa beach the previous night. As soon as his interrogators saw that his forged identity papers listed him as Paul Koch, they arrested him.

Fackenheim was taken to a jail outside Cairo and grilled intently by British intelligence officers. They refused to believe his story that he was but a small-time spy who had agreed to his mission only to escape death at the Dachau concentration camp.

Some of the British officers clung to the notion that Fackenheim was indeed the SS general Erich Koch, who would be tried for espionage and possible execution because he had been wearing civilian clothes.

The trial was rapidly concluded, and it appeared that Fackenheim would be shot. Then, at almost the last moment, the Irish lawyer who had been appointed to defend him somehow located an elderly Jewish woman living in Haifa. She testified that she had known Paul Fackenheim and his parents many years earlier in Germany.

Consequently, the charges were dismissed, and Fackenheim survived the war in a British internment camp.[13]

Part Four

Conflict Spreads Around the World

A Batty Idea for Firebombing Tokyo

DR. LYTLE E. ADAMS, a dentist who lived in Pennsylvania, and his family were driving home from a vacation in the southwestern United States. He was idly mulling in his mind the peculiar sight of millions of small bats he had seen hanging upside down from the ceilings of Carlsbad Caverns, a chain of huge underground caves in New Mexico. A guide had told Adams that this species was known as *Tadarida brasiliensis*. It was December 7, 1941.

Dr. Adams's bat reverie was broken when a news flash blared over the car radio: Pearl Harbor had been bombed. Like nearly all Americans, Adams was outraged and swore to do his part to make the Japanese pay for their sneak attack.

By the time Adams and his family reached home, his fertile mind had hatched a bizarre scheme: Why not develop a technique for using large numbers of bats like those he had seen at Carlsbad Caverns to firebomb Tokyo and other Japanese cities? Most of the houses and many of the buildings there were constructed of flimsy wood, and bats typically head for the rafters in buildings.

Within ten weeks, Adams had drawn up a plan, and through his senator, obtained an audience with President Franklin D. Roosevelt. Beset by gargantuan problems because the United States had been woefully unprepared for war, Roosevelt was eager to hear about any idea that might inflict damage and casualties on a ruthless enemy. Speaking with heartfelt enthusiasm, Adams convinced the president that the project should be pursued.

Consequently, the National Defense Research Committee, as well as a similar group in the U.S. Army Air Corps, began conducting experiments on what was labeled the Adams Plan. Some of the more eager technicians envisioned that the war against Japan could be won for the cost of a few million bats.

From more than nine hundred species of bats, *Tadarida brasiliensis* was chosen for the testing, mainly because there were some one hundred million of them in caves in the U.S. Southwest and readily available to be drafted into the armed forces.

Scientists came up with a plan to refrigerate the bats into hibernation, then strap a tiny amount of napalm and a minuscule parachute onto each one. The combat-ready bats would be hauled aboard Army Air Corps planes and dropped onto Tokyo and other Japanese cities. Many persons involved in the

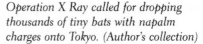

*Operation X Ray called for dropping
thousands of tiny bats with napalm
charges onto Tokyo. (Author's collection)*

Adams Plan gleefully reflected on how much "face" the Japanese would lose to be outsmarted by a bunch of furry bats.

Under the strictest security conditions, Lytle Adams and a group of scientists conducted the first field experiments at a small, remote airport in California on May 15, 1943. As with most tests, problems rapidly surfaced—in this instance, mainly because the bats failed to cooperate. They refused to go into hibernation on demand, nor would they be aroused from sleep on cue.

Another group of bats had the napalm containers strapped to them and, while being loaded into an airplane, escaped from their handlers and flew speedily toward the nearest buildings, which it was hoped they would do. Only the idea was for the structures to be in Japan, not at a small California airport.

Within moments, two hangars and other smaller buildings were raging infernos. Presumably seeking a hiding place, several of the bats flew through the open windows of a parked general's car. It burst into flame and exploded when the fire reached the fuel tank.

Perhaps understandably, the irate general no doubt was a key figure in getting the Adams Plan promptly canceled.

Disappointed but undaunted, Dr. Adams collared U.S. Navy brass, and more bat firebomb experiments were laid on at the Dugway Proving Grounds in Utah. The project was given the code name Operation X Ray.

The tests proved to be quite encouraging, and the navy scientists were enthusiastic. One study indicated that bats loaded with napalm charges could be more productive than any other bomb dropped from the air. It was estimated that a planeload of bat bombs released over Tokyo could set some four thousand fires, as opposed to perhaps three hundred blazes ignited by a planeload of regular incendiary devices.

Major production and subsequent launching of the bat bombs were set for May 1944. However, for no announced reason, the entire project was scrapped—some two and a half years after Dr. Adams had conceived the idea while driving home from New Mexico.[1]

The FBI Nabs a Honolulu "Sleeper"

EVEN AS THE THICK, OILY, BLACK CLOUDS of destruction mushroomed above the shattered U.S. Fleet at Pearl Harbor on December 7, 1941, Robert L. Shivers, special agent in charge of the Honolulu office of the Federal Bureau of Investigation, telephoned FBI headquarters in Washington, more than five thousand miles away. Much to his astonishment, there was only a brief delay before the connection was made. It was about 2:30 P.M. in Washington.

The telephone operator at FBI headquarters in the Justice Department Building switched the urgent call to New York City, where Director J. Edgar Hoover had gone for the weekend. "The Japanese are bombing Pearl Harbor!" Shivers exclaimed. "It's war! You may be able to hear the explosions yourself. Listen!"

Shivers gave Hoover a quick rundown on the sketchy reports of the death and disaster. The FBI director ordered Shivers, a twenty-one-year veteran of the agency, to put into effect the war plan that had been formulated months earlier and that called for rounding up nearly one hundred espionage suspects, most of whom were of Japanese ancestry.

Shivers promptly contacted an old friend with whom he had been working closely in recent months, Honolulu Chief of Police William A. Gabrielson, and asked him to put a guard of his men around the Japanese consulate. The action was for "the protection of the consul general, his staff, and the consular property," Shivers explained.

Gabrielson and Shivers knew there was a far more cogent reason for sending Hawaiian policemen to the consulate. The two law officers had long known that Consul General Nagao Kita, who dressed well, played an enthusiastic game of golf, and considered himself to be a social lion, was the principal spymaster in Hawaii. Gabrielson's cordon of policemen could keep him and other spies in the building from escaping or continuing espionage activities.

In the past, Bob Shivers had often paid a "social" visit to Kita, mainly as a subtle means of impressing the consul general that the FBI was watching. They traded banter and sipped *saki* like two old golfing buddies after eighteen holes on the links. Shivers was always the portrait of affability during these curious sessions in the Japanese consulate. Kita inevitably responded with his toothiest grin.

FBI Special Agent Robert L. Shivers, who led the capture of Japanese spies at Pearl Harbor. (FBI)

"Go ahead, Mr. Kita," the FBI agent said on one occasion in a mocking but polite tone. "Cruise around the island and see what you can see."

"Oh, no," the consul general replied with a chuckle. "Then your men would follow me and chase me."

Those days of cat-and-mouse between two foes now were over. Honolulu Captain of Detectives Benjamin Van Kuren and Lieutenant Yoshio Hasegawa, who was of Japanese ancestry, were assigned the task of "guarding" the consulate. They rushed to the building with a few colleagues, and soon uniformed policemen with sawed-off shotguns fashioned a cordon around the structure. Van Kuren and Hasegawa knew the consulate layout by heart: they had been surveilling the building for many months.

With war breaking out, the Honolulu policemen were unconcerned with diplomatic niceties. Captain Van Kuren and his men smashed open the rear door and barged in. Van Kuren headed immediately for the code room and threw open the door. On the floor was a large washtub in which two Japanese consulars were feverishly burning their secret codebook and messages that had been sent to and received from Shigenori Togo, the foreign minister in Tokyo.

Bulk paper burns slowly, so Van Kuren and his men were able to grab the codebook and a thick sheaf of messages. Although outwardly calm and collected, Consul General Kita protested that his diplomatic status was being violated.

The retrieved papers were turned over to FBI special agent Bob Shivers at his office in the Federal Building. He handed them to the navy's intelligence branch to be decoded. When Shivers received the deciphered messages back, he exclaimed to his staff, "My God, if we'd only had this earlier! Look at these!"

FROM: KITA   December 5, 1941

TO: Foreign Minister, Tokyo

1. The three battleships mentioned in your X239 of Friday morning, the 5th entered port. They expect to depart port on the 8th.

2. On the same day the [carrier] *Lexington* and 5 heavy cruisers
   departed.

3. The following warships were anchored on the afternoon of the
   5th:

   8 Battleships
   3 Light cruisers
   16 Destroyers

Coming in were 4 cruisers of the Honolulu type and 2 destroyers.

                                                        KITA

FROM: TOGO, FOREIGN MINISTER   December 6, 1941

TO: CONSUL, HONOLULU

Please inform us immediately of any rumors of the movements of
warships after the 4th.

                                                        TOGO

Another decoded message to Foreign Minister Togo clearly indicated that
the wily Nagao Kita had arranged for one or more parties to notify Japanese
submarines offshore about movements of U.S. warships. The FBI promptly put
the finger of suspicion on Bernard Julius Otto Kuehn, who had joined the Nazi
Party in Germany in 1930. Since 1936, he and his wife, Friedel, and their offspring had lived in Honolulu, where he first tried the real estate field and then
the furniture business and was a flop at both endeavors.

Despite his commercial failures and having no visible means of finan-
cially supporting his family, Otto Kuehn had two homes, one at Kalama and
the other at Lanikai. Flashlight signals at night from either point could easily
be seen by Japanese submarines.

In late 1935, while still in Germany, he had contacted Captain Tadao
Yokoi, the Japanese naval attaché in Berlin, and signed a contract for his
"services" after he moved to Hawaii. Kuehn would be well paid by Japanese
intelligence: two thousand dollars per month (equivalent to twenty thousand
dollars monthly in 1999), plus a six-thousand-dollar bonus at the end of each
year.

In March 1939, an officer of naval intelligence in Tokyo stopped over in Honolulu to give Kuehn a portable radio and instructions to keep a low profile. When war erupted between Japan and the United States, the German native was to use the radio to send messages to submarines offshore. The underwater vessels would relay the information to naval intelligence in Tokyo.

Kuehn was to be a Japanese "sleeper," a planted espionage agent who would lay low until notified that it was time to act. His Japanese code name was "Ichiro Fujii." However, Kuehn apparently was unhappy with a sleeper role, and he began strolling around the U.S. Fleet anchorage at Pearl Harbor and even drew up a plan for a sneak attack by the Japanese Navy against the bastion. All of this activity did not go unnoticed by the FBI or the local U.S. Office of Naval Intelligence (ONI). Both agencies were undermanned, but on occasion they put tails on Kuehn to keep track of his actions.

After Consul General Kita had taken up his duties in Honolulu in March 1941, he and Kuehn worked out a covert contact scheme. When Kita wanted to see the German, he did so by mailing him a postcard signed "Jimmie" to Kuehn's post office box 1476 in downtown Honolulu.

FBI suspicions that Kuehn was a Japanese spy had intensified after his wife returned from a trip to Tokyo and deposited twenty thousand dollars in a Honolulu bank.

In the wake of the Japanese sneak attack, the FBI hauled in Kuehn for questioning. He was shown the Kita/Togo message referring to signaling Japanese submarines offshore. Finally, the German confessed that he was the one who was to signal the underwater vessels, but he swore that he had never done so. The FBI was unimpressed with his disclaimer.

A few weeks later, a board of U.S. Army and Navy officers, convened under martial law, tried Kuehn and sentenced him to be shot to death as a spy. Later, however, the sentence was commuted by higher authority to fifty years at hard labor. Apparently the sentence reduction had been ordered by the White House so the Nazi regime in Berlin would not seize on Kuehn's execution to kill any U.S. spies who might fall into German hands in Europe.[2]

A French Counterfeit Traitor

LIEUTENANT DE VAISSEAU JEAN PHILIPPON was one of the ten French Navy officers and fifteen hundred French sailors the Germans had kept on active duty at the Kriegsmarine arsenal at the port of Brest after the 1940 armistice. German Navy officers were impressed by Philippon, who clearly held an enlightened view that accepted the Nazi occupation of much of France.

Friendly and personable, the Frenchman had no qualms about fraternizing with German officers at the port, three hundred miles west of Paris at the tip of the Brittany Peninsula, and he often drank with them late into the night. There were times when the Germans, their tongues loosened by Calvados, would reveal secret information to their congenial young French friend.

It was through these late-night drinkfests that Philippon (code-named Hilarion), a highly productive spy for the French underground, learned that the Germans were building U-boat shelters at Lorient, a small port on the southern coast of Brittany. The pens would serve as homes for the submarine wolf packs wreaking havoc in the Atlantic Ocean.

Hilarion belonged to a network called Confrérie Notre-Dame (CND), and he was operating in one of France's most closely watched cities. The Gestapo, the Abwehr, and the Milice (French traitors who were policemen under the Germans) were everywhere.

Radio detection vehicles were highly active in and around Brest. Hilarion and the operator assigned to him to send messages to London bicycled about the city with dismantled radios in their pockets, for no two transmissions were made from the same house or building.

In late December 1941, Hilarion radioed more information about the work the Germans were doing on the submarine pens at Lorient. Construction had just gotten under way, but when completed the pens' twenty-two-foot-thick roofs would be able to withstand the heaviest bombs the British had in their arsenal.

Hilarion insisted that the Royal Air Force Bomber Command attack these new pens immediately, but he received back a haughty reply: "The base will be attacked when it is finished."

This decision would prove to be a disastrous one.

In Lorient, the name of Jacques Stosskopf was hated by the patriotic citizens. A skilled engineer, the Frenchman had accepted a German invitation to continue in charge of the Lorient shipyard, where the submarine pens would be built. He became a trusted collaborator of the Germans.

Equally despised by Lorient people were the handful of French engineers who had worked for Stosskopf in the navy yard prior to the war and who remained when the Germans took over. What the townsfolk did not know was that Stosskopf and his engineers were all loyal Frenchmen who risked their lives almost daily to keep the British informed about the arrival and departure of German U-boats from this important base.

Because he was trusted by the Germans, Stosskopf easily gathered secret information that would not be available to other spies. He knew the number of British and neutral ships sunk by each submarine returning from a prowl into the Atlantic Ocean. And he knew the names of the U-boats that never returned to Lorient and presumably had been sunk.

Stosskopf was regarded so highly by the Germans that when they began combing France for workers to ship to the Third Reich, he was able to retain most of the 4,500 French civilian employees at the yard. Only 147 were forced to depart.

Impregnable to air bombardment, the U-boat pens at Lorient. (National Archives)

One night a British submarine surfaced off Brittany, and Stosskopf was there to greet the team of commandos who paddled ashore in a rubber dinghy. They had come on a reconnaissance mission, and Stosskopf briefed them on details about the region. He was even able to sneak one commando into the U-boat base, presumably to get firsthand information for a forthcoming RAF bombing attack on the pens.

A few months later, an agent in the Confrérie Notre-Dame was captured by the Gestapo, and under excruciating torture he betrayed Stosskopf, who was immediately arrested.

When the townspeople of Lorient learned that the hated Stosskopf had suddenly vanished, they told one another that his cronies in the Kriegsmarine had rewarded the Frenchman with an even more illustrious post elsewhere.

After the liberation of Brittany by American forces (with the substantial aid of armed members of the French underground) in August 1944, the new boss of the Lorient shipyard held a mass meeting of the workers. They were flabbergasted to hear that General Charles de Gaulle, leader of the Free French forces, had posthumously awarded to Stosskopf the stars and decorations of a commander of the Legion of Honor.

After the war, the Lorient facility would be renamed the Jacques Stosskopf Navy Yard.[3]

Their Weapons Were Words

SOON AFTER THE VEIL OF NIGHT FELL over France, a battered old car chugged up to a roadblock on the outskirts of Clermont-Ferrand in central France. The lone occupant, a member of the resistance, felt a cold chill race up his spine. Piled in the back and on the passenger seat were many bundles of illegal underground newspapers that he was carrying to a distribution point in the basement of a patriot's home. It was April 1942.

Two men wearing the gray-green uniform of the Wehrmacht and swinging lanterns approached the car. Despite the terror in his heart, the Frenchman kept his poise. He held up one of the carefully wrapped bundles and declared calmly, "These are government circulars announcing new rationing procedures and I'm taking them to German headquarters in Clermont-Ferrand."

Suspicious, one German held his lantern to be able to read the top sheet of paper, then said, "All right, you can go on."

The sheet the German had scanned was indeed a government piece, and the French producers of the underground newspaper had taken the precaution to place one of the sheets atop each bundle for just such situations that had now confronted the driver.

Immediately after the signing of the armistice in June 1940, the Germans had taken over the media, and it was produced largely by French collaborators. Much of the space in these German-controlled newspapers and magazines was devoted to propaganda and the printing of orders and regulations. The lack of genuine news distressed the French people, so within a few months, covert publications began to spring up, and soon their circulation soared.

As the underground press became ever more powerful, building civilian morale and exasperating the German masters in France, efforts were made repeatedly by the Gestapo and the French Milice to wipe out this menace. But their task was difficult, much like trying to swat flies in a dark room.

Physical obstacles to covert publishing were daunting. Collectively, hundreds of tons of newsprint had to be found, and the Germans had made it illegal to sell that commodity. Some paper was bought on the black market. Underground members were planted in the so-called legitimate press, and they arranged to pilfer some newsprint.

Once a group had located newsprint and ink, a search was launched to find a press, which would have to be located in a small print shop in remote locales not patrolled by the Germans or the Milice. In these instances, the print shop owner either participated in the production of the publication, or he left a key to his place when he departed for the day.

At about midnight, a small resistance group would stealthily enter the building, set the type, and make the press run. Hidden outside in the shadows would be lookouts to warn of approaching danger. Once the papers were printed, the type was rapidly put back in cases and the plates were melted down. The next day, the shop returned to its normal routine, often printing pamphlets and circulars for the Germans.

Not all of the clandestine newspapers were printed in small shops. One publication was run off the press of a large Paris hotel that was entirely occupied by Germans. Wehrmacht officers idling in the plush lobby paid no attention to the faint rumble of the basement press, which was used to print the hotel's menus. Eventually the secret operation was moved for fear that the Germans would recognize that the battered type on their dinner menus was identical to that of the "terrorist" newspapers they had seen on occasion.

Perhaps the trickiest venture of all by an underground publisher was the launching of a German-language newspaper called *Unter Uns* (Among Ourselves). Its target was the occupying Wehrmacht, and mainly it printed graphic stories of the horrors and agonizing deaths being inflicted on the German Army in savage fighting in the Soviet Union.

In late March 1942, *Unter Uns* published a lengthy account of a daring raid by British commandos in which they stole a top-secret German radar from its site at Bruneval, France, on the English Channel coast. The German-controlled French press had ignored this blockbuster story.

One week later, disaster struck: the two publishers of *Unter Uns* were approached by several Gestapo agents, and in the ensuing gun battle, the two Frenchmen were killed.

Distribution of the clandestine newspapers was as dangerous as the printing, and could result in execution for those involved. However, there was no shortage of eager volunteers to take the papers door to door: housewives, students, merchants, doctors, priests, laborers. Circulation techniques became so ingenious that copies even reached inmates in prisons and jails.

Two years after Adolf Hitler took control of most of France, there were many covert newspapers and magazines being printed and distributed, with a combined press run of some three hundred thousand weekly. Perhaps two million French men and women read the sheets.

The underground publications were not journalistic works of art. Yet to French citizens, in whose breasts the flame of resistance was burning ever brighter, the outlaw publications were beacons of hope. At this stage in the war, the covert newspapers and magazines were more important to the French underground than sabotage or other violent acts, for the resistants needed recruits, money, and information.

Most of the underground newspapers and magazines developed their own character, especially those produced by occupational groups. France's doctors fought back through their covert journal, *Le Médecin Français*. Scathing editorials declared that the Germans were deliberately trying to wipe out vast segments of the French population by denying physicians sufficient gasoline,

French underground newspapers fought the war with words quite effectively. (Author's collection)

especially in rural areas. Soon the fuel ration for doctors was hiked by the German authorities.

Large numbers of young French males were being rounded up and shipped to Germany to work in war plants. Before leaving, each worker had to have a certificate stating that he did not have a contagious disease (which might spread to German citizens). *Le Médecin Français* urged doctors of France to reject almost every man presented to them for examination and to make certain that known French collaborators were certified for immediate shipment.

French educators had their own vocal press, *l'Université Libre*. Its editorial thrust was to protect the standards of French education from encroachment by the German authorities. It howled loudly that a campaign had been launched by the occupying power to dilute French schools by cutting back sharply on supplies of books and papers and, more importantly, by badgering and arresting teachers and professors whose lectures were not consistent with Nazi views.

Le Palais Libre, the newspaper of the lawyers, called attention to the repeated abuses by German authorities of the French legal system, including jailing French judges who refused to hold in custody people the Gestapo had arbitrarily arrested and had not charged with crimes.

La Terre, the farmers' clandestine newspaper, gave these natural-born resistants suggestions to conceal harvests from the Germans and send the crops to resistants hiding in the mountains and forests. Moreover, the farmers should delay threshing if their property had been taken over by the Germans.

Even humor, the most slashing editorial weapon of all, went underground. *Le Gaullois* concentrated on comical and sarcastic articles and anecdotes. Cartoons focusing on the Germans as buffoons were received with glee by French readers and with anger by the occupying authorities.

For the eight hundred thousand railroad men, their *Bulletin des Chemins de Fer* carried ringing exhortations for them to prevent the Boche (Germans) from applying their strategy to carry France's precious manpower, goods, art, and metals to Germany "by paralyzing his troop movements, isolating his units, immobilizing his supplies, breaking his power, and precipitating his defeat."

The *Bulletin* described techniques for sabotage without causing permanent damage, and listed the names of the tiny percentage of railroad workers known to be currying favor with the Nazis. It suggested that a heavy packing case "accidentally" dropped on a collaborating coworker's toes would put him out of action for a considerable length of time.

There was a bit of closing advice: As soon as the collaborator had recovered and returned to work, greet him by repeating the above technique—on his other foot.[4]

Peculiar Demise of a Captured Plane

FORTY MILES UP THE OLD NORTH ROAD from London, just outside the ancient village of Tempsford, snuggled a top-secret airfield and a complex of Nissen huts, collectively called Gibraltar Farm. This was the covert base of the Royal Air Force Moon Squadrons, so named because most of their flying was done over Nazi-occupied Europe in periods of moonlight, when conditions were favorable for clandestine operations.

Flying mainly Lysanders—small, maneuverable airplanes capable of landing and taking off in short spaces—the mission of the Moon Squadron pilots was to deliver spies to France and to bring back espionage agents. These male and female agents had been recruited and trained by the Special Operations Executive (SOE), which Prime Minister Winston Churchill had created early in the war with this stirring directive: "Set Europe ablaze!"

SOE, under its "D" (code for the chief), Charles Hambro, had offices at 64 Baker Street in London, not far from the fictional home of the legendary Sherlock Holmes. From its beginning in mid-1940, the agency was cloaked in secrecy. There were no markings or signs anywhere in the building to indicate that a government agency was housed there.

The true name of the spy agency, its correct address—even its existence—were known to but a handful of high-level officials. The Air Ministry knew SOE by a different set of initials, the Admiralty knew it by yet another set. Both thought the agency was located at an address other than the correct one.

By early 1942, about two and a half years after Great Britain went to war against Nazi Germany, Chief Hambro had created a widespread and sophisticated organization to provide intelligence and to conduct sabotage. Each country in Europe that had been overrun by Adolf Hitler's war machine had its own section in SOE, which directed espionage and sabotage operations within its own country and which recruited, trained, and infiltrated its own agents. The SOE-dispatched agents, in turn, would recruit their own spies and organize them into clandestine networks.

Known inside the agency as The Firm, SOE landed some spies in rubber dinghies, others parachuted from Whitley bombers, but the main infiltration source comprised the Moon Squadrons. Their Lysanders, called Lizzies, had been stripped of guns, armor, and other equipment to provide room for one agent passenger, known as a Joe.

All of the Moon Squadron pilots were exceptionally skilled. Their task was incredibly demanding. They were invariably confronted with an operation fraught with peril—not the least of which would be savage torture by the Gestapo and eventual execution if a flight was betrayed and Germans were waiting on the ground for the Lizzie.

Without benefit of a navigator, a Moon Squadron pilot had to locate a flyspeck field in the vast darkness of occupied Europe, using only a map and whatever landmarks—villages, roads, rivers, lakes—he might detect in the moonlight. He would have to avoid Luftwaffe fighter planes searching the skies, ack-ack guns, and searchlights. It was not a job for those with faint hearts and weak knees.

All the time the Moon Squadrons had been running an espionage shuttle service across the English Channel, top officers in the German secret service were giving a high priority to its activities. A few hundred Abwehr agents in France and the Low Countries had been sent in recent months to try to break up the underground networks that were being aided and abetted by the Lizzies.

A directive went out from Berlin for every effort to be made to capture one of the Lysanders so that Nazi aeronautical engineers could study it and perhaps devise countermeasures to thwart its actions. Snaring a Moon Squadron pilot also would be most desirable, because the Abwehr knew very little about the covert organization, or even where it was based.

In the middle of March 1942, one of the ace Moon Squadron pilots, Flight Lieutenant John "Whippy" Nesbitt-Dufort, was at the controls of a Lysander while winging across the blacked-out countryside of northern France. An hour earlier, he had taken off from Gibraltar Farm with the mission of dropping off the Joe with him and picking up another.

*Lysander aircraft used by the British to drop off and pick up agents in German-held Europe.
(National Archives)*

Whippy Nesbitt-Dufort, a lean, congenial officer with an engaging sense
of humor and a buoyant personality, had no qualms about imbibing when off
duty. He would tell a fellow pilot, "Let's go into the village and have a drink
or six!"

Whippy was a free spirit, and he had had his share of close calls while
on missions. On one occasion his Lizzie touched down on a dark pasture, skidded and bumped along the grass wet with dew, and ground to a halt. The
plane's door flew open, the Joe leaped out, raced away, and was swallowed up
by the night.

Moments later, Whippy heard shots ring out. As it developed, the Joe he
was supposed to pick up was pedaling frantically toward the pasture on a bicycle and being pursued by Gestapo agents.

Perspiring heavily from the exertion, the Joe leaped off the bicycle, hur-
tled over an earthen hedgerow, and ran out into the pasture. Nesbitt-Dufort
already had the Lizzie rolling when the Joe, gasping for breath and with bullets whizzing past the Lizzie, sprawled into the cramped space vacated minutes
earlier by the other Joe.

Always irrepressible, Whippy called out cheerily, "Good evening to you,
sir. And a beautiful evening, indeed!"

Now, on his current mission, Whippy knew he was in big trouble. A thin
coat of ice had formed on the wings, causing the Lizzie to steer erratically. As

a result, he became lost, was nearly out of gasoline, and was gliding downward for a crash landing in a field. This could be a disaster, he knew. The pasture could be saturated with tree stumps and ditches.

"Hold your hat!" Whippy called out to the nervous Joe moments before the Lysander crunched onto the wet field, skidded for more than fifty yards, thudded into a ditch, and nosed over with its tail pointing upward. Miraculously, perhaps, neither man was hurt, and they scrambled out of the aircraft.

For several moments, Whippy calmly stood and viewed the Lysander, then exclaimed, "My goodness, I could do with one or six drinks!"

Following instructions, the flight lieutenant began preparations for destroying the Lysander. He exploded the SFF (Secret Identification Friend or Foe apparatus), which sent "friendly" signals of distress to British radar stations, then fired a Verey pistol at the fuselage, setting the plane afire.

Nesbitt-Dufort and the Joe raced to an empty building to hide and contemplate their next move. Whippy thought that the Lizzie was cremated, but the plane had been nearly out of fuel, so the flames could not be fed. The tiny blaze flickered out.

Shortly after dawn, a German motorcycle patrol discovered the Lysander, which was largely intact. Word was flashed up the chain of command. Down from Berlin came precise instructions: The Lysander was not to be dismantled, but rather loaded intact onto a large flatbed truck and hauled—with tender care—to a place where it could be carefully examined by experts.

A German work crew, admonished by officers to be extremely gentle, used a crane to hoist the plane onto the flatbed. Knowing the value the brass in Berlin had placed on the Lysander, the German captain in charge of the recovery operation perspired freely as the truck began to inch cautiously across the rough field and onto a dirt road. No doubt the officer breathed easier when the flatbed truck reached a smooth, hard-surfaced road.

Some three miles along, the crawling truck neared a level railroad crossing and, snail-like, edged onward. Suddenly the escorting Germans heard a frightening sound—that of a train racing toward the crossing at fifty miles per hour. Moments later, the locomotive hit the truck broadside, smashing the vehicle and the Lysander into smithereens.

German commanders were furious over the loss of this prized booty and ordered an all-out search to be launched for the British pilot. Unaware of the slapstick scenario unfolding around his Lizzie, Whippy Nesbitt-Dufort had been taken in tow by members of the French underground, furnished native clothing, and hidden about fifteen miles from where thousands of pieces of the Lysander were strewn. Five weeks later, Whippy was able to contact England by radio, and a Lysander was dispatched on the first moonlit night to pick him up.

Returning to Gibraltar Farm after nearly two months, Whippy breezily greeted welcoming comrades: "What I need is one or six drinks!"[5]

A Bishop in Disguise

Soon after Adolf Hitler sent his booted German legions to take over peace-ful Norway in April 1940, a notorious collaborator, Vidkun Quisling, founded Nasjonal Samling, the Norwegian Nazi Party. Nearly two years later, the traitor was appointed "minister president" by the führer and became the most hated man in Norway.

The German occupation force had long been trying to gain control of Norwegian churches by enlisting clerics to support a "holy crusade against communism." When Quisling took power on February 1, 1942, one of the few native clerics with Nazi sympathies announced that he would hold a special service in the cathedral at Trondheim to celebrate the new regime. Not a single person showed up.

That same afternoon, however, at the regular service conducted by the dean of the cathedral, hundreds of Norwegians crammed into the building, and scores of others spilled outside. A day later, the dean was removed from his post by Quisling. In protest, nearly every other pastor in Norway resigned. However, they would continue to perform their duties before relatively small gatherings, but Norway's churches would remain empty throughout the war.

Infuriated by the defiance of the clergy, Quisling ordered the arrest of Bishop Eivind Berggrav, primate of the Norwegian Lutheran Church and a key leader in the underground. To intimidate other clergy and bring them into line, Quisling planned to try Berggrav before a kangaroo court and have him executed.

Berggrav's arrest became known that same day to Lieutenant Colonel Theodor Steltzer, a staff officer at German headquarters in Oslo. Since reaching Norway in late 1940, Steltzer had been playing a dangerous game. He belonged to the Schwarze Kapelle (Black Orchestra), the secret group of high-ranking German military and government leaders whose goal was to get rid of Adolf Hitler and the Nazi regime.

Soon after his arrival in Oslo, Steltzer had established clandestine contact with Bishop Berggrav and the Norwegian underground, and he tipped off the resistants about impending Gestapo raids and other important information. Now he immediately contacted an ally, Helmuth von Moltke, a legal adviser to the Abwehr in Berlin, and asked him to intervene on Berggrav's behalf with the intelligence agency's chief, Admiral Wilhelm Canaris, who was a leader in the Schwarze Kapelle.

Canaris rushed Moltke to Oslo, where the lawyer and Colonel Steltzer argued to the German High Command that executing Norway's most popular cleric would trigger massive unrest among the population. Consequently, Quisling was ordered to release the bishop from prison and put him under house arrest in Oslo.

Bishop Eivind Berggrav continued as a Norwegian underground leader by wearing many disguises, including that of a policeman. (Author's collection)

Norwegian policemen thought to be loyal to the Nazis guarded the house, but they were patriots and looked the other way when the bishop sneaked out the door countless times to meet with the Norwegian underground during the remainder of the war. Because Berggrav's face was widely known to the Germans, he became a master of disguises. At various times he posed as a policeman, as a college professor complete with thick-lensed eyeglasses and fake mustache, and as a junk dealer pushing a dilapidated cart.

After the war, Colonel Theodor Steltzer, who had saved the bishop's life, was honored by grateful Norwegians by being presented to the restored national leader, King Haakon VII, who had been in exile.[6]

The Mysterious Inspector Thompson

IN EARLY JUNE 1940, a secret British organization known as MI-9 began wrestling with an unprecedented and unforeseen problem: How could hundreds, perhaps thousands, of British soldiers cut off from their units and in hiding in France be rescued from under the noses of the Germans?

A week earlier, 850 vessels of all shapes and sizes had begun evacuating some 340,000 British soldiers trapped at the small Channel port of Dunkirk, France, but many men had to be left behind.

The daunting task of locating and evacuating the British refugees fell into the hands of Brigadier Norman R. Crockett, head of MI-9, the War Office intelligence branch. Section IS9(d) was responsible for conducting covert operations in France, Belgium, and the Netherlands to rescue the military evaders.

Section IS9(d) was located at 5 St. James Street in London, and one of its chambers was known as Room 900. So the evade-and-escape organization was called Room 900, and its existence was known only to a select few military and government officials.

Within a month after the Dunkirk debacle, Brigadier Crockett began organizing escape lines. Most of the cut-off British soldiers were hiding near the Channel coast. But German forces were guarding the ports and beaches, making it impossible to smuggle evaders directly across to Britain. Consequently, the escape lines would have to extend all the way from northeastern France westward to the towering Pyrenees Mountains at the French-Spanish border.

In one of its first moves, Room 900 sent Donald Darling (code-named Sunday), an MI-9 agent posted at Gibraltar, to neutral Spain, where he was to forge links at the western end of the escape lines. Bright and energetic, he established safe houses where the escapees could hole up until transportation to Britain could be arranged for them.

Sunday then traveled to Lisbon in neutral Portugal, where he organized a system for the evaders to be carried across the Channel to Britain by boat.

At the same time Sunday was in Spain and Portugal, Room 900 arranged for an unlikely secret agent, Nubar Gulbenkian, to create an operation to escort the escapees over the rugged Pyrenees, where they could be taken in tow by Sunday's agents.

Gulbenkian was in his early thirties, wealthy, and an official in the neutral Iranian legation in London. For whatever his motives, he had sought out British agents and volunteered to carry out undercover assignments in foreign countries.

Disguised as a traveling salesman, Gulbenkian was to go to the city of Perpignan, on the French side of the Pyrenees, and make contact with a garage owner known as Parker, whose real name was Michel Pareyre. He had been recruited as an MI-9 agent by Sunday.

Room 900 officials told Gulbenkian that he was to arrange with Parker for the payment of guides to escort British escapees over the Pyrenees. His Majesty's Treasury would pay forty pounds for each British officer and twenty pounds for other ranks. The plan was for Parker to hide British escapees in his garage, then turn them over to guides. The guides would sneak the escapees into Spain.

As planned, Nubar Gulbenkian met Parker several days later in a café at Perpignan. Neither had seen the other before. As recognition signals, Parker was reading a French newspaper upside down, and the Iranian asked him, "Have you a Parker pen?" The discussion was brief, for the Gestapo in disguise had heavily infiltrated the region. The MI-9 agent told Parker that he would be paid only on results and that money due him would be held in London until the end of the war. The Frenchman agreed to that arrangement.

While Donald Darling in Spain and Portugal and Nubar Gulbenkian along the Pyrenees were creating links at the far end of the escape lines, Captain Ian Garrow had been risking his life almost daily in German-held France organizing a system for getting the evaders to the French-Spanish frontier.

Energetic and resourceful, Garrow had been cut off when his Scottish 51st "Highland" Division was overrun near Dunkirk. Rather than try to get to England, he chose instead to remain in France and help other British soldiers to escape from the Continent.

Garrow was confronted by enormous obstacles, other than the quite real threat of being arrested by the Gestapo and possibly executed for his covert activities. There was a lack of funds, he had no radio communication with London, and he did not speak a word of French.

During the next year, however, the captain organized an escape line from Paris (where evaders were collected from northern France) to the Pyrenees. There the garage owner code-named Parker and the agents he had recruited escorted the refugees across the mountains to Sunday's men.

By mid-1942 Garrow's "underground railroad" was shuttling the evaders for hundreds of miles to sanctuary in Spain. Disguised in civilian clothes, they traveled singly or in tiny groups by foot, bicycle, horse and cart, bus, car, and train.

Finally, Garrow's luck ran out. He was betrayed by a civilian, arrested by Vichy France police, and sent to prison. But he had set the pattern for escape lines for others to follow.

At the same time that Garrow had been marooned at Dunkirk two years earlier, a Coldstream Guards officer, James Langley, was with the rear guard. After most of the British Army had left the fireswept beaches, Langley was seriously wounded. His soldiers carried him on a litter to the shore, where a few small boats were preparing to sail for England. But a Royal Navy skipper explained that he could not be taken aboard because a litter would occupy as much space on a ship as would four men standing up.

A day later, Langley was captured. He was put in a German prisoner-of-war camp, where a British surgeon had to amputate his mutilated left arm. His leg had been so shattered by shell fragments that he could get around only by crawling. Later he was transferred to a hospital in Lille, France.

Despite his physical injuries and weakened condition, Langley managed to escape from the hospital only four months after being wounded. Then he made his way alone to Spain, and he reached England in a small boat on almost the first anniversary of his capture at Dunkirk.

British Army officials were preparing to discharge Langley because of his physical handicaps. But he raised such a protest that he was assigned to active duty in Room 900. In the months ahead he organized the escape of many British soldiers from the Continent.

By now the RAF and the U.S. Eighth Air Force, based in England, had been increasing the frequency and weight of their attacks on facilities used by the German war machine in France and the Low Countries, and fliers were being downed in greater numbers than before.

Soon Langley began hearing reports from his agents across the Channel about the actions of a Briton who was running great risks to help evaders get out of France. On one occasion the mystery man, Harold Cole (his true name), had smuggled six British airmen out of German-occupied France to the Pyrenees. Before departing, the senior officer of the group had asked the escort for his name so that his courage and resourcefulness could be recognized by the Crown at some future date.

"I'm Inspector Thompson of Scotland Yard," Cole replied.

Later, a French woman, who was being sought by the Gestapo for her participation with the resistance, and her family arrived in England. She told authorities that an Inspector Thompson had made their escape possible.

By now, Scotland Yard was curious to uncover the true identity of Inspector Thompson. So the French woman was invited to Scotland Yard to look at photographs of all of the Yard's inspectors. None of them was Thompson. Then, acting on a hunch, a detective showed her a rogues' gallery of wanted felons.

"Why, there is Inspector Thompson!" she exclaimed, pointing to the image of Harold Cole, a fugitive from a murder charge.

Only after the war would British sleuths piece together the full truth about Cole. A few months before the conflict erupted in September 1939, he had disappeared after learning the police were trying to locate him for the homicide. Later, after the British Army had been sent to France to whip Adolf Hitler, he popped up in Paris wearing the uniform of a British soldier, claiming that he had escaped from Dunkirk. In fact, he had never been in the army.

After France surrendered in May 1940 and the Wehrmacht occupied much of the country, a latent patriotic instinct may have been ignited in Cole. Apparently on his own volition, he began assisting British evaders.

Somewhere along the way, Cole was arrested by the Gestapo and, in exchange for not being executed, agreed to continue his work on the escape lines but keep the Gestapo informed in advance of his activities. Although he had previously helped many escapers to get to England, his treachery now resulted in a large number of helpers being arrested and shot by the Gestapo.

Wearing the uniform of a German captain, Cole was in Paris when Allied spearheads approached the city in August 1944, and he fled eastward on the heels of the retreating Wehrmacht. About a year later, a few months after Victory in Europe (V-E) Day, Cole was taken into custody by U.S. authorities in Germany while posing as a captain in British intelligence.

Under armed guard, Cole was brought to Paris and ensconced in a U.S.-operated prison. Within days, he stole an American sergeant's uniform and walked out the front door, unchallenged.

Cole holed up in a cheap rooming house, and the landlady reported him as a deserter. When French police arrived to take him into custody, a shoot-out erupted. The part-time hero, part-time villain was hit in the head by a bullet and died instantly.

During the war, the escape lines had brought back some five hundred British soldiers and perhaps three thousand Allied airmen. Not all the evaders had made it home, however. German and Vichy French prison camps held hundreds who had been apprehended while trying to reach Spain.

The cost of rescuing so many had been heavy. Some five hundred French, Belgian, and Dutch patriots who had aided the evaders were known to have been executed by the Germans. The true figure might have been several times that number.[7]

A Nazi Counterfeiting Plot

MAJOR BERNHARD KRÜGER, youthful, ambitious, hard-driving, was summoned to an office in Berlin in July 1942, and sworn to secrecy by a small group of German intelligence officers. Then a bombshell was dropped on Krüger: He was to take charge of a master plot designed to throw Great Britain's economy into chaos by counterfeiting British currency. Code-named Operation Bernhard, the scheme had been conceived by forty-two-year-old Heinrich Himmler, the one-time chicken farmer who now held the exalted rank of Reichsführer. As chief of the Gestapo and the SS, Himmler was Germany's second most powerful man.

Responding with typical alacrity, Major Krüger tried to recruit skilled experts at the Reichsbank and the Reich Printing Company, but even in wartime and at great personal risk, they declined to get involved in printing another nation's currency.

Undaunted, the resourceful major rapidly rounded up the technicians he needed from concentration camps, whose inmates included large numbers of men who had excelled in civilian life before being judged "enemies of the people." Those selected were transferred to the Sachsenhausen concentration camp, where a counterfeiting plant had been set up in an isolated compound surrounded by electrified barbed-wire fences.

Legitimate money printers around the world would have been envious of the sophisticated plant. Plates were engraved with meticulous care. Craftsmen had been threatened with the gas chamber if they tried some trickery to purposely insert a slight flaw in the plates that could result in the printed currency being detected once it got into circulation.

A German manufacturer, sworn to secrecy under pain of execution, provided the most modern of printing machinery. But perhaps the most crucial contribution of all to Operation Bernhard was the production by a prominent

A counterfeit British ten-pound banknote produced by the Germans. (Author's collection)

German paper company, long known for the high quality of its products, of Bank of England paper, with its elaborate watermarks.

By late 1942, all the kinks had been smoothed out and presses were running at full speed. Some four hundred thousand bogus British banknotes were being shipped out of Sachsenhausen each month, and this counterfeit currency was being used all over the world to finance German clandestine operations.

During the first half of 1943, London bankers became highly alarmed. Something irregular—and no doubt illegal—was taking place in Europe. A flood of fake British banknotes from Madrid, Lisbon, Zurich, Istanbul, and Stockholm, all in officially neutral countries where the Germans were known to have extensive espionage networks, were pouring into London.

Officials of the Bank of England knew that there was only one source for a counterfeiting operation on such a massive scale: Nazi Germany. These British financiers were deeply worried because with so much bogus money afloat around the world, confidence could be lost in the traditionally rock-solid British note, even to a point where the Allied war effort could be jeopardized. Such a calamitous eventuality was precisely what Reichsführer Himmler had envisioned when he hatched the scheme.

Suddenly the Bank of England jolted the financial world by announcing that it was taking from circulation all its notes and would replace them with currency of a new design. This drastic action may well have been taken in the nick of time, just before the British economic system might have been wrecked by the Nazi plot.[8]

A Chance Meeting in a Café

ON A WARM AFTERNOON in early October 1942, Donald Q. Coster, a vice consul at the U.S. consulate in Casablanca, French Morocco, was sitting with a friend at a table in a dingy waterfront café. "Vice consul" was only a cover. Actually, Coster was a spy for the Office of Strategic Services (OSS), and he was in the café, a popular hangout for seamen, to listen for information on ship movements.

In civilian life Coster had been a Madison Avenue advertising firm executive in New York City. When war had broken out in Europe in late 1939, he had given up his cushy job for the challenge of driving an American Field Service ambulance for the French Army. He was captured, spent several quite unpleasant weeks in German hands, was released, and came back home to join the U.S. Navy.

Coster's fluency in the French language resulted in his being assigned to the Office of Naval Intelligence (ONI). With Operation Torch, the Allied invasion of French Northwest Africa, being prepared in mid-1942, Coster discovered that, unbeknownst to him, he had "volunteered" for service with "Wild Bill" Donovan's OSS.

Soon the former advertising executive found himself seated in the Washington office of Bill Donovan and was informed that, effective immediately, he was a "vice consul" in the pay of the State Department. But he would take his orders from the OSS.

"Casablanca is the most important place in the world at this moment," Donovan declared in a mysterious tone. "And you are going to Africa, to Casablanca."

Coster swallowed hard. It appeared that he, a total amateur in the cloak-and-dagger business, was going to be plunged right in the center of intrigue and espionage hijinks.

"French Northwest Africa will be invaded one of these days," Donovan continued, "by either the Germans or the Allies. Your job will be to help strengthen an Allied deception scheme to coerce the French Army in North Africa and German intelligence to believe that if the Allies invade, we will go ashore at Dakar."

"Yes, sir!" replied Coster, who felt the blood draining from his face.

Dakar, a major port in Sénégal on the western coast of Africa, lies 1,440 miles southwest of Casablanca. Dakar was a plausible locale for an Allied invasion. It was directly across the Atlantic from Brazil, which declared war on Germany in August 1942, becoming the first South American nation to do so.

To reinforce the many-faceted Dakar deception plan, Coster was to plant misleading information with Major General Theodor Auer, chief of the German Armistice Mission, whose function in Casablanca was to enforce the terms the Nazis imposed when the French Army had surrendered in the spring of 1940.

"How you accomplish that task will be left to your ingenuity," Donovan added. "Auer is cunning, ruthless, and knows all the tricks to catch spies."

Coster felt a choking sensation. Dancing before his mind's eye were a horde of Gestapo agents, cutthroat assassins, and ingenious Nazi torture techniques.

In Washington, the new OSS recruit was rushed through a quick course of instruction in the code he was to use. And little else. All he knew about espionage was what he had seen in Hollywood movies.

Now, at the disreputable waterfront café in Casablanca only a month before D-Day for Torch, two young men, obviously searching for a table at which to sit in the packed room, meandered near Coster and his friend, also a "vice consul." Coster invited the men to share his table, hoping to gain information on ship movements.

The two strangers accepted and sat down. One, named Walter, was especially talkative. His friend hardly said a word. Walter told Coster that they were Austrians who had been in France when that country was conquered by the Wehrmacht in 1940. A short time later, Walter said, they had been jailed by the Vichy government, the puppet French administration headed by senile, eighty-four-year-old Marshal Henri Philippe Pétain.

"We managed to escape and fled to Casablanca," Walter confided. His companion nodded in agreement.

While the chitchat continued, Walter happened to mention about "running on to Teddy Auer" on a Casablanca street. A chill shot up Coster's back. This, no doubt, was General Theodor Auer, the sinister chief of the German Armistice Commission.

"I knew him [Auer] in Paris before I was interned," the talkative Walter continued. "When we got to Casablanca, my partner here and I made a deal with him. We supply him with secret information and he keeps us out of jail."

Seeing the concerned look on Coster's face, Walter quickly added, "Of course my partner and I are very anti-Nazi."

Coster's mind was in a whirl. Here, by accident, was the pipeline he had been seeking to General Auer. Or had these two friendly Austrians been planted to coerce the vice consul's true role from him? Did they really hate the Nazis? With the specter of being found dead soon in a dark Casablanca alley hovering over him, Coster decided to take a risk. He would pose as a loudmouthed, rich playboy who drank too much and talked too much. While "drunk" he would spill the beans that the Americans and the British were preparing to invade at Dakar.

Coster's assessment of his two new friends proved to be accurate. A few days later, Walter and his companion called on General Auer and told him about the drunken State Department official's revelation that Dakar would be the invasion target. Auer was delighted. He broke open a bottle of champagne and shared it with his two spies, who had just pulled off an intelligence bonanza—or so it seemed.

Just past midnight on November 8, 1942, the Allied invasion of the French colonies of Morocco and Algeria struck at three places—including Casablanca—along one thousand miles of North African coastline. In spite of comic-opera blunders by green and partially trained U.S. Army and Navy units, the assault troops got ashore in strength and pushed inland rapidly.

On the outskirts of Casablanca, a convoy of three German staff cars rounded a street corner and came upon an American platoon. Brakes squealed and the vehicles lurched to a halt. *"Komm heraus, Schweinehunds!"* (Come out, you sons of bitches!) a GI shouted, pleased to have had the chance to use the German phrase he had been honing for weeks. Ten impeccably attired members of the German Armistice Commission emerged slowly with their hands in the air.

At the same time, far to the south, a large number of U-boat wolf packs were circling around Africa's western shore off Dakar, waiting to ambush an Allied invasion convoy that never came.[9]

Hitler's Evil Guardian Angel

FIELD MARSHAL GÜNTHER HANS VON KLUGE, leader of Army Group Central on the Eastern Front, was a favorite of Adolf Hitler and a hero to the German people. A courageous soldier and a skilled tactician, he was one of the few generals who would stand up to the führer. When Hitler telephoned with some new battlefield idea, Kluge would respond condescendingly: "But my dear führer, what you suggest simply is not practicable. You must come down out of *Wolkenkuckucksheim* [cloudy cuckooland]."

Although Kluge recognized the Nazi regime as the lawful government of Germany and had sworn the *Fahneneid* (blood oath), pledging strict obedience to Hitler, by November 1942 the field marshal was convinced that the führer was taking Germany down the road to destruction.

But when Kluge's senior operations officer, forty-one-year-old Colonel Henning von Tresckow, delicately broached the subject of the urgent need to "eliminate" Hitler, the field marshal listened but was noncommittal. "I am a soldier, Tresckow, not a politician!" he replied evenly.

Despite the rebuff, Tresckow was encouraged by Kluge's failure to respond angrily—or even to have the colonel arrested and court-martialed. So Tresckow plunged ahead with his efforts to eliminate the führer.

Tresckow came up with a simple plan of action: Hitler would be lured to Kluge's headquarters and riddled with bullets by guns in the hands of German soldiers especially picked for the task. Lieutenant Colonel Georg von Boeselager, holder of the Knight's Cross with oak leaves and swords, Germany's highest award at the time for valor, eagerly accepted the challenge to

General Henning von Tresckow,
conspirator to murder Hitler.
(Author's collection)

form and lead this commando-type unit. An evaluation report described him as "a spirited cavalry officer who thinks boldly . . . the idol of his men."

Boeselager found that there was no shortage of volunteers. They were selected from his own twenty-two-hundred-man Cavalry Regiment Center, which, according to the plan he and Colonel von Tresckow had painstakingly drawn up, would be assigned to field security around Kluge's headquarters on the day of the führer's visit.

Success of the plot would depend on Field Marshal von Kluge's willingness to invite Hitler to his headquarters on the specious pretext of raising the morale of the troops. Hitler would be shot down not long after he stepped down from his four-engine Condor aircraft and began walking through the towering forest that shielded Army Group Center's command post.

Boeselager's tough combat veterans chosen for his assassination unit, all armed with Schmeisser submachine guns, would then spring forward to engage in a firefight with Hitler's thirty SS bodyguards, all fiercely loyal and pledged to give their lives for the führer if need be.

If Hitler's penchant for erratic schedules and sudden changes in timetables would make it impossible to kill him before he reached the headquarters, then he would be riddled with bullets while eating lunch in the mess hall, presumably with Field Marshal von Kluge at his side. Ten officers from Boeselager's regiment volunteered to do the mess hall shooting.

Now everything was ready for the *coup d'état*. But when Colonel von Tresckow approached Kluge about his role in the plot, the field marshal's nerve failed at the last minute. No doubt the specter of the führer being blasted out of his chair by a group of decorated German combat veterans blazing away with Schmeissers in the middle of lunch was more than Kluge could bear.

Kluge's argument was that "neither the world, nor the German people, nor the German soldier would understand such an act at this time." Consequently, Boeselager and his hit men would have to bide their time.

A half a year later, in the summer of 1943, German conspirators pledged to the termination of Adolf Hitler felt that the time was ready to strike. The Wehrmacht had suffered disastrous setbacks on the Eastern Front, the Americans and the British had invaded and conquered Sicily, and the RAF Bomber Command continued to pulverize Germany's cities at night while the U.S. Eighth Air Force pounded German industrial facilities by day.

Highly decorated Captain Axel von dem Bussche, who had been sent to a hospital near Berlin several weeks earlier after taking a Soviet bullet through the lungs, eagerly volunteered to be an assassin. Twenty-three years of age, Bussche had been determined to get rid of Hitler, a man he earlier had admired as a god, because of an episode in the Soviet Union several months earlier.

Captain von dem Bussche, a devout and compassionate young man, and the infantry company he commanded had just been involved in a bloody fight to capture a key town in the Ukraine. While they were taking a short break near the ruins, Bussche saw a squad of SS soldiers herding perhaps a hundred civilians into a field. While Bussche watched in horror and disbelief, the ragged townspeople were forced to dig a pit, then lie down in their own mass grave. Then the SS men riddled the hapless natives with Schmeisser bullets until all the victims were dead.

Bussche, courageous in battle, was badly shaken for days by the fact that he had not tried to stop the murders. He was ashamed to have once sworn unswerving loyalty to the man he now considered to be a mass murderer—Adolf Hitler. Bussche rejected the oath he had taken to the führer. "He has broken the oath to God a thousand times," Bussche assured himself.

Although still weak from his serious wounds, the captain was released from the Berlin hospital, and while on leave to recuperate his strength, he and other conspirators held lengthy discussions on the technique to be used in killing Hitler. They finally decided on a scheme that called for an excuse for a lowly captain, Bussche, to get close to Hitler, who would be flanked by sharp-eyed SS bodyguards. Bussche would have a bomb with a four-and-a-half-second fuse concealed in his coat. Once he was near the führer, Bussche would activate the fuse, then wrestle with Hitler long enough for the blast to blow them both to smithereens.

In October 1943 the first gusts of Arctic cold whistled over the Russian steppes, and many commanders complained that their men's winter combat uniforms were inadequate. A Berlin manufacturer rapidly turned out a few experimental samples of new winter garb, but the design would need Hitler's approval before mass production could begin.

Learning of the new design, Bussche and his fellow plotters felt that this could provide the perfect means for killing Hitler. It would be arranged for

Bussche to be in charge of five men flown to the führer's battle headquarters, Wolfsschanze, in East Prussia, to model the new gear.

While conspirators at high levels began the subtle task of persuading Hitler to name a firm date for the modeling of the winter clothing, Bussche locked himself in his quarters and began experimenting with the type of bomb he would build. He inserted a fuse from a hand grenade into an explosive charge. Although the fuse would hiss when burning, he would mask the noise by faking a coughing fit moments before grabbing the führer in a bear hug.

During the last week in November, the captain concealed his homemade bomb in a satchel of clothing and flew from Berlin to Wolfsschanze. Checking into an army camp ten miles from Hitler's headquarters, he hid his bomb and waited for a summons to model the uniforms. Meanwhile, the führer had agreed to inspect the new design, but he refused to be pinned down to a specific day or hour.

Bussche's first order of business was to check with an officer at Wolfsschanze to confirm that the experimental uniforms had arrived from the Berlin mill. The new garb could not be found. Checking with the mill, the captain was stunned. A dozen uniforms had been put in a boxcar of a train sitting on a railroad siding in Berlin. But during a heavy British bombing raid that night, the boxcar containing the clothing became a charred, twisted wreck.

The would-be assassin had no alternative but to wait for the mill management to acquire bolts of cloth and produce a fresh consignment. However, Bussche, a battle-tested leader, could not risk drawing attention by loitering around a rear-echelon headquarters. So he concealed the homemade bomb in a musette bag and headed back to the Eastern Front to take command of his company.

Before departing, Bussche was told by another conspirator, Major General Helmuth Stieff, a staff officer at *Führerhauptquartier* (the führer's headquarters), that when Hitler agreed on a new date for the modeling, an excuse would be concocted to pull the captain back from the front so he could carry out the assassination scheme.

Hitler's evil guardian angel continued to watch over him, however. In January 1944 a Soviet artillery shell exploded at Captain von dem Bussche's feet, and the blast knocked him unconscious. A few hours later, surgeons at a field hospital amputated his shredded leg, leaving him alive but unable to proceed with his covert mission.

Despite the assassination-plot failures, Henning von Tresckow, now a general, was determined to persevere. But his subtle search to find someone to murder Hitler proved to be futile until he accidentally discovered a likely candidate in an unlikely place—Captain Eberhard von Breitenbuch, the personal aide to Field Marshal Ernst Busch, one of the few generals still fiercely loyal to the führer.

Busch had succeeded the wounded Field Marshal von Kluge as commander of Army Group Center on the Eastern Front. Back in 1938, when General Ludwig Beck tried secretly to have the army High Command go on record as opposing Hitler's march to war, Busch and another senior officer had been the only ones who declined to endorse the proposal.

Early in March 1944 Busch was ordered to fly to southern Germany and report to Adolf Hitler at Berghof, the führer's large and ornate retreat perched on the Obersalzberg, 6,208 feet above the picturesque village of Berchtesgaden. Busch was supposed to present a briefing on the situation along the Army Group Center front and explain why the Wehrmacht was suffering one defeat after another.

Busch promptly called in Eberhard Breitenbuch and told him to prepare for the flight to the Berghof. Within the hour, the captain was in touch with General von Tresckow and suggested that this could be a golden opportunity to "liquidate" Hitler inside the retreat. Tresckow suggested that the field marshal's aide use a new type of bomb with a one-second fuse, but the captain refused the suggestion. He explained that he was an expert marksman, and if he could smuggle a pistol into the führer's presence, he could not miss a shot to the head.

Breitenbuch collected the documents that Busch would need for briefing Hitler, left behind an envelope with a letter to his wife in case the plot was successful, and slipped a pistol into a trouser pocket. Soon the field marshal and his aide were in a four-engine Condor winging toward Berchtesgaden. They reached the Berghof at noon on March 11.

As was his custom, the fifty-four-year-old absolute master of eighty million Germans kept Field Marshal Busch cooling his heels in an anteroom to the fifty-by-sixty-foot chamber where visitors were received. Breitenbuch struggled to mask his anxiety, and he wondered if any of the SS guards had noticed the bulge in his pocket where the pistol was concealed.

After a lapse of what seemed to be an eternity, an SS lieutenant colonel said that Hitler would now receive the field marshal. Busch headed for the door, followed closely by his aide, lugging Busch's heavy briefcase. The young captain grew even more tense. In moments the führer, whom he considered to be the scourge of Germany, would be dead with a bullet in his head.

Busch reached the heavy double doors leading into the great room and was about to enter when an SS major stepped in front of Breitenbuch. This is the end, the captain reflected. But the SS man merely said, "No aides permitted inside, by the führer's order."

Shrugging, the field marshal took the briefcase from his aide and walked into the room, where Hitler greeted him warmly. Busch sank into a plush, oversized chair surrounded by large oil paintings, ornate tapestries, and classic statuary and soon launched a lengthy presentation on why things had gone wrong on the Eastern Front.

Outside, in the empty anteroom, Captain Breitenbuch was undergoing the torments of the damned. Had the Gestapo tapped General von Tresckow's telephone? Was the murder plot known? At any moment, the captain expected

SS men to barge into the anteroom and arrest him. He wondered nervously how he could get rid of the incriminating pistol in his pocket.

At midafternoon, after Breitenbuch had suffered mental agony for three hours, Busch strolled back through the two doors, and soon he and his aide were flying in the Condor back to the Eastern Front.

General von Tresckow and Captain Breitenbuch discussed the curious scenario at the Berghof. Why had the aide suddenly been barred? Neither could broach a reason. They could only conclude that the führer had exercised the *Fingerspitzengefühl* (intuition in the fingertips, or a sixth sense) for which even his staunchest enemies in Germany had long given him credit.[10]

Roosevelt's Guest a Nazi Spy

IN THE POSH MIRAMAR HOTEL in Fedala, Morocco, U.S. and French military leaders gathered to smoke the peace pipe. Lieutenant General George S. Patton Jr. and other American officers were in high good spirits, elated to have the fighting halted. So were most of the Frenchmen. However, Admiral François Michelier, the commander at Casablanca and a diehard supporter of the German puppet government in Vichy, France, was grim, even sullen. It was November 11, 1942.

Three days earlier, American and British forces, sailing from the United States and the United Kingdom, had stormed ashore at several key points along a twelve-hundred-mile stretch of coastline in French Northwest Africa. Code-named Operation Torch, the invasion had been launched to confront Adolf Hitler with a second front, thereby taking some of the heat from Josef Stalin's hard-pressed armies in the Soviet Union.

After a two-day fight with French forces whose commander, Admiral Jean Darlan, was loyal to the Vichy government, a cease-fire was called. It was not a French surrender, as General Dwight D. Eisenhower, the Allied commander, was quick to point out. Rather, it was a halting of the bloodshed so the French armed forces in Northwest Africa could join with the Americans and the British in battling "our common enemy, Nazi Germany," Eisenhower declared.

After the peace parley in Fedala, General Patton returned to his headquarters in Casablanca, the major objective his Western Task Force had seized. With time on his hands, Patton traveled to Rabat to call on the sultan, the traditional military and political leader of Morocco.

After entering the sultan's grounds of several hundred lavishly manicured acres, Patton and his aides reached the palace itself, a huge, three-story white building of Moorish architecture. The Americans were met by the grand vizier, who wore a white robe with a hood and had a scraggly beard and an enormous set of gold-inlaid teeth. The general pondered that he must have been at least ninety-two years of age.

الى كل عربى كريم

١. السلام عليكم ورحمة الله وبعد فحامل هذا الكتاب من ،
جيش الولايات المتحدة وهو صديق لكل الشعوب العربية
فنرجو أن تحسنوا معاملته وتحافظوا عليه من كل الأضرار
وأن تقدموا له الطعام والشراب وترشدوه إلى
أقرب معسكر أمريكى أو بريطانى وسنكافئكم
بسخاء على خدماتكم والسلام عليكم ورحمة
الله وبركاته .

FRANKLIN D. ROOSEVELT

رئيس الولايات المتحدة الأمريكية

**To all Arab peoples greetings and peace be upon
you. The bearer of this letter is a soldier of the
United States Government and a friend of all
Arabs. Treat him well, guard him from harm,
give him food and drink, help him to return to the
nearest American or British soldiers and you will
be liberally rewarded. Peace and the mercy of
God be upon you.**

FRANKLIN D. ROOSEVELT,
President of the United States of America.

U.S. troops carried this two-language leaflet ashore. (Author's collection)

The ancient one announced in cracked English that the sultan had graciously consented to see Patton, which, the general reflected, was the reason he had made the dusty jaunt from Casablanca. Patton, his aides, and an entourage of the sultan's confidants walked up three flights of stairs, then entered a long room covered with thick, beautiful, and obscenely expensive rugs. At the end of the long chamber on a raised platform sat the sultan, who was a man in his midthirties with a mostly clean-shaven face, as opposed to the bearded legacy of scores of predecessors over the centuries.

As instructed earlier by his protocol aide, Patton walked briskly up the room, then halted before the platform and bowed from the hips, much to his consternation but in the interest of good relations with the Moroccan leader. The sultan rose regally, shook hands with Patton, and both men sat down.

During their conversation, the sultan spoke in Arabic, so there were long pauses while an interpreter translated the words into French, a language Patton spoke fluently. This procedure annoyed the general, for the Americans knew the sultan spoke French and English quite well. Rumor had it that he had graduated under an alias from Oxford University in England.

Patton masked his irritation, feeling it was important to have the leader of millions of North African Muslims regard the invaders favorably. What the fiery general did not know was that the gracious and friendly sultan was a spy for Nazi Germany.

A few months before the invasion, Admiral Wilhelm Canaris, the head of the Abwehr, and one of his top aides, General Erwin von Lahousen, a tall, astute Austrian, had flown from Berlin to Morocco, where they recruited the sultan as a secret agent. Now the ruler presumably would provide the Abwehr with details of his long talks with General Patton. It was a high priority with Adolf Hitler that the military intentions of the Western Allies be learned so that countermeasures could be taken.

On January 13, 1943, just over three months after the sultan had hosted Patton, President Franklin Roosevelt and Prime Minister Winston Churchill, along with their chiefs of staff, began a conference (code-named Symbol) at Casablanca to discuss future strategy. Perhaps through the sultan, the Germans seemed to know that the two Allied leaders were coming and that the discussions would be held at the fashionable seaside resort Anfa, four miles outside the city. On the first night after the arrival of the president and the prime minister, the moans of air-raid sirens caused lights to be extinguished at the Anfa.

For a half hour, the heads of state, generals, and admirals engaged in chitchat by candlelight that illuminated the whiskey bottles on the table. The all-clear was sounded. No bombs fell. Presumably a lone German reconnaissance plane had flown over to scout the situation around the Anfa.

Two nights before President Roosevelt was to depart from Casablanca, he played host at a lavish banquet to "my good friend the sultan of Morocco." Much to the dismay of Winston Churchill and Roosevelt's closest civilian confidant, Harry Hopkins, no alcoholic beverages were available, in deference to the sultan's Muslim religious beliefs.

On January 25 Symbol broke up, and President Roosevelt and his entourage left Casablanca in his personal airplane, *Sacred Cow*. In Berlin that same day, General von Lahousen wrote in the diary at Abwehr headquarters: "Orders have been received [from Adolf Hitler] that the letter received from the sultan of Morocco should be kept top secret. It contains information of the highest strategic and political importance."

The letter was the sultan's detailed recollections of his conversation with President Roosevelt at the Casablanca banquet. What the Moroccan leader had learned would never be known, but it was likely that his lengthy communication contained reference to a factor of utmost importance to Berlin: that the British and Americans would continue operations in the Mediterranean in 1943, rather than launch a cross-Channel assault from England against northern France, as the German leaders had feared.[11]

Ruse in a Berlin Brothel

TWO OF THE BRIGHTEST STARS in the Nazi hierarchy were SS General Reinhard Heydrich, the thirty-six-year-old chief of the Sicherheitsdienst (SD), the intelligence branch of the Schutzstafel (SS), and his top deputy, SS Major General Walther Schellenberg. At thirty years of age, Schellenberg was the youngest general in the German armed forces.

Both men had been selected for their posts by Reichsführer Heinrich Himmler, who, as head of the Gestapo and the SS, was the second most powerful man in the Third Reich. No doubt Himmler saw in the two young men reflections of his own character: a blend of keen and innovative minds with the ruthless instincts and morals of gangsters.

Tall, slim, and blond, Reinhard Heydrich was a first-class fencer, an excellent horseman, and a talented violinist. Extremely ambitious, he envisioned the day when all German espionage services would be united under one leader: himself.

Walther Schellenberg, equally ambitious, had studied to be a physician for two years, but he changed his mind and earned a law degree at the University of Bonn. He first came to Himmler's attention by giving a lecture on German law in which he castigated the Roman Catholic Church, a primary target of Nazi leaders.

Boyish and charming, Schellenberg hoped to one day replace Heydrich as chief of the SD, but that goal did not interfere with the close relationship the two men had. They complemented one another perfectly. All one of them had to do was to throw out a vague idea—such as kidnapping two British spies in the Netherlands, or planting an agent in the home of the British ambassador in Turkey—and the other would elaborate on the scheme and carry it out to perfection.

One day in 1942, Schellenberg was seated in a comfortable chair in Heydrich's ornate Berlin office, and the two men were discussing possible Machiavellian operations. Suddenly Heydrich hit on a novel espionage plot: Establish a place in Berlin where foreign notables could come and relax amid attractive company and, involuntarily, give up information important to the Third Reich.

Schellenberg took that thread of an idea and embroidered on it without further consultation with his boss, Heydrich. Heydrich's brainstorm would be known as the Kitty Salon, and it would become quite famous and popular among notables, foreign and domestic, in Berlin.

A large number of the prettiest and most vivacious prostitutes were rounded up and sworn to secrecy. Their task was to "entertain" the foreign dignitaries, subtly ply them with alcoholic drinks, and extract information from them. Also recruited as "hostesses" for the Kitty Salon were a number of Berlin women who had high social standing. They claimed to have volunteered for the undercover duty through patriotism, to help the führer.

The scheme exceeded the fondest expectations of the two SD leaders. A large number of foreign diplomats and high-ranking military officers in civilian clothes spilled out secrets in this paradise filled with hidden microphones, tape recorders, and cameras.

One visitor to this posh brothel was Count Galeazzo Ciano, who was married to the only daughter of Italian dictator Benito Mussolini. To the surprise of no one, after the 1930 nuptials Ciano rose rapidly in the foreign service, and in 1936 the thirty-three-year-old count reached the top: foreign minister.

Ciano dealt often with Nazi leaders, and he had signed the Pact of Steel in an elaborate ceremony in Berlin on May 22, 1939. If either Germany or Italy were to go to war, the pact stated, "the other power will immediately come to its partner's aid with its full military strength."

If Count Ciano had any moral scruples, he kept them concealed. To him, morality in international relations was a fairy tale. Morals in his private life were equally nonexistent. Despite these flaws, many women found him to be witty and charming and were attracted by his classic good looks.

In February 1943, after the war began to turn against the Axis Powers (mainly Germany and Italy), bombastic Benito Mussolini began reshuffling his government in what would be a losing effort to retain power. Son-in-law Ciano was appointed ambassador to the Vatican. Four months later, after the Western Allies had conquered the island of Sicily and were preparing to leap across the Strait of Messina and invade mainland Italy, mild little King Victor Emmanuel III summarily booted out Adolf Hitler's good friend Mussolini from the post he had held for twenty-one years. The monarch then had Mussolini arrested and locked up at an undisclosed locale.

A short time later, Count Ciano—quite wisely, no doubt—vanished from Rome, leaving his wife, Edda, behind. Soon he popped up in Berlin, a curious place for him to take refuge in light of the fact that his opposite number in the Third Reich, Joachim von Ribbentrop, detested him. So did Heinrich Himmler, the SS chief.

No doubt Walther Schellenberg's SD agents were monitoring the hidden bugs in the infamous Kitty Salon when their ears must have perked up: one of

*In happier times, Count
Galeazzo Ciano (left) and
German Foreign Minister
Joachim von Ribbentrop.
(National Archives)*

the "guests" that night was Count Ciano. Before he could leave the ornate establishment of pretty young women, the Italian was pounced on by Schellenberg's men and put in jail.

Now began a cat-and-mouse game between the incarcerated Italian count and top Nazi officials in Berlin. Since 1940, Reinhard Heydrich's agents had known that Ciano kept a voluminous diary, and they learned that he had shown portions of it to friends that disclosed Adolf Hitler's double dealings with foreign dignitaries.

That diary had to be tracked down. Foreign Minister von Ribbentrop offered to free Ciano in exchange for all copies of his diary. Apparently the proposal was either refused or Ciano insisted on time to think it over. No doubt he realized that his best chance of escaping the firing squad or the hangman's noose was his incriminating diaries.

A German woman known only as "Frau Beetz" had been assigned as Ciano's interpreter. She visited him in his cell almost daily. Actually, Beetz was an SD agent whose task was to coerce Ciano into disclosing the location of the diary. In a curious twist, the woman apparently became enamored of the handsome, charismatic count, and she became more interested in helping the Italian get out of jail than she was in Nazi goals.

Ciano, growing more desperate each day, took a gamble and put his faith in Frau Beetz. Had his judgment been wrong, he could have been signing his own death warrant. He told her where the diary was hidden, and she found an excuse to go to Rome, recover the document, and turn it over to Edda Ciano.

Edda contacted German authorities in Rome, handed over six volumes of transcriptions of harmless conversations between her husband and German leaders over the years, but refused to give up the diary unless the count was released.

Meanwhile, Ciano had been taken to Scalzi Prison in Verona, a city in northern Italy. On instructions from his father-in-law, Benito Mussolini, who had set up a caretaker government after being rescued from captivity by German commandos, the count was charged with treason.

Dragged from Cell 27 on January 11, 1944, Galeazzo Ciano was shot to death in the courtyard of Scalzi Prison. Had he not succumbed to the lure of the Kitty Salon, he might have escaped to neutral Switzerland and survived the war.

Prolonged efforts by Reinhard Heydrich and Walther Schellenberg to locate and confiscate the Ciano diary proved to be in vain. On the day before her husband was riddled with bullets, Edda Ciano reached Geneva with the diary. Soon she released it to the *Chicago Daily News* for global publication in serial form.[12]

A Spy Spies on the Spymaster

NIGHT HAD CAST ITS VEIL over Bern, the medieval, picturesque Swiss capital, as the hulking figure ambled up to the building at Herrengasse 23. Squinting in the dim glow of a streetlight, Hans Bernard Gisevius, an Abwehr agent under the cover of a German vice consul, discerned the lettering on a small sign next to the door: "Allen W. Dulles, Special Assistant to the U.S. Minister."

The sign was merely part of the games that those involved in international intrigue play. Dulles, as nearly all of the one hundred or so German spies roaming about neutral Switzerland knew, was actually the OSS station chief in Bern, a hotbed of espionage.

Gisevius rapped on the door and was greeted by Dulles himself. It was a strange rendezvous indeed: the American spymaster and a key figure in the Abwehr, the Nazi intelligence agency. It was February 1943, and the war's fortunes had begun to turn against Adolf Hitler after more than three years of largely battlefield successes.

Despite his deceptively mild appearance, Dulles was tough-minded and cagey. He was fond of tweed jackets and bow ties. He wore rimless spectacles and was a stereotype of Hollywood's version of a kindly college professor.

During World War I he had gained experience in undercover activities doing the same job he was now performing a war later—collecting intelligence from inside Germany. In the earlier conflict, his cover had been as an employee of the U.S. State Department.

Dulles's guest on this night, Hans Gisevius, who had a stiff Prussian bearing, had joined the Gestapo in 1933, shortly after Adolf Hitler came to power, only to be ousted six months later because of his lack of enthusiasm for the Nazi cause. Then he became a member of the Berlin Police Department, but he was fired for criticizing the elite SS, the führer's bodyguard.

In 1939, just before the outbreak of war, the 270-pound Gisevius joined the Schwarze Kapelle, the small conspiratorial group bent on ousting Adolf Hitler and the Nazi regime. Admiral Wilhelm Canaris, chief of the Abwehr and a leader in the Schwarze Kapelle, took Gisevius as an agent and assigned him to the consulate in Zurich to be the eyes and ears of the German anti-Hitler conspiracy in Switzerland.

Gisevius first had tried to establish a covert contact with the British secret service in Switzerland, but he had been rejected. However, Allen Dulles had decided to take a chance on this incomparable pipeline into the highest levels in Berlin.

After a secret meeting with the big German, held on a dark side street, Dulles had been impressed with his sincerity. Subsequently, Gisevius made numerous nocturnal visits to Herrengasse 23, and plans were worked out between the two men for Gisevius to recruit couriers to bring high-grade intelligence out of Berlin to Dulles.

One evening, as the two men were dining at Herrengasse 23, Dulles's female cook cracked the kitchen door a few inches and listened. She had not seen Gisevius before and did not know who he was. However, she was surprised that Dulles and his guest were conversing in German.

Her curiosity aroused, the woman sneaked into another room and inspected the guest's hat. In it were the initials H.B.G.

Within an hour, the cook left the premises and headed for the German consulate, where she informed an official about the hulking man with the closely cropped hair who was meeting secretly with the American master spy in Switzerland.

For the previous few weeks, Dulles's cook, a Swiss, had been on the German embassy payroll and assigned the task of reporting on "suspicious" visitors at Herrengasse 23.

When Vice Consul Gisevius reported for work the next day, he was confronted by two consulate officials, who accused him of treason. A quick-witted man, Gisevius feigned deep indignation and loudly rebuked the two men. Of course he had visited Dulles, and there was good reason for his doing so: The American was providing him with secret intelligence about the Allies.

Glowering down on the now subdued consulate officials, the six-foot-five Gisevius said that he was willing to forget their impertinence, but if they valued their jobs, they had better forget what Dulles's cook had told them.

Before the day was out, Gisevius made secret contact with Dulles, and the American master spy promptly fired his cook, learning for the first time that she was a Nazi spy. For his part, Hans Gisevius learned a valuable lesson: A secret agent must never display his initials inside his hatband.[13]

Part Five

The Tide Turns

A Female Resistant Tricks
the Gestapo

ALTHOUGH THIRTY-YEAR-OLD LUCIE AUBRAC had a two-year-old son and was pregnant again in mid-1943, she and her husband, Raymond, had been active members of the French underground movement Libération for nearly three years. The couple lived in the large city of Lyon, in southeastern France, but Raymond had been almost constantly traveling around the country as one of the leaders in the resistance.

A mining engineer, Aubrac stole explosives from the Germans for his specialty—planning and leading missions to blow up railroad facilities that were aiding the German war effort—and occasionally "eliminating" a French collaborator.

Lucie's role as a history teacher and homemaker was a perfect foil for her activities with the resistance. She had helped scores of men on the run from the Gestapo and downed Allied pilots to escape from France.

Although the Gestapo apparently had never suspected that Lucie was involved with the resistance, Raymond had been suspect, but he had escaped with the aid of other resistants. Then his luck ran out: He was one of the eight members of the Lyon underground who had been captured in a Gestapo raid in a house where a meeting was in progress.

Raymond was hurled into a thick-walled, closely guarded prison from which no one had ever escaped. Although tortured for a week, he refused to disclose the names of other underground members. He was sentenced to be executed.

Lucie learned of her husband's predicament, and she knew that a raid by resistants to free him would be futile. Although several months pregnant, she concocted a unique scheme to gain his freedom. Armed with forged papers that identified her as a staunch collaborator, she marched boldly into Gestapo headquarters in Lyon.

There she put on a rousing performance that would have turned Sarah Bernhardt green with envy. Claiming to be an unwed mother-to-be, she demanded to see the German captain in charge, then screamed at him that her honor was at stake and demanded that he do something about it.

Lucie loudly declared that the lousy, no-good "terrorist" (Raymond), who was being held in prison, had been her lover, but she had known nothing of his underground activities. Pointing to her pregnant condition, she vowed that he was the father of her unborn child, and that unless he married her, the offspring would go through life as a "bastard" and she as a scarlet woman.

The Gestapo leader pondered her story for several seconds, then apparently decided that a highly favorable propaganda bonanza could result, proving how kind and humane the Nazi police force truly was. So he agreed to bring in a French priest to marry the couple in Raymond's cell. "No! No!" Lucie cried out hysterically. Such a scenario could bring only shame to her. So the Gestapo leader agreed to bring the condemned man to her at the headquarters.

As Lucie and Raymond had discussed countless times in the past, if either one was arrested, the other would give no indication that they were husband and wife. So when the bearded, haggard prisoner entered the room, she embraced him and whispered, "The truck carrying you back to jail will be attacked by friends."

Then the wedding ceremony was performed by the unknowing priest, presumably making the unborn child legitimate and salvaging Lucie's honor. Afterward, Raymond was hustled outside and put in a truck that held several other French "terrorists." Two German soldiers armed with Schmeisser machine pistols guarded the prisoners, and a third Feldgrau sat next to the driver. By now, darkness had descended.

With a grinding of gears, the truck pulled away. The bored Germans failed to notice that four cars were trailing in the traffic. Suddenly one car whipped around the truck, and a bullet was sent through the head of the driver, causing the truck to careen wildly and crash into a pole.

Before the German guards could bring their weapons to bear, the Libération men gunned them down. Raymond jumped into one of the cars, and the remaining prisoners fled into the night.

Three weeks later, the Aubracs were in England—just in time for Lucie to give birth to baby Catherine.[1]

An Owner Blows Up His Factory

THE STRIDENT SOUNDS OF AIR RAID SIRENS split the night over the Paris region, and minutes later, a large flight of Royal Air Force bombers was over the huge Peugeot plant that was building airplane engine parts and tank turrets for the German Wehrmacht. Soon there was the eerie rustling noise of hundreds of bombs racing to the earth, then a firecrackerlike series of ground-jarring explosions. It was July 1943.

After dawn, an RAF reconnaissance plane winged over the Peugeot plant at a high altitude and snapped photographs. Back in England, the film was processed, and RAF leaders were stunned. The bomb concentration had missed the factory by a mile and had killed scores of French civilians in their homes.

While dazed townspeople dug loved ones from the ruins, Henry Rée, a Frenchman who had been parachuted into the region by the British Special Operations Executive (SOE) several months earlier, sensed opportunity from the tragedy. He covertly approached Rudolphe Peugeot with a bizarre proposal: If Peugeot would arrange to sabotage his own factory and render it useless, Rée would make sure that the RAF did not return to do the job again, probably causing more civilian casualties.

For long moments, Rudolphe stared at the visitor. What kind of game was he playing? Was he an agent provocateur, sent by the Gestapo to trap him into some illegal action? Finally Peugeot demanded that Rée provide proof that he was in league with the Allies and could halt a second bombing raid. Rée told Peugeot to tune his radio to BBC from London at nine o'clock that night and hear a short phrase that the factory owner suggested.

SOE long had had a working arrangement with BBC whereby that government broadcasting station would flash over the air at a designated time an innocuous statement provided by a spy in the field.

Rée hurried back to his home, took his radio transmitter from its hiding place in the basement, and asked London to have the BBC announcer read the phrase. The BBC complied.

When Rée contacted the shaken Peugeot the next day, the company owner suggested points where explosives should be placed to achieve the most damage and assigned two trusted employees to do the job. Forty-eight hours later, a gigantic blast shook the region as the Peugeot factory blew skyward in thousands of pieces.

Although German engineers were rushed in to try to restore production of the crucial war items, they did not succeed. So effectively had the plant been sabotaged that it would never be operational again during the war. Although the Gestapo grilled Rudolphe Peugeot, he feigned such anguish over the loss of the factory that they went away convinced of his innocence.

Henry Rée tried the same formula on the Michelin tire family but failed. The Michelin plant kept on churning out high-quality tires for the Wehrmacht at Clermont Ferrand, about two hundred miles from Paris. A few nights later, a Royal Air Force bomber force flew over and the Michelin family watched from a hill as the huge plant was blown to smithereens.

In mid-1943, seventy-five RAF Lancasters took off from southern England for Lyon, to bomb the Schneider-Creusot factory, which was producing weapons for the German Army. The Lancasters barely damaged the French-owned works but killed a large number of civilians.

Rather than risk another slaughter of innocents, the RAF commanders decided to knock out sources of electric power that fed the Schneider-Creusot factory and a number of satellite factories around Lyon. However, it would not be the bombers, but secret agents on the ground who would perpetrate the power-complex sabotage.

In August 1943 Raymond Basset (code-named Mary) and André Jarrot (code-named Goujon), two Frenchmen, parachuted into the Lyon region. Acting quickly, they recruited sabotage teams, provided each with explosives that had been dropped at night by the RAF, and drew up plans for a coordinated sabotage attack.

The saboteurs, stealing through the night, blew up four power stations and set fire to their oil and coal dumps. The Schneider-Creusot complex was inoperable for many months due to lack of electricity.

All over France in late 1943 and early 1944, many resistance men employed in factories producing war materials for the Germans created sophisticated techniques to halt production. At Toulouse, in the South of France, an engineer put subtle changes into blueprints, or wrote in a reversal of tolerance indications, or made deviations of a fraction of a millimeter in a mold. As a result, there were malfunctions of components, just enough to badly damage German engines or guns after short use. Because the components were already being used, it was impossible for the Gestapo to pin down just where in the production and distribution processes the sabotage had occurred.

Another technique was created by Britain's Political Warfare Executive (PWE), to destroy or seriously damage French factories producing items for the Wehrmacht. Pamphlets, printed in several languages because so many foreign workers were in France, were dropped by the millions from British bombers over German-occupied France. The pamphlets contained many drawings that explained how to drop pebbles into delicate machinery, pour sand into fuel tanks, and screw manufactured parts on loosely.

"These actions can never be traced to you," the factory workers were assured.[2]

A Plan to Bomb the United States

REICHSMARSCHALL HERMANN GOERING, chief of the Luftwaffe and number two man in the Nazi pecking order behind Adolf Hitler, was under heavy criticism in mid-1943. The pompous, 290-pound World War I fighter ace once had boasted publicly: "Not a single [Allied] bomb will ever fall on the Third Reich." Now droves of British and U.S. bombers were rapidly turning the Greater Reich into a greater wreck.

In a desperate effort to slow the daily and nightly onslaught, Goering decided to implement a tactic put forward by an ace fighter pilot, Major Hans-Joachim (Hajo) Herrmann, who was widely known in the Luftwaffe for his innovative ideas. Herrmann's plan was to oppose the British bombers at night with day fighter planes.

German flying boats like this one were to be used to leapfrog the Atlantic and bomb New York City and Washington. (National Archives)

Instead of relying on radar and ground-control radio messages to intercept the bombers on the way to targets, the Focke-Wulf 190s would hover high above a city while the attack was taking place. The German pilots could look down on bombers silhouetted against the bright glare from marking flares, searchlight beams, and burning structures. Then the Fw-190s would pounce on the intruders with all cannons blazing. These roving fighters came to be called Wilde Sau (Wild Sows).

By the fall of 1943, the Wild Sow tactic had inflicted gargantuan losses on the night-flying British bombers. During three major raids on Berlin, German pilots shot down 123 bombers and badly damaged another 114.

In the months ahead, however, the round-the-clock Allied bombings reduced most major German cities to piles of rubble, and the Luftwaffe fighter planes had been virtually wiped out. Across the Third Reich there were incessant demands that means be found to bomb cities in the United States.

Reichsmarschall Goering knew that his scientists were developing long-range bombers that, hopefully, could eventually reach targets in the United States. But it would be many months before these revolutionary aircraft could go into production. In the meantime, Goering decided to give the green light to an ingenious plan conceived by the bold thinker, Major Hajo Herrmann, to drop bombs on New York City and Washington.

The Luftwaffe chief knew that the relatively few explosives that might fall on New York City and Washington would cause only minimal destruction. However, he was convinced that the adverse psychological impact on the United States home front would be gargantuan, while the morale of the German *Herrenvolk* would soar.

Conventional land-based Luftwaffe bombers could not be used for the project because their longest range was only a few hundred miles. So Hajo Herrmann's idea was to develop a "bridge" of U-boats carrying containers of aviation fuel stationed at specified intervals along the thirty-five-hundred-mile air route across the Atlantic Ocean.

Flying boats would take off from bases in western Europe with the customary amount of fuel and leapfrog along the air route. They would land beside the first surfaced submarines, which would refuel the aircraft. Then the flying boats would lift off on the next leg of the flight and continue this procedure nine or ten times.

When the flying boats reached the final U-boats hovering perhaps two hundred miles off the coast of the United States, bombs carried by the submarines would be fitted into racks that had been designed and attached to the underbodies especially for this mission. Then the planes would wing the last leg of the leapfrog pattern to New York City and Washington.

These unique missions would be one-way. After dropping their lethal cargos over the targets, the flying boats would land off the coast of the United States and the crews presumably would be taken prisoner.

In Germany, feverish efforts were launched to implement Major Hajo Herrmann's stratagem. But the Third Reich was steadily being pressed from east and west by Allied forces, manpower and resources had dwindled, and the plan could not be realized.[3]

The Princes and Seven Thousand Danish Jews

NIELS BOHR HAD ENORMOUS PRESTIGE in Denmark and in the global scientific community. A nuclear physicist, he was president of the Royal Danish Academy and a confidant of King Christian X, who was seventy-three years old in 1943 and ailing. Since Hitler's legions overran helpless Denmark in 1940, the king and Bohr had tried to save their people by avoiding an open confrontation with the Gestapo.

In Copenhagen, Bohr experimented at the Institute for Theoretical Physics. President Roosevelt was told by scientists in Washington that Bohr's work was dangerously like atomic projects secretly under way in the United States.

The Gestapo knew what Bohr was doing, and no doubt was waiting until he had succeeded in his project—a theory to build an atomic bomb—before arresting him and seizing his information. The Danish underground was well aware that Bohr was engaged in revolutionary work that might be of value to the Germans. So underneath his laboratory, in a sewer, resistants had stealthily laid dynamite charges—just in case.

Meanwhile, King Christian remained in his castle and made every effort to protect the Danish people. During the German occupation both the angular, distinguished monarch and Professor Bohr had been handled gently by the Nazis, who were biding their time until the physicist had finished his work in atomic energy.

For two years, Bohr had been playing a dangerous game, communicating on a regular basis with British physicists in London. In the spring of 1943 he cautioned his London contacts that the Germans were seeking large amounts of uranium and heavy water that, theoretically, could be used to develop atomic bombs.

Bohr's disclosure triggered a flap in the British government. Prime Minister Winston Churchill's scientific adviser Frederick Lindemann (Lord Cherwell) suggested that the Danish underground should ignite the explosives under Bohr's institute laboratory.

In Copenhagen, the Gestapo chief recommended to Berlin that King Christian be taken into custody and Bohr's project be brought overtly under the control of the Germans.

A few days later, a thousand German troops, led by a general, stormed the Royal Palace and overpowered the fifty guards armed with swords, and the king became a virtual prisoner. While the Germans were still in the palace, Christian managed to scribble a note that was delivered to Niels Bohr, urging him to escape to England. The physicist knew that he would be arrested and sent to Germany. So he sealed his papers in a large metal tube and buried it in the garden of his residence.

In the days that followed, a wave of terror swept through Denmark. Jews were rounded up by German soldiers and Gestapo agents, herded into railroad freight cars, and shipped to the Third Reich.

Bohr knew that it was time to go. His laboratory now was so closely guarded that Danish resistants could not blow up the facility. In mid-September he was spirited away by the underground and took a boat at night over the narrow waters between Copenhagen and the neutral Swedish port of Landskrona. A few days after his fifty-eighth birthday, Bohr, one of the world's foremost nuclear scientists, was escorted to a dark pasture outside of Stockholm. Soon he climbed into a Mosquito airplane sent by the Royal Air Force, and moments later he was winging toward London.

In the meantime, about two hundred members of the Copenhagen Synagogue listened fearfully as Rabbi Chaim Melchoir disclosed: "Last night I

received word that tomorrow the Germans plan to raid Jewish homes throughout the city to arrest all Danish Jews for shipment to concentration camps." It
was Friday morning, September 10, 1943.

"The Germans know that tomorrow is Rosh Hashanah and our families
will be home," Melchoir added. "By nightfall tonight, we must all be in hiding."

It seemed to be an impossible task. Where could the remaining seven
thousand Danish Jews hide?

The rabbi knew that his frightening information was accurate: it had
come from "The Princes"—the action arm of the Danish underground. As
resistants to Nazi tyranny, the Danes had no equal in Europe. The Princes were
divided into "The Priests," who sabotaged and surveilled harbors; "The Barris-
ters," in charge of action against German telecommunications; "The Brewers,"
whose job was to wreak havoc with the Germans' electrical system; and "The
Painters," who blew up railway lines and locomotives.

On Rosh Hashanah, hundreds of Germans launched a dragnet to scoop
up Denmark's seven thousand Jews for deportation. None could be found; they
were being sheltered in Christian homes.

That weekend, The Princes had been busy. They had rounded up one
hundred small boats, which were used to carry the threatened Jews to safety in
Sweden.[4]

Eisenhower's Secret Weapon

WAR-WEARY LONDON was gripped by cold early on the morning of January 14,
1944, when General Dwight D. Eisenhower's private coach *Bayonet* rolled into
a railroad station. His train had whisked him through the thick fog from Prest-
wick Airport in Scotland, after he had spent two weeks in Washington for con-
sultations on Operation Overlord, the looming invasion of Normandy.

Within a few days of taking over at Supreme Headquarters Allied Expeditionary Force (SHAEF) on Grosvenor Square, the affable, chain-smoking
Eisenhower was staggering under the tremendous burden. Never in history had
one man been called on to direct such a gargantuan endeavor.

Anxiety constantly gripped SHAEF because the stakes were enormous.
British General Frederick Morgan, who had drawn up the original invasion
plan, warned, "If the Germans have even a forty-eight-hour advance notice of
the time and place of the landings, we could suffer a monstrous catastrophe."

Increasing the chances of Eisenhower avoiding such a bloody debacle was
the existence of several top-secret storage houses holding a vast amount of information on the Wehrmacht and topographic features on the far side of the English Channel. This conglomeration had been collected by British spies and
other clandestine sources.

At the War Office in London, an Oxford professor, Eric Birley, and a small staff constantly analyzed the German Army's deployment in France. This picture changed almost daily, sometimes hourly. Birley kept track of the location, components, and experience of all units of the Wehrmacht. His reports and files would be the keys to deducing the enemy's capabilities and intentions.

Tucked away in a time-worn building at staid Oxford, the oldest university in England, located about fifty miles northwest of London, Fred Wells, a classicist, and his staff of geologists, hydrographers, geographers, economists, photographers, and draftsmen operated the Inter-Services Topographic Department. They collected a wealth of detailed information about beaches, tides, and currents in and around western Europe and built models of the shorelines and German strong points.

On the top floor of a major department store in the heart of London, another Oxford educator, John Austin, chaired the Theater Intelligence Organization. For four years, since the British Army had been evacuated from France, Austin and his scholars had painstakingly been collecting a wide array of information that was obtained from many sources: radio intercepts, spy reports, press clippings from Allied and German newspapers and magazines, aerial photographs, captured documents, results of sand tests on beaches, and interviews with prisoners and refugees. All of these data were carefully cataloged and indexed so they could be readily pulled out for use by Eisenhower or other commanders as needed.

As the date for Overlord, set for the first week in June 1944, approached, activity was hectic at one of the most closely guarded facilities in Great Britain—the Martian Room. Located just outside London, the chamber contained a mammoth, detailed master map of Adolf Hitler's vaunted Atlantikwall, along a 125-mile stretch of the Normandy coastline.

Updated daily, the map displayed an amazing assortment of German defenses. Plotted in were the precise locations of coast and field artillery batteries, their caliber, ranges, and fields of fire, and the thickness of their protective concrete covers; radar sites, machine-gun posts, tunnels, signal communications, barbed-wire entanglements, barracks, supply dumps, vehicle parks, flamethrowers, tank obstacles, and minefields; blockhouses, command posts—even the positions of small units deployed along the Atlantic Wall, together with the names of their captains and lieutenants.

This colossal map achievement was made possible mainly because of the courage and resourcefulness of hundreds of French men, women, and youngsters of the Normandy underground network Centurie. The espionage apparatus of amateurs was created by forty-one-year-old Marcel Girard (code-named Moureau), who was a traveling salesman for a cement firm in Caen, the historic capital of Normandy.

Girard's job permitted him to travel freely throughout northern France, but peddling cement was a cover. Only his patriotic boss in Caen and a few others knew that he never sold a pound of cement, that his almost constant journeys were for the perilous task of recruiting spies.

Almost daily, bits of information on German defenses and troop positions along the Atlantic Wall arrived at Centurie's central collection point in Caen. There skilled cartographers tediously incorporated the data on thousands of notes, rough diagrams, and drawings provided by Girard's amateur spies into a series of maps of sectors along the wall.

These map sketches were collected by couriers and carried, usually by train, to a dingy suite of rooms in an old building in a run-down section of Paris. This dilapidated structure was headquarters for the Battle of the Atlantic Wall, as the French underground called it. There, dedicated checkers daily sifted through a mountain of material collected by the men, women, and children spies in Normandy and bundled it for transfer to England.

Small, nimble Lysanders, piloted by Royal Air Force pilots, landed under cover of night at predesignated pastures outside Paris. The pilots taxied up to signaling flashlights held by French underground members, gathered the bundles of Centurie maps and data, sped down the grassy field, and lifted off for England.

Most of the hundreds of Centurie spies in Normandy lived in or near the Zone Interdite (Forbidden Zone). It was set up by the Germans and was several miles deep along the Atlantic Wall. An outsider had to have a legitimate reason for getting into and lingering around the restricted area. But this problem was solved when Centurie agents were furnished with a set of German identity papers and passes—all very carefully counterfeited by a thirty-eight-year-old Caen housewife.

Centurie agents risked their lives solely on faith. None knew if the Allies would ever invade France, or, if they did, that they would land in Normandy. Scores of Girard's agents were caught by the Gestapo, tortured, and executed.

One of Centurie's boldest and most productive spies was Jacques Bertin, a member of the French aristocracy with the exalted title Comte de la Hautière. On a cold, raw day in March 1944, he was pedaling furiously on his old bicycle northward along the eastern coast of the Cotentin Peninsula, bound for Cherbourg. Six-feet-two, blond, and handsome, the twenty-five-year-old count had urgent business to attend to in the bustling, Nazi-occupied port.

Bertin's code name was Jacques Molines, to protect his family, who lived in a large château near Cherbourg. He had no way of knowing that within a few months the port would hold the destiny of the Allied world. Unless Cherbourg could be rapidly captured after the invasion of Normandy, Eisenhower's forces might be bottled up on the beachhead and destroyed.

Molines was in charge of Centurie operations on the Cotentin Peninsula, which juts northward into the English Channel. For nearly three years, the count had been a man without a home. He was constantly on the go, always in danger of being trapped, seldom sleeping in the same house two nights in a row.

Of all the regional leaders in Centurie, Molines's task was the most diffi-cult—and perilous. Cherbourg, and some sixty square miles around it, were sat-urated with fortifications. German vigilance was intense. There were nearly forty thousand troops in and around the port, which Adolf Hitler had ordered to be defended to "the last man and the last bullet."

If the Germans were vigilant, the count was doubly so; his life depended upon it. On entering a bistro, he had to loiter inconspicuously until he learned if local residents were ordering alcoholic beverages that day. On arbitrary occa-sions, the Gestapo, seeking to identify outsiders, would suddenly forbid cafés and bistros to sell alcoholic drinks, a fact known to natives of the community but not to outsiders.

Molines always entered Cherbourg wheeling his bicycle, because on cer-tain irregular days, the German authorities would forbid riding two-wheeled bicycles (pushing one was acceptable).

Admiring Centurie agents swore that Jacques Molines was devoid of nerves. One night, he slept soundly on a cot in the back room of a dingy Cher-bourg bistro, a rough drawing of an Atlantic Wall gun position in his pocket, as German soldiers in the front room drank boisterously into the early morn-ing hours.

One factor kept him from capture and a slow, agonizing death in a Ges-tapo torture chamber: despite incessant efforts to trap the "terrorist" named Jacques Molines, the Germans did not have a clue as to his true identity. Cer-tainly a playboy member of the French aristocracy would not have the courage and ingenuity for such a perilous and demanding venture.

Meanwhile, in London, as D-Day grew closer, all of the colossal amount of information—from Eric Birley's order of battle group, Fred Wells's Inter-Services Topographic Department, John Austin's Theater Intelligence Organi-zation, and Marcel Girard's Centurie network—was stitched into policy by the Joint Intelligence Committee (JIC). Chaired by V. F. W. Cavendish-Bentinck of the British Foreign Office, the five-man committee had representatives from the Admiralty, the Air Ministry, the War Office, and the Ministry of Economic Warfare.

The JIC reviewed, revised, and finalized intelligence appreciations and estimates. Once each week it met with the British Chiefs of Staff to review and discuss its analyses.

Taken as a whole, these various entities formed an imposing structure for intelligence and clandestine operations. When the mighty Allied force assem-bling in Great Britain was ready to charge across the Channel, General Eisen-hower would have a powerful secret weapon available: more detailed infor-mation on the Atlantic Wall and the Wehrmacht in the West of France than would German commanders in France and Berlin.[5]

A Call for Nazi Suicide Pilots

ON THE LAST DAY OF FEBRUARY 1944, Hanna Reitsch, an ardent Nazi and famed as a derring-do test pilot, called on Adolf Hitler at the Berghof, the führer's luxurious retreat perched on a mountaintop in Bavaria. In essence, Reitsch had come to tell the German leader how the war could still be won despite months of disastrous military debacles.

Attractive, blue-eyed, fair-haired Reitsch had been a famous stunt pilot when a Luftwaffe general selected her in 1937 to test military aircraft. He had been impressed by the fact that she was courageous to the point of foolhardiness. She was only one of two German women, and the only civilian, to be awarded the Iron Cross First Class for gallantry.

Reitsch knew that German scientists were rapidly developing a revolutionary secret weapon known as the V-1, for the first vengeance weapon. Designed to be launched from concrete ramps 150 feet long, the V-1 (later known to the Allies as a buzz bomb) was an unmanned airplane packed with one ton of explosives. It could fly at a maximum speed of 440 miles per hour at an altitude of 4,000 feet. Its engine would be preset to cut off over a target— mainly London. A single robot would be capable of leveling an entire city block.

Hanna Reitsch knew that the führer was counting on the V-1 to bring at least a negotiated peace by demolishing British cities. However, the test pilot, one of the few Germans who dared to contradict Hitler, told him at the Berghof meeting that the robot would be too inaccurate.

What was needed to alter the course of the war was to convert the V-1 for manned flight as a suicide weapon, she insisted. When Hitler expressed skepticism, she volunteered to prove that a converted V-1 could take off and be landed by a pilot. If tests proved successful, the pilot, instead of landing, would crash the V-1 into the target in England, blowing himself to bits in the process.

Famed German test pilot Hanna Reitsch proposed recruiting "suicide pilots." (National Archives)

British soldiers inspect a captured suicide aircraft, a modified V-1 buzz bomb. Nearly two hundred were built, but none was flown operationally. (National Archives)

Finally the führer gave permission to launch experimental work on the V-1 conversion project as long as he was not pestered during the development stage.

After two pilots crashed on attempting to land the modified craft (carrying a payload of sand in lieu of explosives), Reitsch climbed into one of the vehicles and made a successful flight.

"Those other two simply didn't know how to bring down fast planes," she explained.

Despite Reitsch's most strenuous efforts, the project failed, mainly because there was no discernible rush of volunteers for suicide missions. When the V-1s began raining down on London on June 13, 1944—one week after the Allied invasion of Normandy—there were no Nazi "kamikaze pilots" aboard.[6]

A Plot to Murder Two
Allied Generals

FOUR FIGURES carrying a small boat and explosives were stealing through the darkness near the Italian village of Foss Incastro, outside Rome. The men were highly trained saboteurs and hit men of the Gestapo who had been assigned

*U.S. General Mark W. Clark (left) and British General Harold R. L. G. Alexander were
targets of German assassins. (U.S. Army)*

an important task—sneak onto the Anzio beachhead, thirty miles to the south,
and murder the Allies' two top commanders in Italy, British General Harold
R. L. G. Alexander and U.S. General Mark W. Clark. It was about 10:00 P.M.
on March 9, 1944.

The Gestapo scheme was for the assassins to sail southward along the
coast of the Tyrrhenian Sea to the Anzio beachhead, held by a hundred thousand British and U.S. troops, and slip ashore near the mouth of the Moletta
River inside Allied lines. The hit men would have little difficulty in reaching
the Allied headquarters building on the beachhead, the Gestapo felt, because
all were Romans who knew the region well and, if halted, could pass themselves off as natives.

Provisions had been made for the Gestapo in Rome to radio to the assassins on the beachhead when Clark and Alexander were both at the headquarters (information presumably to be obtained from spies at Anzio).

As the assassination team shoved off from dark Fossa Incastro, a young
one-armed man named Michelle Coppola, despite his physical handicap,

insisted on steering the small boat. The others did not protest: Coppola was highly regarded by his Gestapo masters in Rome and was recognized by them as a zealous agent with a deep hatred for the Americans and the British.

Curiously, Coppola, instead of hugging the shoreline, as planned, steered the craft in a sweeping arc, almost as if he were trying to be spotted by Allied vessels known to be patrolling the region. His three comrades had grown uneasy. Had it not been for Coppola's stupidity in steering the boat off course, the hit team would have been ashore by now.

The boat burrowed on through the black waters. "When are we going to land?" the others asked Coppola with increasing frequency.

"Soon," was the repeated reply. "Very soon."

Now the others had grown mutinous. This idiotic Coppola was lost and would get them all captured and executed, they muttered to one another.

Finally, Coppola steered the boat toward shore and onto the beach at the designated spot near the mouth of the Moletta River. Then, with quick movements, he removed a grenade from his belt, pulled the pin, and hurled the missive onto the shore, where it detonated with a roar that echoed across the dark landscape. As if on cue—and that was precisely what the grenade blast was—a group of dim figures, armed with rifles and submachine guns, emerged from the darkness and took the three men with Coppola into custody.

Coppola had long been working as a British spy in Rome and had connived his way into the confidence of the Gestapo to the degree that he was one of its most trusted agents.

Allied intelligence had been aware of the Gestapo plot to murder Generals Alexander and Clark. After learning of the scheme, Michelle Coppola had insisted to his German controllers that he be allowed to join in the mission. Then he had slipped away from the Gestapo on a pretext and told an underground leader of the plan. In turn, the underground alerted Allied headquarters at Anzio by secret radio communication, and a reception committee had been set up to capture the hit team when it landed.

For several weeks after the aborted murder mission, the Gestapo in Rome was in a quandary, trying to determine what had happened to the hit team—it had simply vanished.[7]

Hitler Warned by a Female Spy

EXTREME NERVOUS TENSION gripped those at Supreme Headquarters, Allied Expeditionary Force (SHAEF), who knew all about Neptune, code name for the assault phase of Overlord, the mammoth invasion of Normandy set for the first week in June 1944. The diarist for Allied Supreme Commander Dwight Eisenhower wrote: "Ike looks worn and tired. The strain is telling on him. He looks older now than at any time since I have been with him."

Eisenhower himself wrote to a general in Washington: "Because of the stakes involved, the atmosphere is more electric than ever before. We are not merely risking a tactical defeat, we are putting the whole works on one number."

Indeed, everything was on the line: it had taken the entire military, economic, and intellectual resources of the United States and Great Britain four years just to mount this cross-Channel assault.

As D-Day drew closer, the Allied high command was confronted by a haunting mystery. Why was there generally silence and inactivity on the part of the Germans? The only Luftwaffe actions during the ten days prior to the Normandy invasion were an occasional reconnaissance flight over England and the dropping of a few bombs on London to awaken everyone.

The conventional wisdom at SHAEF was that Adolf Hitler was nursing his strength and would hurl everything in the Wehrmacht's arsenal at the Normandy invaders on D-Day. Then jitters struck Eisenhower and his planners when information was received that the führer would unleash poison gas or bacteriological weapons on the Allied assault troops.

Alarmed intelligence officers at SHAEF promptly contacted one of their cleverest and most productive spies, a beautiful, cerebral young Argentine woman code-named Bronx. Actually, she was a double agent, having first been recruited by the Abwehr when she paid a visit to Vichy, France, in 1942 to visit her father, an employee of his country's embassy there.

When the Abwehr officer had suggested that she might like to be stationed in England, where her father had had significant connections prior to the war, she eagerly accepted. However, on reaching Madrid en route to London, she contacted British officers and told them her story. They arranged for her to be met by undercover security agents when she reached England from neutral Spain.

Early in 1943, the British XX Committee, a secret group that plotted to mislead the Germans, took control of the woman, gave her the code name Bronx, and put her to work. She began as a secret ink letter writer, providing her Abwehr controller in Hamburg with information carefully concocted by the XX Committee. There were elements of truth to boost her credibility with the Germans, and misinformation to mislead the Oberkommando der Wehrmacht. Her secret letters reached Hamburg through the Bank of the Holy Ghost in Lisbon, Portugal, a neutral nation.

In Berlin, the Abwehr chief, Admiral Wilhelm Canaris, was so delighted with her production that he authorized paying her a monthly retainer of the equivalent of $120, a tidy sum in that era, plus expenses and periodic bonuses.

Now, as the Normandy invasion approached, the XX Committee had Bronx write a letter to her controller in Hamburg stressing that the Allies had huge stocks of a germ warfare agent that could cause a widespread epidemic like the bubonic plague and from which victims died horrible deaths.

This tale was intended to warn Adolf Hitler that if he loosed poison gas or bacteriological weapons against the Allied forces on D-Day, retaliation in kind would be swift and gargantuan. The führer, indeed, had a large stockpile of poison gas, but far less than the Allies had.

Bronx's machination may have paid off. Whatever may have been Hitler's earlier intentions, neither poison gas nor bacteriological weapons were used by either adversary during the war.[8]

An Alarming Breach of Security

SPRING OF 1944 was perhaps the most peculiar time in the history of England. As D-Day drew closer and the mightiest land, sea, and air force ever assembled was poised to leap the Channel, a thick blanket of fog covered Great Britain— a fog of strict security. If Adolf Hitler were to learn the time and place of the June invasion, a bloody debacle could be inflicted on the Allies.

Never before had Britons been so suspicious. Informers and busybodies flourished, keeping their eyes and ears open for German spies. Security was an obsession with Allied forces. Supreme Commander Dwight Eisenhower, Prime Minister Winston Churchill, and even King George VI were unaware that U.S. Brigadier General Thomas J. Betts, who was in charge of security, had placed tails on them.

Britain became, temporarily, a police state, isolated from the rest of the world. Overseas cabling privileges were taken away from journalists. Unbeknownst to those involved, each telephone call made by a soldier or an official, each letter in most of England, and every telegram were monitored. Travel into and out of Britain was cut off. Soldiers' mail was delayed, sometimes confiscated.

Tight restrictions on military matters were even more severe. Eisenhower told his commanders: "[You] will ensure that the highest standard of individual security discipline is maintained, and that the most stringent disciplinary action is taken in all cases of the violations of security."

One of the basic security measures was that no one in uniform with knowledge of the invasion be sent on operations where they might be captured. The Gestapo had ways of prying secrets from even the strongest men. However, on May 7, about a month before D-Day, British Air Commodore Ronald Ivelaw-Chapman was lost on a bombing mission against a target near Le Mans, a French city about one hundred miles inland from the Normandy beaches.

General Betts, the security eagle, asked the Air Ministry to find out if Ivelaw-Chapman had knowledge of Overlord. As a commander of a bomber base at Elsham Wolds in Lincolnshire, the missing officer would have no knowledge of invasion plans, the Air Ministry report stated. However, the second part of the document sent shock waves throughout Supreme Headquarters, Allied Expeditionary Force (SHAEF) in London's staid Grosvenor Square.

Before being assigned to Elsham Wolds, Ivelaw-Chapman had been on the planning staff at the Air Ministry, and he had had extensive contact with General Frederick Morgan, the architect of the original invasion plan. Moreover, the Air Ministry said, the commodore had some knowledge of paratroop operational plans for Neptune, code name for the assault phase of the invasion.

Word that Ivelaw-Chapman had not been authorized by the Air Ministry to make the flight over German-held territory compounded the nervous tics that had erupted in SHAEF. A crucial ingredient of Neptune would be a strike by eighteen thousand paratroopers and glidermen of the U.S. 82nd and 101st Airborne Divisions and the British 1st Airborne Division behind the Normandy beaches to prevent German reinforcements from attacking the amphibious invaders. Conceivably the Gestapo could learn from Ivelaw-Chapman crucial intelligence that would result in disaster for the airborne operation, thereby leaving the seaborne troops vulnerable to destruction as they came ashore.

Now the information SHAEF security anxiously sought was whether Commodore Ivelaw-Chapman was dead or alive. Betts's sleuths began interrogating the crews of the fifty RAF bombers that had been on the mission and learned that the commodore's plane had been intercepted by Luftwaffe fighters on the homeward trip—the only aircraft shot down on the raid. Most of the crewmen of the stricken bomber were seen to bail out over open countryside, so it was considered likely that Ivelaw-Chapman had survived.

A radio message from the leader of a French underground *réseau* (unit) code-named Donkeyman and operating near Paris was the first clue London received that Ivelaw-Chapman was alive. But the source of the information, Roger Bardet, leader of Donkeyman, sent shivers up the spines of SHAEF intelligence. Bardet, it was known, had been captured by the Gestapo months earlier. He had returned to his réseau and told a hair-raising story about how he had escaped from the Gestapo.

However, Special Operations Executive (SOE), the cloak-and-dagger British agency responsible for organizing and directing underground units on the Continent, had learned from other sources that Bardet had gone over to the enemy. But in the games played between competing sides in undercover machinations, SOE chose to pretend it was not aware that Bardet had sold out his country and his comrades.

So if Donkeyman had Commodore Ivelaw-Chapman in its "protection," in what scheme was Bardet involved? No doubt it had been orchestrated by the French traitor's friend the Gestapo. Whatever may have been the case, SHAEF concluded that an all-out effort must be launched to spirit Ivelaw-Chapman out of France.

SHAEF promptly contacted Lieutenant Colonel Airey Neave, who, from his office in London, directed a section of MI-9, an escape organization with lines running throughout Europe. The British had formed the network after the Dunkirk disaster in 1940 for the precise purpose of recovering downed Allied airmen. Could Neave's organization recover the missing RAF commodore?

Neave got in touch by radio with Bergundy, code name for a Frenchman who, at enormous personal risk, had established an escape line that carried Allied soldiers, airmen, and agents from the Paris region to a small port in Brittany, southwest of Normandy. Bergundy agreed to try to locate Ivelaw-Chapman and fly him out in a short-takeoff-and-landing Lysander aircraft.

Two weeks later, near the end of May, Bergundy located the commodore. Somehow he had left—or fled from—Donkeyman and was hiding in civilian clothes with a loyal underground réseau about fifty miles from Le Mans. A Lysander was scheduled to pick him up on the night of June 8–9.

In the meantime, on June 6, the Allies struck in Normandy, and the Germans were especially alert in northern France. Fewer than ten hours before the Lysander was to pick up the commodore, the Gestapo raided the house where he was hiding and hauled him off to jail.

Ivelaw-Chapman was convinced that his days—or hours—were numbered. The Gestapo would try to torture intelligence out of him about the invasion, then kill him. Fortunately for the Briton, the Gestapo agents who grilled him never mentioned the invasion. Instead, they demanded to know who had provided him with his phony French papers.

Then, when the commodore was taken to a Luftwaffe post near Frankfurt, Germany, his interrogator only wanted to know about Royal Air Force bomber tactics. An accommodating fellow, Ivelaw-Chapman gave the Luftwaffe colonel a long rundown on the topic—all of the information being false.[9]

The Wizard and the Mushroom Man

IN THE EARLY-MORNING HOURS of darkness, an elderly volunteer of the Royal Observer Corps stood on the roof of a four-story building in southeastern England and turned his binoculars toward a strange object streaking through the sky toward London. Its dim contours resembled those of an airplane, but it was unlike anything he had studied on the silhouette charts of Luftwaffe craft. Its exhaust was belching reddish-orange flame, and it gave off a sputtering sound.

Onward the flying object raced at what seemed to be a speed the sky-watcher had never seen by any airplane. A few minutes later, far out of his line of sight, its preset timer cut off the engine; the entire object crashed into the sleeping village of Swanscombe, some eighteen miles short of its intended target, the Tower Bridge in London. The ensuing explosion, which had the impact of a four-thousand-pound blockbuster bomb, hurled terrified citizens from their beds. It was shortly after 4:00 A.M. on June 13, 1944—precisely one week after Allied forces had stormed ashore in Normandy.

England was under attack by lethal robots—pilotless aircraft packed with explosives that could fly at speeds of 440 miles per hour, far faster than any Allied plane could fly. Called the V-1 by the Germans, these fiendish flying devices would be known as buzz bombs or doodlebugs by the British and the Americans. Hitler had ordered fifty thousand of them to be built.

In the days and the weeks ahead, Target 42, as the Germans code-named sprawling London, lived in constant fear and chaos. Hundreds of buzz bombs rained on the city, killing and wounding tens of thousands of civilians by early July. Three hundred thousand London houses and hundreds of other buildings had been destroyed.

The British government was desperate. Great pressures were brought to bear on General Dwight D. Eisenhower, the Normandy invasion commander, to scrap long-standing tactical plans to advance toward Germany and, instead, to send his forces northeastward along the English Channel for some 150 miles to the Pas de Calais, from where the buzz bombs were being launched.

A fateful decision was reached. Frightful as was the carnage, Hitler's vengeance-weapon barrage was not greatly affecting the prosecution of the war. So London would have to endure, and an all-out effort would be made to break out of the Normandy bridgehead at the earliest possible time and overrun the launching sites along the Pas de Calais while sticking to the tactical scheme for bringing the war in Europe to a conclusion.

Eisenhower had to make another crucial decision in an effort to halt the deluge of lethal robots. A large portion of the powerful U.S. and British bomber forces would be diverted from pounding key industrial targets in Germany and would begin attacking the buzz-bomb launching sites along the Pas de Calais coast.

At the same time, W. J. Savy (code-named Wizard), a British agent who had parachuted into northern France prior to D-Day, had established himself underground in Paris. One day on a scouting trip to Creil in the Pas de Calais region, Wizard, a prosperous lawyer in peacetime, engaged in casual conversation in a restaurant with a Frenchman, who mentioned that he had grown mushrooms in huge caves at Saint Leo d'Esserent, a short distance away. Wizard drew out the mushroom man and learned that the Germans had evicted him and said they were taking over the caves to raise mushrooms for the Third Reich.

The Frenchman went on to say that the Germans had built a railroad line leading up to the caves. Wizard's ears pricked up. It seemed strange enough that in the heat of a war the Germans would divert manpower and money to raising mushrooms. But it seemed even more odd that they would construct a railroad just to transport the produce.

What's more, the Frenchman added, the roofs of the caves had been lined with concrete and braced with steel pillars. These caves have to be some kind of an ammunition or weapons dump, Wizard reflected.

A few days later, at great risk to his life, Wizard stole a look at the landscape leading up to the caves, made cautious inquiries among French civilians living in the region, and discovered that the Germans were storing in the caves perhaps as many as two thousand buzz bombs—all of them ticketed for London, no doubt.

This information was radioed to London by Wizard. On the night of July 4, 227 Royal Air Force bombers dropped blockbusters on the caves and the rail line leading up to them. Luftwaffe fighters rose to challenge the attack and to protect the precious stash of buzz bombs. Swarming around like angry bees, the fighters shot down 13 bombers.

This RAF mission was followed by another group of four-engine Lancasters, each carrying a six-ton "earthquake bomb." Eleven of the earthquakes hit at or near to the targets.

A day later, Wizard's mushroom man reported that the entrances to the caves had been blocked but that the Germans already had started digging them open. Within twenty-four hours the arduous job was completed. Buzz bombs could again be removed and taken to launching ramps.

Wizard flashed this latest development to London. On the night of July 7–8, a force of some 330 Royal Air Force heavies paid a return call to the caves. The sky armada winged in extremely low and deluged the entrances and parked buzz-bomb dumps nearby with a mass of high explosives.

This time the job had been completed. The Wizard's one-man intelligence coup, which would have been rejected by Hollywood scriptwriters as implausible, denied the Germans much of their buzz-bomb stockpile in France and vastly diminished the robot assault on London.[10]

Warning: Your Submarine May Explode

MORE THAN TWO YEARS after the poorly equipped, outmanned, partially trained, and starving force of General Douglas MacArthur had been wiped out in the Philippines by Japanese invaders, the flame of armed resistance in the islands continued to burn brightly. Thousands of Filipino guerrillas, many of their bands lead by U.S. military officers who had escaped capture, had been steadily making life miserable for the Japanese conquerors.

After breaking through a Japanese sea and air blockade and reaching Australia by PT boat and aircraft in early 1942, MacArthur, despite meager manpower and resources, began conducting what he called a "hit 'em where they ain't" campaign of speed and surprise, leapfrogging from one island to the next on the jungle road to the Philippines.

The "underground" war in the Philippines was also an "underwater war." Hundreds of thousands of weapons of all types, millions of rounds of ammunition, hundreds of tons of explosives, vast quantities of radio equipment, and piles of medical supplies were being slipped into the islands surreptitiously by a few submarines.

MacArthur's man in charge of orchestrating the shipments of war accoutrements to the guerrillas was Major General Courtney Whitney, who had been a pilot in World War I and who had practiced law in Manila for twenty years prior to the outbreak of hostilities. So important was Whitney's task that he was assigned an office next to MacArthur's in Australia.

In July 1944 Whitney had more than a professional interest in his cloak-and-dagger assignment. His eldest son, Courtney Jr., would soon be deeply involved. Young Whitney, nicknamed Sonny, had left Yale University to join the army and reported for duty in the Southwest Pacific. Hearing of his arrival, MacArthur arranged to have the younger Whitney assigned to his father's organization.

Shortly after he arrived, young Whitney heard that a small group was being formed for a secret mission to Luzon, the most important and most heavily populated island in the Philippines, and he promptly volunteered for the mission. The officer who would approve or deny his request was his father. It was an anguishing decision for the general, who was fully aware of the hazards involved. Despite the peril, there were far more volunteers than could go, so whatever choice he made, it would be viewed by some as tainted by favoritism.

General Whitney took his dilemma to MacArthur, who replied simply, "Let him go."

Young Whitney and his comrades departed for Luzon. Shortly after their submarines cast off, the elder Whitney's headquarters received an urgent warning from an intelligence group in London: certain sabotage materials manufactured in Great Britain had been found to be in danger of spontaneous combustion and should be destroyed immediately.

The cable sent a surge of fear through Courtney Whitney Sr. Some of the defective explosives were at that moment on board the submarine heading for the Philippines with his son. But radio silence was in effect during daylight hours, so no warning signal could be transmitted. The interminable wait for darkness was agonizing for the father.

When the submarine surfaced en route that night to recharge its batteries, word was received that the faulty explosives should be dumped overboard immediately. But U.S. Navy Commander Charles "Chick" Parsons, leader of the landing party, refused to obey the order. The explosives would be needed on Luzon, he declared.

Commander Parsons was well known to the Kempei Tai, the dread Japanese secret service, after having been involved in many espionage activities on Luzon and the neighboring island of Leyte during the past eighteen months.

There was a price on his head: fifty thousand U.S. dollars in gold, a huge fortune to poverty-stricken natives. Yet Filipinos had regularly provided the swashbuckling American with food and lodging, risking death if the Kempei Tai discovered him in their homes.

On his espionage escapades, the most-wanted American "terrorist" wore what he called his "business suit": old, dirty, and torn trousers and shirt, along with a tattered, sawtooth straw hat. He went barefoot and had a two-week growth of beard. Parsons never carried a gun, preferring to use his agility—mental and physical—to evade the Kempei Tai. If caught with a weapon, he would be shot.

Now, on his ninth mission to the Philippines, Parsons, Sonny Whitney, and members of the submarine crew perspired heavily and rode in almost total silence. An explosion of the defective materials could occur at any moment. Each slight noise set hearts thumping furiously.

Finally, the submarine reached a dark beach on Luzon. Whitney and Parsons silently paddled ashore in a rubber dinghy and were met by Filipino guerrillas. Before dawn, the weapons, ammunition, and supplies had laboriously been lugged ashore and hidden at an island guerrilla base. Twenty-four hours later, the presumably defective explosives were used to blow up a Japanese ammunition dump.[11]

A Puzzling Episode in Normandy

FOUR WEEKS AFTER THE ALLIES STORMED ASHORE in Normandy, savage fighting raged in the treacherous swamps and earthen hedgerows the Normans called the *bocage*. As frightful as were the American casualties, the Germans were suffering "the most monstrous bloodbath, the like of which I have not seen in eleven years of war," exclaimed Lieutenant General Dietrich von Choltitz, a German commander in Normandy.

Field Marshal Erwin Rommel, whose task was to repel the Allied invaders, had warned the führer repeatedly that "the dam is bound to burst at any minute." He pleaded to pull his army back to the first natural defensive barrier, the Seine River.

"Hold your ground!" an angry Hitler barked.

"The man is mad!" Rommel exploded to his staff, convinced that the führer was mindlessly butchering German soldiers in a hopeless cause in Normandy.

In the early-morning haze along the U.S. 1st Infantry Division sector near Caumont, the battlefield was quiet. Suddenly, weary Germans heard an American voice speak fluent German over an amplifier: "*Achtung! Achtung!* (Attention! Attention!) We call the German commander in this sector. We have important news for him!"

A short time later, when it was indicated that the German commander was listening, the voice explained that the Americans wanted to hand over a group of German women, mostly nurses, who had been captured when Cherbourg fell a week earlier. Would the Germans accept the women?

It was the beginning of one of the strangest battlefield episodes of the war between Nazi Germany and the Western Allies. After the German commander consulted with his superiors, they in turn contacted General Hans Speidel, Rommel's trusted right-hand man, who gave orders for the nurses to be accepted.

A truce took effect at 3:00 P.M. GIs and Feldgrau alike edged warily from their holes burrowed into the earthen hedgerows, stood up, and watched in amazement as three American officers walked down the middle of the road. Carrying a white piece of cloth on a long pole was Captain Quentin Roosevelt, an intelligence officer in Big Red One (as the 1st Division was known), and Captain Fred Gercke, a prisoner-of-war interrogator. Trailing along were seven German women.

From behind a hedgerow into the road stepped Major Hans Heeren, the commander of the Reconnaissance Battalion of the 2nd Panzer Division. There was a brief conversation, the nurses joined Heeren, and the Americans returned to their lines.

The transfer had taken only ten minutes—but firing did not resume again for more than four hours. Why had the truce lasted so long? Could this whole affair have been arranged secretly by German emissaries to cloak the passing of a letter written a few days earlier by Colonel Walter Bargatzky, a lawyer on the staff of General Karl-Heinrich von Stuelpnagel, the military governor of France? It was composed in precise English to be signed by Field Marshal Rommel and was addressed to the Allied ground commander in Normandy, British General Bernard Montgomery.

Six German officers were to carry the letter through the lines. It outlined conditions for a permanent truce in the West: Rommel would pull his troops to the Siegfried Line on the western frontier of the Third Reich, and the Allies would cease bombing German cities. Then the Wehrmacht would continue to fight the Red Army to "keep the Russian barbarians from overrunning Germany."

Curiously, a second strange interlude took place a week later in the same sector, near the hamlet of Sept Vents. Captain Quentin Roosevelt and two other officers came out of their lines waving a white flag. The guns on both sides immediately went silent as the three Americans walked down the road shouting, "Hello!"

Again, the time was 3:00 P.M.

A German sergeant and two Feldgrau, all looking surprised, edged onto the road from some bushes. Roosevelt told the Germans that they wished to turn over nine more women, two nurses and seven secretaries, who had been captured at Cherbourg. Confused (they presumably knew nothing about the deliverance of the seven nurses a week earlier), the sergeant sent for a captain, who arrived within minutes. He said that he would accept the women.

A short time later, U.S. army ambulances came down the road with the seven captives, and they were turned over to the Germans. The women lifted their arms in Nazi salutes to the German captain and snapped, "Heil Hitler!" The captain did not respond.

Before departing, the German officer said in a friendly tone to Quentin Roosevelt and his party, "What a pity it is that we are fighting Americans instead of us joining to fight the Russians!"

It had taken fewer than twenty minutes to complete the handover of the German women, yet again, it was nearly four hours before the guns began to roar.

Why had this second truce also lasted so long? Had the silent interlude been arranged so that some sort of reply by the Allies could be slipped through the lines in response to the letter drafted by Walter Bargatzky and signed by Erwin Rommel that may have passed between the sides during the truce a week earlier?

Rommel sent the führer a blistering report a few days later. "The situation on the Normandy front is growing worse every day and is now approaching a grave crisis. Against the enemy's enormous concentration of artillery, tanks, and airplanes, even the bravest army will be smashed piece by piece. It is urgently necessary for the proper conclusions to be drawn from this situation."

Hitler was infuriated by Rommel's pointed suggestion that the führer should seek an armistice with the Western Allies. Later he sharply told Rommel to "take care of your front and I'll take care of the war."

Had Field Marshal Rommel actually been in touch with General Montgomery or other Allied leaders during the two inexplicable battlefield truces, ones that lasted far longer than the few minutes required to transfer the German nurses and secretaries? There were clues that this might have been the case. If the Allies had wanted only to return the German women, the logical means for achieving that goal would have been through the International Red Cross, standard procedure in such cases.

These questions will never be answered for certain. Only educated conjecture survived the war. Before he could negotiate a separate armistice in the West, Field Marshal Rommel was gravely wounded when his speeding staff car was shot up by two British fighter planes on a Norman road, and he was evacuated to Germany.[12]

A Poison "Treatment" for Hitler

ADOLF HITLER WAS RACKED by agonizing pain. Forty-eight hours after members of the Schwarze Kapelle conspiracy had exploded a time bomb at the führer's feet during a strategy conference at Wolfsschanze, his battle headquarters behind the Eastern Front, aides summoned Major Erwin Giesing, an eye, ear, nose, and throat physician from a nearby field hospital. It was July 22, 1944.

After the explosion, flames had shot up and a hail of glass splinters, timber, and plaster rained down. Smoke erupted in the room. Hitler miraculously escaped death. Trousers in tatters, face blackened by soot, he staggered from the building.

Doctors and rescue workers were in action minutes after the blast, and ambulances rushed the seriously wounded military officers to a hospital in nearby Rastenberg. A physician bandaged the führer's burns and put his badly sprained right arm in a sling.

Hitler refused to rest. After eating lunch, he was driven to the railroad platform adjoining Wolfsschanze, where he greeted his longtime crony Italian dictator Benito Mussolini, known as Il Duce.

"Duce," the German leader remarked evenly, "a few hours ago I experienced the greatest piece of good fortune I have ever known!"

Now, at his living quarters at Wolfsschanze, Hitler was examined by Dr. Giesing, who found that an eardrum was badly ruptured and the inner ear damaged. A day later, the doctor performed a drum cauterization to stop the bleeding.

During the next month, Major Giesing examined Hitler almost daily. The führer began to express gratitude to the doctor, gratitude that ripened into deep faith.

"*Mein doktor*," Hitler said, "you are one of the few around me that I still trust!"

Each examination was followed by long discussions on a variety of topics: the future of the Third Reich, the postwar world, the evils of drinking and smoking. All the while, Giesing was conducting a subtle, and primitive, psychological test. He diagnosed the führer as "a neurotic with Caesar-mania."

On October 1, about two months after the bomb explosion, Hitler was again suffering from an excruciating headache and summoned Giesing. When the doctor entered the führer's spartan living quarters, Hitler was lying on his bed in a nightgown. He tried to raise himself, but was too weak, and he complained of heavy pressure in his head.

While Giesing was making a thorough examination of his patient, Hitler's longtime valet, Heinz Linge, left the room in response to a knock on the door. Moments later, Hitler's words began to fade. Giesing felt the führer's pulse. It was weak. Then Hitler passed out, apparently from a dose of cocaine that he had insisted the doctor give him.

Giesing now was struck by a startling thought: unconscious and alone before him was a tyrant who had brought enormous grief and suffering to millions of people. As Giesing would later write in his diary: "At that moment I did not want such a man to exist and exercise the power of life and death in his purely subjective manner."

Some inner force caused Giesing to stick a swab stick with cotton into the cocaine bottle from which he had given Hitler a dose only minutes earlier. A second dose would be fatal. He began painting the interior of the führer's nose with the substance. Just as he was preparing to do the second nostril, Heinz Linge walked back into the room.

Just then Hitler's facial muscles began to twitch, and he drew up his legs as though in pain. Linge said that the führer was having yet another of his periodic intestinal cramps, and he suggested that the best treatment was bed rest.

Coolly composed, Dr. Giesing picked up his medical black bag and left the room, returning to his base at the field hospital. Had he killed Hitler? Almost in panic, he cooked up an excuse to return to Berlin the next day.

Giesing phoned Wolfsschanze from the capital and learned that Hitler, amazingly, was alive, chipper, and out of bed. No one suspected the double-cocaine treatment that the man the führer trusted so highly had administered.

Returning to Wolfsschanze, Giesing was greeted warmly by Hitler, who thanked him profusely for his tender care and promoted him in rank on the spot.[13]

Belgian Resistants Steal a Locomotive

SOON AFTER ADOLF HITLER had launched Case Yellow, the invasion of the Low Countries and France, on May 10, 1940, Belgian patriots began organizing an underground network. During the four years of German occupation, the Armée Secrète grew steadily, and by August 1944, when the Allies were racing eastward across France in pursuit of the retreating Wehrmacht, the Belgian underground had grown into a potent force of fifteen networks.

London retained operational control of the fifty-four thousand resistants, while a Belgian, Major General Ivan Gérard, was in command.

Things had been and were especially difficult for the Belgian underground because of geography and supply. The country was ill suited for guerrilla warfare, so most of the action was carried out in the cities, making it easier for the Gestapo to track down the resistants. Parachute drops were tricky, because the Germans had concentrated ack-ack batteries in Belgium to fire on the Allied bomber streams that were winging toward Germany.

Despite these handicaps, the Belgian underground wreaked havoc on the German occupiers, cutting rail lines, derailing trains, and blowing up bridges, pumping stations, watering points, telephone and cable lines, waterway lock gates—and two floating cranes.

Masterminding much of this clandestine mayhem was Groupe G, an intelligence and sabotage unit directed by twelve professors at the University of Brussels. They were transformed almost daily from seemingly mild-mannered educators into devious plotters against the forces of Adolf Hitler. They applied their academic know-how to identify important sabotage targets, checking out their suggestions with Special Forces headquarters in London, then selecting specialized underground groups to destroy the objectives.

Resistants discovered that the Germans had hidden thirty-six railroad tank cars loaded with precious fuel in a tunnel. This was standard practice, to protect valuable materials from marauding British and American fighter planes.

Fuel was especially important to the thirsty German war machine, because that commodity had long been in short supply in the Third Reich. In most cases, the trains were parked in tunnels in the daytime; then they continued to their destination—or the next tunnel—cloaked by darkness.

A hurried reconnaissance disclosed that heavily armed German soldiers were standing guard at both ends of the tunnel. So an ingenious plan was hatched. Somehow the resistants managed to steal a locomotive, then "requisitioned" two empty freight cars parked on a siding. A huge amount of explosives was rapidly loaded onto the freight cars, and the locomotive was hitched to them.

With an experienced engineer at the throttle and two other railroad workers in the cab with him, the dynamite train chugged down the track toward the tunnel. As it neared, the German guards frantically waved their arms for the engine to halt. When only a hundred yards from the mouth of the tunnel, the three Belgians leaped from the cab.

Moments later, there was a colossal roar, and the blast rocked the hill and ignited a monstrous fire in the tunnel. Despite desperate efforts by the Germans to extinguish the blaze, it burned for more than two days, until all the fuel had been consumed.[14]

A German General Cuts
a Strange Deal

ROGER LANDES eyed the German Army sergeant with a mixture of suspicion and interest. Landes, who had parachuted into the region near Bordeaux in southwestern France months earlier, had been trained and sent in by the Special Operations Executive (SOE), Britain's secret agency. Its task was to organize, equip, and control the politically divided French resistance and to guide those acts of sabotage and guerrilla warfare against German lines of communication and transportation.

Disheveled, red-eyed from stress and lack of sleep, Sergeant Franz Stahlschmitt had fought with distinction in Russia and elsewhere. But he had become disillusioned with Adolf Hitler's voracious appetite for spilling the blood of young German men when the cause was already hopeless. So he had deserted from his post at the port in Bordeaux and sought out the leader of the French resistance, Roger Landes, to make a daring proposal. It was August 20, 1944.

Five days earlier, Allied armies, spearheaded by an airborne assault, had stormed ashore along the fabled Riviera in southern France, some three hundred miles east-southeast of Bordeaux. When the crack 11th Panzer Division, which had been guarding the city, was ordered to head for the Allied landing beaches, Sergeant Franz Stahlschmitt and other army men were left to their fate in Bordeaux, with orders to blow up the port.

Now the German was briefing Landes on a scheme to destroy the explosives before the commander in Bordeaux had time to carry out his orders. The deserter said he could slip back into the city, obtain keys to the bunker where the explosives were kept, and ignite the dynamite.

What did Stahlschmitt want in return for the sabotage deed? Nothing, he replied. Only protection by Landes's resistants. Landes was finally convinced of the German's sincerity.

Two days later, on August 22, Stahlschmitt was back inside Bordeaux. After opening the bunker, he laid a fuse, lit a match, and stealthily departed. About twenty minutes later, Roger Landes and his men, a few miles from the port, felt the earth tremble from a tremendous blast.

Bordeaux lies in the heart of the Aquitaine Basin, a region covered with vineyards, so most of the resistants working under Roger Landes had been in the wine trade. Ironically, the German port commander, a reserve naval officer, had been in the wine business in Berlin before the war, and he knew most of the leaders of the area's underground. During the past two years, he had often held friendly talks with these Frenchmen, unaware that they were resistants.

Meanwhile, Landes had obtained copies of German orders that called for the army commander in Bordeaux to destroy bridges across four rivers. Now the underground learned that the German general in charge had concealed other explosives, enough to blow up the four bridges.

Several of the French wine industry leaders, at great personal risk, slipped into Bordeaux and contacted their old friend from his Berlin days, the German port commander. The Frenchmen pleaded with him to put pressure on Major General Hans Nake, the army commander in the city, not to blow up the large bridges or port facilities.

No doubt realizing that German armies in France were now pulling back hell-bent toward the Third Reich and that the garrison in Bordeaux had been left to wither on the vine, the former wine merchant agreed. He approached General Nake, who went along. But to salvage his personal honor, Nake insisted on scuttling three ships to block the entrance to the harbor, denying access to it to Allied ships for at least two weeks.

Nake's deal was passed along to Roger Landes and his resistant leaders. It was the best they could hope for, so the proposal was accepted.

Two days later, on August 24, a curious chain of events began. General Nake and French officials agreed to publish the terms of the deal, in which the local population was warned not to attack German military men or to sabotage their vehicles and equipment.

A second, secret agreement set the date for the Wehrmacht to begin pulling out of Bordeaux, and by midnight of August 27, the last of the German occupiers had left the city, leaving the port and the bridges intact.[15]

Part Six

Allied March to Victory

The Armée Secrète Saves Antwerp

THESE WERE HEADY DAYS in the ivory towers of Supreme Headquarters, Allied Expeditionary Force (SHAEF). Two German armies had been virtually wiped out in Normandy, a powerful Anglo-American force had invaded southern France along the Riviera, and Paris had been liberated. It was late August 1944.

Despite taking a horrific beating, the Wehrmacht in France was withdrawing eastward in orderly fashion—with tank-tipped Allied spearheads nipping at its heels. The Germans would make a stand at the Siegfried Line, a concrete-and-steel fortification that stretched just inside the Third Reich for some three hundred miles from the Switzerland border northward to the Netherlands.

General Dwight D. Eisenhower's plan for ending the war in Europe was to push his thirty-six divisions up to the German frontier, then launch a full-blooded offensive for a drive into the Third Reich. This plan offered a massive logistics problem. Twenty thousand tons of supplies were devoured daily by the advancing divisions, and most of this cargo had to be hauled overland from Cherbourg, some four hundred miles from the front.

Suddenly Antwerp, Europe's largest port, had become the most important one in the world. If it were captured, and if its facilities were usable, Eisenhower would no longer have to rely on supplies being hauled long distances by road and rail, and he could continue the advance into Germany.

Two years earlier, in 1942, Adolf Hitler had recognized how crucial European ports would be to an invading Allied army. So he had proclaimed several major ports in France and the Low Countries, including Antwerp, "fortresses" and gave them the highest priority in manpower and materials for building "impregnable" defenses. He required commanders to sign declarations that they would defend the fortresses "to the last man and the last bullet" and then destroy the harbor facilities to render them useless to the Allies.

There was one colossal worry at SHAEF. Would Antwerp be able to unload ships once it were captured, or would the port be left "a field of devastation," as Hitler had ordered?

When the Americans had captured Cherbourg three weeks after D-Day in Normandy, Major General Cecil R. Moore, chief engineer of SHAEF, saw to

Lieutenant Urbain Reniers (code-named Reaumur) (center) discusses with other Belgian resistance leaders plans for saving the crucial Antwerp docks. (Centre de Recherches et d'Études Historiques)

his dismay that the Germans had carried out the führer's orders with great skill and thoroughness. "They knocked hell out of the port!" he told Eisenhower.

Colonel Alvin G. Viney, who prepared the original plan for rehabilitating Cherbourg Harbor, had been aghast. "The demolition was masterful, beyond a doubt the most complete, intensive, and best-planned demolition job in history," Viney declared.

Now, with Allied armies pounding on his front door along the western border of the Third Reich, it seemed logical to SHAEF that the führer would order Antwerp harbor to be devastated, as Cherbourg had been. That was precisely what the Germans prepared to carry out. And they might have succeeded had it not been for the vision, courage, and ingenuity of the Armée Secrète.

A year earlier, in 1943, leaders of the Armée Secrète had set up a committee that operated out of Colonial University in Antwerp and that was to form a separate "save the port" command with a Belgian Army officer, Lieutenant Urbain Reniers (code-named Reaumur), in charge. The group established a list of six objectives that would be necessary to keep the port from being sabotaged by the Germans—if and when Allied armies ever reached Belgium. At that time, the resistants were risking their lives solely on faith. There was no assurance that the Allies would eventually invade the Continent.

Soon a small group, Le Comité Clandestin de Coordination de la Resistance d'Anvers, was formed to implement the objectives. By July 1944, when

With the aid of the Belgian underground, the British Second Army captured Antwerp almost intact. German prisoners are marched through the city. (National Archives)

the Allies broke out of the stalemated Normandy beachhead, some thirty-five hundred armed resistants were available in Antwerp.

Eugene Colson (code-named Harry), a merchant marine officer, was put in charge of forces operating in the immediate harbor area. His was the most crucial task, for which he had assembled such specialists as pilots, merchant seamen, dock workers, ship maintenance crews, harbor policemen, and employees in the harbormaster's office.

Along the six miles of docks, quays, water towers, locks, and other facilities there were numerous German harbor offices. Colson managed to place one or more of his resistants in each office, and they provided him with weekly detailed, up-to-the-minute reports on German plans for the destruction of the port.

From among the fifteen hundred Belgians in Colson's harbor force, special squads were formed and trained to deactivate booby traps, time bombs, explosives, mines, and incendiary devices. Heavily armed combat teams were organized to protect crews involved in antidestruction operations. Resistants were assigned to guard specific bridges and to seize tugs and other small vessels.

On September 3, the British Second Army, under capable General Miles C. Dempsey, captured Brussels, Belgium. In Antwerp, thirty miles to the north, jubilant members of the Armée Secrète celebrated the event by blowing up the signal box at Central Station, thereby blocking German troop movements by train.

An hour later, the Armée Secrète leaders got orders from a coded phrase broadcast over BBC in London to spring into action at Antwerp. Like a well-oiled machine, resistants rushed to bridges, tunnels, wharves, and other installations slated for demolition.

Every move the Germans made was immediately reported by the Belgian moles in the harbor offices. For each action the Nazis took, the resistants, who knew the installations better than the Germans, launched a countermeasure. Two cement plants were blown up. Electric cables were cut to make certain that drawbridges over canals and rivers would remain shut, preventing the Wehrmacht from rapidly moving troops to confront the approaching British.

Teams of resistants leaped on barges, disarmed the crews, and dumped overboard the tons of explosives that were going to be used to destroy harbor facilities.

Among the resistants playing active roles in the Antwerp action was Robert Vekemans, a Belgian officer who had just been released from a concentration camp in Germany. Learning that the British spearhead was nearing, he decided to reconnoiter the region south of the port. He realized that Dempsey's spearheads would have a major problem in forcing a crossing of the Willebroek Canal and the Rupel Stream at Boom, ten miles south of Antwerp.

At Boom, Vekemans put his military background to use in assessing the situation. He discovered that the Germans had mined the two major bridges across a canal and a river. From a lookout house above one of the bridges, German soldiers had a clear view of the southern approaches, so they could spot British tanks in time to blow up the spans.

Continuing to sneak around the Boom area, always in danger of capture and execution, Vekemans came upon the century-old bridge, the Pont van Entischodt, that crossed Willebroek Canal a half mile east of the other two bridges. Concealing himself in a large clump of bushes, the Belgian saw that a few Germans were guarding the ancient bridge, and it appeared that demolitions had been planted on the span.

Vekemans mulled over the situation, then decided that if he could make contact with the British before they were spotted by the guards on the bridge roof half a mile to the west, he could escort the tanks to the Pont van Entischodt. There the view of the Germans to the south was blocked by several buildings, so he was convinced the British could reach the Pont van Entischodt undetected. Then the German guards could be dealt with, the explosives ripped out, and the tanks could barrel across the bridge and race on to Antwerp.

Early the next morning, Vekemans was in the village of Breendonk, sipping tea in a crossroad café, from where he could look south down the road and spot the British tanks before they came into the view of the Germans on top of the bridge at Boom. Soon he heard the rumble of approaching armored units, and he rushed outside to flag down the leading tank.

After being convinced of Vekemans's bona fides, the British commander was concerned that a century-old bridge would not hold heavy tanks. The Belgian, based on his experience as an army engineer officer, stressed that it would do so.

Two tanks and support vehicles were rushed to the Pont van Entischodt. Just as the Belgian had projected, the German guards were surprised and "neutralized" before they could set off the explosives, and the entire tank squadron crossed the canal.

Without loss of momentum, the British commander led his tanks down the northern bank of the canal to the first of the Boom bridges. Not expecting an attack from that direction, the confused German sentries quickly surrendered. But they refused to disclose the demolition firing point. Vekemans drew his pistol, cocked it, and put its muzzle against the head of a German sergeant, who had a sudden change of mind, and the wires were cut.

Just then, the other Boom bridge was blown into the sky, but its demise was of no consequence. British spearheads were already on their way to Antwerp.

Meanwhile, Eugene Colson's harbor resistants had been methodically going about their business—saving the port of Antwerp from destruction. By the afternoon of September 4, only a day after the BBC had flashed word for the Armée Secrète to strike, the key locks, bridges, and docks were in the hands of the resistants. Rather than the world's third-largest port being a "field of devastation," as Hitler had ordered, the facilities were intact. The action was one of the most spectacular underground feats of the war—but 150 resistants had paid with their lives.[1]

Machinations at a Dutch Hotel

ON A DARK, STORMY NIGHT in October 1944, the civilian press corps attached to Lieutenant General William H. "Big Simp" Simpson's U.S. Ninth Army moved into Maastricht and took over the Hôtel du Lévrier et l'Aigle Noir (the Greyhound and the Black Eagle). Only four hours earlier, Simpson's foot sloggers and tankers had captured the city of some seventy thousand hard-working and devout Dutch citizens. Maastricht had been a heavily traveled crossroads for centuries. Tucked away in the southeastern corner of the Netherlands, the city is only a few miles from Germany on one side and Belgium on the other.

With the arrival of the Allied war correspondents, the Dutch hotel operator, Mynheer van Egerschot, found himself host to a new set of guests. Since May 10, 1940, when Hitler's legions stormed into Maastricht, his 125-room hotel had been used as a billet for German officers. Over the fifty-one months of Wehrmacht occupation, Egerschot and his son Willem had catered to the needs of their Teutonic guests.

Willem, in his early twenties, had long been groomed to take over the operation of the hotel one day from his father. He had been sent to elite hotel schools in Germany and Switzerland, and he was well versed in the business. Willem was friendly, outgoing, and he hit it off well with the German officers.

Over the years there were angry mutterings against the father and son, who, townspeople were convinced, had become traitors to the Netherlands. Citizens wearing threadbare clothes and being short on food would walk down the Boschstraat past the large dining room windows of the Hôtel du Lévrier and see Mynheer van Egerschot and his son Willem bowing and scraping as they escorted German officers to tables. The angry Maastricht citizens also had glances at the hefty amounts of steaming food the guests were consuming with their wine.

During the occupation, Willem married Yvonne Ramakers, a beautiful, charming belle of Maastricht, whose father was a leading businessman. Convent-educated, Yvonne spoke German, French, English, and her native Dutch. If she didn't seem to especially cater to the German hotel guests, townspeople growled angrily, she made no effort to show her disapproval of them.

Now, in the fall of 1944, in the first exultant relief from their oppressors with the arrival of the Americans, the people of Maastricht vented their wrath on collaborators and those suspected of collaboration. Women who were thought to have been too friendly with the hated Boche (Germans) were seized by angry mobs, had their heads shaved, and were paraded naked through the streets. Male collaborators were beaten and, in some instances, summarily shot.

A day after the Ninth Army journalists arrived, three men in civilian clothes stalked into the lobby of the Hôtel du Lévrier. "We are black market police," one told Major Barney Oldfield, the Ninth Army press officer who had made lodging arrangements for the correspondents. "We will make a search of this hotel."

Oldfield was annoyed. For the time being, the U.S. Army had requisitioned the inn. "For what reason?" the major barked.

"The Egerschots have been German-friendly."

"What do you mean by that?"

"All during the occupation, they had Germans in this hotel."

Mulling over the Dutchman's remarks, Oldfield gave his approval for the search. But he insisted that one of his sergeants accompany the three men.

When the three black-market sleuths reached the third floor, Willem van Egerschot happened to be coming out of a room at the end of the corridor.

"Police!" one of the Dutchmen shouted, and all three, manacles in hand, started toward him. Willem knew that many of his countrymen, armed with forged identity cards and official-looking documents, were looting and taking revenge on those they disliked. Presumably thinking he was about to be dragged off and shot, Willem bolted past the trio and hurdled the guardrail at the head of the stairs to leap across the first landing. His jump was short. He hit the chandelier and plunged head over heels to the ground floor.

Miraculously, the younger Egerschot was not killed. He was dazed, but conscious. Bounding down the stairs, the three detectives looked at the bleeding, prostrate form. One said triumphantly: "See, he tried to escape. That proves he is guilty!"

An ambulance arrived and Willem was carried out on a stretcher and hurried to the hospital. His father, Mynheer, distraught and weeping, had tried to climb into the ambulance, but he was forcibly restrained by a policeman. "No one can go with the guilty man," he declared.

Two weeks later, Willem was on his road to recovery, although months of medical treatment and physical therapy would be required.

Meanwhile, the true story of the Egerschots spread through Maastricht like a wildfire across a dry prairie. Far from being German collaborators, they had risked their lives for the Netherlands.

Yvonne, the beautiful young wife, had purposely stayed away from the Hôtel du Lévrier to avoid any untoward incident with some amorous German officer that might rupture the comradeship between the Egerschots and the guests. Instead, she lived at the family's comfortable home.

Each night she had listened avidly as husband Willem told her in great detail of everything the German hotel "guests" had said that day. What did their jobs appear to be? What military units were passing through Maastricht? Where were they going?

With these bits and pieces of information, Yvonne had climbed onto her bicycle the next day and pedaled to the homes of friends—who happened to belong to the Dutch underground. She related what Willem had told her, and the information was radioed to an Allied headquarters. If there had been any questions Willem could not answer, his father, Mynheer, often was able to casually extract the information from his good "friends," the German guests.[2]

"Gift-Wrapping" a Kidnap Victim

WITH THE ARRIVAL OF FALL 1944, Adolf Hitler learned from his intelligence services that the Third Reich's ally Hungary was preparing to defect. Admiral Miklós Horthy, the nominal ruler of Hungary, who called himself the regent of the Kingdom of St. Michael, had covertly sent envoys to Moscow to beg Soviet dictator Josef Stalin for an armistice. The advancing Red Army was fewer than one hundred miles from Budapest, the capital.

Hungary had a habit of backing the wrong horse. In World War I, it was the German Kaiser; now it was the führer. Anxious to regain the territories Hungary had lost after World War I, Horthy joined the Axis camp in 1941 and sent two Hungarian armies into the Soviet Union on a "holy crusade" with the Wehrmacht.

When nearly an entire Hungarian army was destroyed in the German debacle at Stalingrad in 1943, Admiral Horthy began casting out peace feelers to the West. Strangely, the British responded by announcing over BBC's Hungarian Service that Allied bombers could now easily reach Hungary.

On May 19, 1944, Hitler, concerned about the looming defection, sent powerful forces into Hungary to take over operation of the government. Admiral Horthy now became a figurehead, a king without a kingdom. But when the führer got word that Soviet emissaries had sneaked into Budapest to finalize a surrender pact in late October, he sent for his favorite commando, Sturmbannführer (SS Major) Otto Skorzeny, a folk hero in the Third Reich, a villain in the Allied world. Hitler gave the 6-foot-3, 250-pound Skorzeny one of the war's strangest secret missions: Kidnap Admiral Horthy and his son Niki and bring them to Germany.

A day later, Major Skorzeny left for Budapest to launch the kidnapping operation, aptly named Mickey Mouse. He entered Budapest wearing civilian clothes and posing as "Dr. Wolf" from Cologne. He rented a room in a modest hotel and took on the role of a tourist, meandering about the° city and inspecting various government buildings where Horthy might be located.

Skorzeny learned from Gestapo agents that the regent's son Niki, a notorious playboy, was meeting with Yugoslav partisans who were acting as intermediaries in negotiating Hungary's surrender to the Soviets. The SS officer decided that the surest way to keep Admiral Horthy, a doting and indulgent father, in line would be to also kidnap his son.

Meanwhile, a contingent of Skorzeny's commandos had bivouacked on the outskirts of Budapest. On October 15, the day Niki was to confer with the Yugoslavians, the German soldiers stole into the city and concealed themselves near the house where the meeting would be held. At about noon, "Dr. Wolf" drove up and parked his automobile in front of the structure.

Suddenly Skorzeny, weapon in hand, barged into the house where Niki was discussing final details of the surrender with three partisans. Several German commandos were on the heels of their leader.

Young Horthy, taken by total surprise, vigorously waved his arms in protest. However, the huge German simply grabbed the Hungarian, rolled him into a large handy rug (he got the idea from George Bernard Shaw's play *Caesar and Cleopatra*), trussed the rug with a rope, heaved it into a truck, and rushed to the airport for same-day delivery to Berlin.

Meanwhile, the seventy-six-year-old Admiral Horthy was taken into custody by Skorzeny at the towering citadel where the regent lived. The SS major escorted the senior Horthy to Germany in style—aboard the Hungarian ruler's luxurious private train. There Horthy would spend the remainder of the war in comfortable "protective custody" in a Bavarian castle.[3]

An Ingenious German
Deception Plan

AMID GREAT SECRECY, Adolf Hitler and his entourage boarded a train in bomb-battered, blacked-out Berlin and headed for the Western Front. After a ride of a few hundred miles, the führer established himself in a huge concrete bunker called Adlerhorst (Eagle's Nest) twenty-five miles behind the battle line. It was December 10, 1944.

On the following day, sixty field marshals and generals, who had received mysterious—and unprecedented—orders to report alone to the bunker, were relieved of their sidearms by stern-faced SS junior officers when they entered the structure. Then they were seated in a large conference room in chairs that had been arranged in rows, much like those in a children's classroom.

Only a handful of Hitler confidants knew the purpose of this strange activity, and they had signed statements pledging total secrecy—under pain of being summarily shot.

Minutes later, a door at the front of the room opened and through it walked the führer. To those who had long known him, his haggard appearance came as a shock. Now he seemed a broken man, with an unhealthy color and trembling hands. To them, the fifty-five-year-old Hitler was a man grown old.

An eerie hush fell over the room. Then Hitler began to speak in a low voice. For more than an hour, he rambled on about great warriors in Germany's past and of the goals and triumphs of the Nazi Party he had founded. He ranted at British Prime Minister Winston Churchill as the "instigator of a holy war" against the Third Reich.

Although most of the field marshals and generals had heard all of this many times, they dared not fidget in the hard wooden chairs or reach for a handkerchief for fear that such gestures might be interpreted by the SS soldiers lining the room as going for a concealed pistol.

Suddenly, Hitler paused. Silence ensued for long moments. Then he stated: "I have made a momentous decision. I will take the offensive in the West!"

The field marshals and generals were thunderstruck. For nearly five months, the Allies had been advancing toward Germany, and now they were aligned along the Reich border preparing to launch a mighty offensive to end the war in Europe.

Breathing the fire of bygone days of triumph, the führer pointed to a locale on a wall map of the Western Front, and said, "I will strike the enemy here—in the Ardennes!"

Again the commanders were stunned. This sixty-mile sector in Belgium and Luxembourg was known as the Ghost Front. Both sides thinly manned it, and each used the region to "blood" (lightly test in combat) green troops and to rest veteran outfits exhausted from earlier battles. Hilly and forested, the Ardennes would force German panzers to traverse narrow, twisted roads on surfaces that would be coated with ice, making maneuvering highly difficult or even impossible.

The brilliance in the führer's choice of a locale in which to launch a final, desperate roll of the dice for victory or a negotiated peace in the West was that the complacent Allied High Command, already intoxicated by looming victory, was convinced that an attack through the Ardennes in winter would be out of the question.

Hitler's plan was for powerful spearheads to smash through disorganized American lines and charge two hundred miles to the northwest to seize the crucial port of Antwerp, on which the Allies relied for supplying most of the Western Front.

There would be two keys to success, the führer stressed: secrecy and speed. Secrecy would be obtained by an ingenious deception plan, which, hopefully, would permit German commanders to move up to the Ghost Front, from ten miles to the rear, two panzer armies without the Allies detecting the massive activity. This feat would be equivalent to relocating the population of Cincinnati, Ohio, or Liverpool, England, together with their cars and trucks, without neighbors knowing about it.

O-Tag (attack day) would be December 16, only five days away. The code name for the operation was Wacht am Rein (Watch on the Rhine), a designation intended to convey a defensive posture.

After the German commanders left Adlerhorst and rushed back to their posts, Field Marshal Karl Gerd von Rundstedt, commander of forces in the West, launched the deception plan. Sending a radioed order in a code that Allied wireless eavesdroppers could easily break, the seventy-year-old, ramrod-straight leader instructed his generals on the Western Front to halt all attacks and prepare for a last-ditch defense of the Reich.

Forty miles north, in the Aachen area, where the Americans were massing units for a looming offensive, the Germans set up a fake radio network that simulated the presence of the nonexistent Twenty-fifth Army. This ploy was intended to convey to Allied wireless monitors that the only remaining German reserves were being brought up there to confront the expected U.S. onslaught.

On the night of December 13, only seventy-two hours before the assault phase, code-named Herbstnebel (Autumn Mist), thousands of tons of straw that had been collected was brought up from rear areas and spread over the roads to muffle the sounds of tanks and vehicles moving forward. Some artillery pieces would be drawn by horses shod with specially padded shoes.

Marking of the roads of approach marches behind the lines, a normal procedure in all armies, was strictly forbidden. An Allied spy spotting such markings might realize that large troop units were being moved to the front.

Any travel by vehicles during the day was prohibited. Orders had been given to shoot out the tires of any conveyance detected moving, whatever the rank of the occupants.

Supplied with prime movers, winches, and sand, a special road service had been organized to assist tanks or vehicles in distress and get them off the roads before daylight.

Selected officers were designated as road commanders with stern orders to enforce camouflage measures and, in flagrant cases of abuse, they were authorized to arrest or even shoot the violator, be he general or private.

As troop formations, tanks, vehicles, and artillery pieces edged closer to the front in stages on succeeding nights, Luftwaffe planes flew up and down the front lines as though on combat missions but actually to help to cloak telltale sounds.

Charcoal was issued to assault troops so that smoke from wood-cooking fires would not betray the presence of large units. By midnight on O-Tag minus 1, every German soldier, tank, assault gun, ammunition truck, and artillery piece had reached their precise assigned place. Not an iota of suspicion had been aroused with the Americans, from outposts along the Ghost Front back to Supreme Headquarters outside Paris. Adolf Hitler's masterful deception plan had paid off.

In the meantime, German spies had been slipping behind American lines. Some of them had infiltrated into the Ardennes two weeks earlier. Because several German dialects were spoken by the natives in the frontier areas of Belgium and Luxembourg, it was easy for secret agents to blend with the population. The spies were to report back by radio the movements of American troops.

As the inky blackness of the cold winter night of O-Tag commenced to dissolve into a gray overcast, the two German armies, spearheaded by panzers, struck with fury behind a cacophony of colossal noise from nineteen hundred artillery pieces. Tons of explosives rained onto American positions, barracks, and headquarters that had been pinpointed earlier by German spies.

Before being halted after six weeks of bloody fighting in the bitterest winter cold in a quarter century, German forces had plunged sixty miles into Belgium. Known as the Battle of the Bulge, Hitler's audacious gamble came within a hairbreadth of phenomenal success. Instead, Wacht am Rein ended in disaster that would soon doom the Third Reich, which the führer had often boasted would last for a thousand years.[4]

Spies Swarm into the Third Reich

TWO DAYS BEFORE CHRISTMAS 1944, when it appeared that Adolf Hitler's legions were about to inflict a crushing and bloody defeat on the Americans in the Battle of the Bulge, Navy Lieutenant William J. Casey, at only thirty-one years of age, was appointed chief of secret intelligence for the European Theater. In an action growing out of desperation, the Allied brass gave Casey blanket authority to concentrate all of the resources of his Office of Strategic Services (OSS) to extract fresh intelligence out of Germany.

Casey, a wealthy New York lawyer with all the right connections, had been recruited into the OSS by its founder and director, "Wild Bill" Donovan. Now Casey plunged into his new task with customary energy and wisdom. His "battle" headquarters was his OSS offices at 72 Grosvenor Street in London.

Casey's new status was unique. Although a lieutenant in the U.S. Navy, he had the clout to give orders to colonels and navy commanders, and he would be dealing directly with American and British generals.

It was recognized by the brass in London that Casey was confronted with a protocol problem, and it was decided that the situation could best be resolved if Casey became a civilian once again. So he was put on inactive duty by the U.S. Navy and told to go out and buy some civilian suits.

Because of the Allied race across France and into Germany after the July 1944 breakout from the Normandy bridgehead, the OSS in Europe had been ready to put up a going-out-of-business sign. The agency had only two spies planted in Germany, but neither had the means to send back intelligence.

Now Casey rapidly recruited nondescript agents—anti-Nazi German deserters and prisoners of war, and Belgian, Polish, Dutch, and French refugees from German-occupied Europe. As each assignment was laid on, Casey appointed an OSS operations officer to coordinate training, documents, clothing, the cover story, communications, and the flight plan. When agents had been prepared, those leaving for Germany from London awaited takeoff at Area O, a mansion outside the city, which was operated by British enlisted men.

Casey realized that these covert agents were under enormous pressure. He issued orders to give them anything they wanted so they would depart in an upbeat frame of mind, and an OSS lieutenant was assigned to each two-man team to cater to the spies' final needs and whims.

After a two-hour drive to a secret airfield at Harrington, the OSS conducting officer took the agents to a hangar, where they were given a meticulous last-minute security check. Pockets were turned inside out in a search for train-ticket stubs, matchbooks, or other evidence that disclosed a recent life in London. Then the spies were taken to another room, where a second OSS officer performed an identical inspection.

Finally, a third OSS officer carefully examined the fake German identification, ration, census, and work cards that had been crafted by OSS technicians at a large house in London.

Before climbing into an airplane, each agent was handed a set of pills: benzedrine sulfate to battle excessive fatigue, knockout drops to put a person out for six hours, and a cyanide pill in case the agent had to kill himself.

Later in the war, spies and resistants in Europe used such small radio receivers that the devices could be carried in pockets. (National Archives)

These weeks were incredibly hectic ones at 70 Grosvenor Street, with a seemingly endless round of conferences on a wide array of topics: cover stories, available aircraft, targets, briefings, intelligence reports, drop zones, enemy anti-aircraft batteries, communications arrangements. The OSS operational map showing bomb lines as well as friendly and enemy troop positions had to be changed almost hourly because of the rapid advance of Allied spearheads. Casey's war room, in his words, was organized chaos.

On April 10, 1945, with the Western Allies closing in on Berlin and the Soviet armies to the east only some sixty miles from the capital, thirty-one-year-old Adolf Buchholz, a native German, parachuted into a huge park beside Wannsee Lake outside Berlin. During the late 1930s, Buchholz had served more than two years in a German prison for treason against the Nazi government. Early in the war, he managed to escape to England, where he was recruited by the OSS.

It was an especially hazardous mission. Buchholz, who had been a well-known sports director in Berlin before the war, might run onto numerous people—including the Gestapo—who would recognize him. His orders were to report on the military defenses in and around Berlin.

Buchholz was to communicate with the OSS by means of an ingenious new electronic system code-named Joan-Eleanor, which had been perfected by two OSS scientists especially for the use of secret agents dropped into Germany.

Earlier spies parachuting or infiltrating into Nazi-occupied countries customarily lugged along transmitter-receivers weighing as much as thirty pounds. In Germany, a nation saturated with Gestapo agents and informers, a spy carrying a heavy set in a suitcase would most likely be rapidly detected.

Consequently, Buchholz landed with a radio only six and a half inches long and weighing only three-quarters of a pound. It was powered by long-lasting batteries and fit snugly into a coat pocket. The radio was the Joan part of the system.

Eleanor was the forty pounds of complicated equipment that had been installed in a Mosquito, a swift, highly maneuverable British airplane. To accommodate Eleanor and her operator, much standard equipment, including all guns, had to be ripped out.

The procedure was for the unarmed Mosquito to circle overhead (at night), and the spy on the ground could speak directly to the operator in the Mosquito by way of a radio beam so narrow that it would be almost undetectable by German direction finders.

On two occasions, the specially equipped Mosquito flew to Berlin and circled overhead, then returned to its base without contacting Buchholz. Back in London, OSS officials regarded the agent as "lost."

By mid-April, sixty OSS teams had been parachuted into Germany, some having departed from England, others from France, a few from Italy. One two-man team (code-named Chauffeur) consisted of André Renaix and Michel Dehandtshutter, a former Gestapo employee. When they arrived at a supposed safe house in the major city of Regensburg, they discovered that the occupant had left six months earlier. So the agents spent the next two weeks concealed in a thick woods, getting by on only eight days' worth of food they had brought with them.

When they decided to come out into the open, Renaix and Dehandtshutter talked with the driver of a milk truck at Abensberg, a small town twenty miles southwest of Regensburg. After selling them some milk, the driver explained that he was a Belgian who had been assigned to work in a nearby dairy and that his name was François.

Trusting the Belgian, they gave their true identities, described their mission, and asked for his help. He agreed, and took them to his dairy.

François was one of twelve Belgian and French prisoners of war working in the dairy. The manager was gone most of the time, and the German sergeant ostensibly in charge was a buffoon. After François described the mission of the two agents, the other POWs agreed unanimously to aid them.

It turned out to be an undercover agent's dream, a perfect operation to spy on Regensburg. Each morning before dawn, ten or twelve trucks rolled out of the dairy to collect milk from farms that formed a virtual circle around Regensburg. Disguised as dairy workers, Renaix and Dehandtshutter rode along and collected information on artillery and antiaircraft emplacements and other targets. This intelligence was sent back to England on a radio transmitter.

One day, the two agents were told by the POWs that two French women, although loyal to their country, were working in a German brothel in Regensburg. Dehandtshutter promptly located the two young prostitutes and, at considerable personal risk, asked if they would help him in his espionage work.

They eagerly agreed, asking only that the Americans help them get back to France after the war. The OSS agent gave the two women a crash course on how to draw information from German officers, who were the brothel's principal customers, without raising suspicions.

Each day, one of the agents would visit the brothel and collect the information gathered by the two women. Within a few hours, this intelligence was radioed to London.

On another mission, two Belgian agents, Emil Van Dyck, who had been captured by the Germans in 1940, escaped, and joined the underground, and François Flour, who had been a foreign student in the United States when war broke out in Europe, arrived in Munich and obtained jobs as mechanics at a garage used extensively by the SS and the Gestapo.

Six weeks after they had parachuted near Munich, the team (code-named Painter) was confronted one night by two Gestapo officers at a laborers' shack where they lived. The Belgians felt surges of fright. However, the Germans said that they had been tailing the agents for many days, hoping to uncover the spies' allies in Munich. Now they had a deal to offer.

The two Germans turned over to Flour and Van Dyck a list of the entire Gestapo organization in the Munich region, plus all double agents and informers, including their addresses and code names. In return, when the Americans arrived, the two Germans wanted the OSS to arrange to send them and their families to South America with a good-size sum of money to get started in a new life.

Van Dyck and Flour, knowing that they had no authority to guarantee such a proposal, took the documents and assured the Gestapo men that their wishes would be carried out.

On May 7, 1945, four days after Adolf Hitler committed suicide in his Berlin bunker, General Alfred Jodl, the führer's closest military confidant since 1939, surrendered what remained of the Wehrmacht. OSS operatives soon began scouring the hospitals in Berlin in search of Adolf Buchholz, who had parachuted near the capital two months earlier, then vanished. No trace of him could be found. Had he been captured and killed by the Gestapo? Whatever may have been the case, Buchholz was presumed to be dead.

In August, Lieutenant Joseph Gould, who had recruited and trained Buchholz for the perilous mission, was eating in a Berlin mess hall when a soldier informed him that two Soviet soldiers wanted to see him. Going out into the corridor, Gould saw standing between the Soviet soldiers a thin, emaciated man who greeted the OSS officer warmly.

Gould was shocked. Who was this man? Then it dawned on him: It was Adolf Buchholz, who had lost sixty-five pounds since bailing out over Berlin four months earlier.

While Buchholz ravenously devoured a meal, he told Joe Gould of his ordeal. Because of the chaos and other factors, he explained, he had never found a place from where he could make the Joan-Eleanor communications rendezvous with the circling Mosquito airplane.

Buchholz's OSS cover had been as a Gestapo agent, and while he was in the act of disposing of the Gestapo medallion he was carrying, the Soviets took him into custody. He was thrown into a prison camp one hundred miles from Berlin, had been nearly starved by his captors, and it took him many weeks to convince the Soviets that he was an OSS agent.

During the war, the OSS had infiltrated some two hundred agents, including many women, into Germany. Most of them operated in the major, militarily significant cities. War, including its clandestine aspects, is never cheap. Thirty-six OSS agents were listed as killed, captured, or missing.[5]

Blasting Doomed Resistants to Freedom

SVEN TRUELSON, the soft-spoken, unflappable chief of intelligence for Denmark's underground, arrived in London in his customary manner, casually and without warning, in early March 1945. For three years he had managed to evade the Gestapo and shuttle between German-occupied Copenhagen and the British capital.

Now Truelson presented the British Air Ministry with an astonishing request. He wanted a flight of Royal Air Force bombers to rupture the foundation of Gestapo headquarters in the Shell building in Copenhagen so that some forty Danish secret army chiefs being held on the top floor could escape. Among those awaiting execution were the political chief of anti-Nazi operations, Dr. Mogens Fog, and a renowned scientist, Professor Brandt Rehberg.

Truelson's fantastic request was studied and debated by the War Cabinet, which said it couldn't be done. The target was at the extreme range for Mosquito bombers carrying the special explosives required. Pilots would have to fly for a long distance just above the sea to avoid German radar and then swoop into Copenhagen's streets at full speed at rooftop level to get in one-shot strikes.

Then the War Cabinet heard the other side of the story from Sven Truelson. Unless the raid were launched, the leaders of the Danish resistance would be wiped out by the Gestapo, and Denmark's secret army would disintegrate. In that case, the two hundred thousand German troops occupying the country to fight guerrilla operations could be released to oppose Allied forces.

Despite this plea, the War Cabinet stood firm: It was an "impossible" mission.

Persevering, Truelson took his request to the highest level of the British government: Prime Minister Winston Churchill. He listened intently, mulled over the pros and cons, then gave the green light to the raid.

Preparations for the operation began immediately. But now it was decided to send a Danish underground veteran, Ole Lippmann, who had escaped to England six months earlier with the Gestapo on his heels, back into Copenhagen to make a fateful decision. Could the bombing of the Shell building be justified when there was only a fifty-fifty chance for success and the lives of British airmen and Danish civilians might be taken?

After slipping back into Copenhagen, Lippmann strolled about the city as casually as possible to assess the mood of the people. Then he discovered that the Gestapo had made much progress during his absence and clearly was in control of what had been the underground network. He telephoned members of the resistance cells, and in every case, a Gestapo agent answered.

From a resistance leader he met face to face, Lippmann learned that an effort had been made to smuggle suicide L-pills to the men being held on the sixth floor of the Shell building as a favor to them. The effort had been thwarted.

Lippmann thought, if L-pills were regarded as a favor, why not bombs now?

Before returning to England, Lippmann reconnoitered the Shell building once more. Adjoining it was a convent school filled with hundreds of children. The sidewalks were jammed with passersby. So even if most of the bombs hit the target, heavy civilian casualties were bound to occur. However, he concluded that he must ask for the raid.

Eighteen Mosquitoes were diverted from the battlefronts. They and their crews would be spared for no more than forty-eight hours. If the bold mission were to fail, there would be no repeat raid.

Flight Lieutenant Ted Sismore, who had been the pathfinder in previous low-level missions, was assigned to solve the tricky navigational problem. He asked Sven Truelson if it would be possible to obtain a photograph of the Shell building from the sea approach.

Truelson replied that he would try to get a picture. Ten days later, the underground leader handed Sismore a perfect target photograph, just as the navigators and bombardiers would see it when zooming in at wavetop level.

Sismore was quite curious about the source of this tailor-made photograph. Truelson said he had sneaked into Copenhagen, stolen a small boat, snapped the picture from the right angle, then returned to England.

The first briefing for the thirty-six British airmen was attended by Truelson. Group Captain Robert Bateson, who would lead the mission, wanted his men to comprehend the operation in human terms, that it was crucial that the resistants in the Shell building be helped to escape.

"If the prisoners are not killed in the raid, they are going to die slowly and terribly," the Dane declared. "If they can escape, their value will be enormous. And if the Gestapo files on the first floor can be destroyed also, it will mean that a secret army in Denmark will continue to fight the Germans."

Dawn was starting to break on March 21, 1945, when the eighteen Mosquitoes lifted off from England and set a course for Copenhagen. The planes carried eleven-second-delay bombs, which would provide each aircraft with time to get out of its own bomb blast in the low-level attack. A gale was blowing across the North Sea, threatening to plunge into the water the Mosquitoes racing at wavetop level.

Flying on the port side of the leader, Group Captain Bateson, was a pilot carried on the mission orders as "Lieutenant Smith." Actually, he was a stowaway of sorts: Air Marshal Basil Embry, who had been forbidden to take part in the dangerous mission by his superiors but who had insisted on going along. Embry directed special operations for the RAF, and he knew most of the Allied military secrets, including about Ultra, the British device that intercepted and decoded German wireless messages. If he were shot down and survived, the Gestapo would have on its hands a potential intelligence bonanza. So "Smith" carried a suicide pill.

Protected by an escort of thirty Mustang fighter planes, Robert Bateson's bomber flight hit the Danish coast right on target. Minutes later, the Shell building was in view. Unwittingly, German efforts to "hide" the structure had made it stand out like the proverbial sore thumb. It was the only building painted in brown-and-green camouflage.

Bombs were released at the last moment and plunged into the base of the target. Tremendous blasts rocked the large structure. Inside, the Danish underground prisoners, not knowing what was taking place, were terrified. Walls crumbled. Ceilings crashed down. Cell doors were wrenched loose. One Dane grabbed the keys of a German guard who had been dazed by the explosions.

The wing of one Mosquito struck a pole and crashed into the convent school, killing and maiming children and Catholic nuns.

Meanwhile, the Danish resistance leaders, although dazed, staggered through gaping holes in the walls into the street, which was blanketed by thick black smoke, aiding in their escape.

From a military point of view, the pinpoint bombing attack, which the War Cabinet had decided was impossible, had been quite successful. Thirty secret army leaders had escaped, and the Gestapo files on Denmark's underground had been destroyed before they could be acted on. However, the cost had been heavy: the lives of ten British airmen, twenty-seven teachers, and a large number of civilians.

After the war in Europe ended seven weeks later, Lieutenant Ted Sismore made a pilgrimage back to the virtually destroyed school. He would try to explain why the raid had been necessary. Much to his astonishment and relief, the parents of the dead children said that they understood, that heart-wrenching sacrifices had been necessary to free Denmark from the Nazi yoke.[6]

The Plot to Surrender a Nazi Army

AS THE EXPRESS TRAIN FROM MILAN sped through the cold night on the five-hour trip to Zurich in neutral Switzerland, a group of seven civilians identified on their passports as members of a German-Italian trade mission occupied two compartments with drawn shades. These businessmen were going to discuss with Swiss government officials the use of the facilities of the port of Genoa, in the northern industrial rectangle of Italy controlled by the Wehrmacht. It was March 6, 1945.

Actually, the trade commission was a phony designation to provide a cover story. The traveling party included Obergruppenführer (four-star general) Karl Wolff, who held the highest rank in the Schutzstaffel (SS), and three of his aides, all wearing civilian suits. Also in the group were Major Max Waibel, a top officer in the Swiss Secret Service; and a wealthy Italian industrialist, Baron Luigi Parilli, a slight, energetic man with ingratiating manners, who had many contacts in the German Armed Forces.

Karl Wolff, who had been awarded the Iron Cross for gallantry in World War I, had been sent to Italy in September 1943, and given the long-winded title: *Bevollmächtigter General der Wehrmacht für das Rückwärtige Frontgebiet Italiens* (General of the Armed Forces for the Rear Combat Areas of Italy). His task was to safeguard the northern part of Italy controlled by the Germans.

After his arrival, the congenial, forty-two-year-old Wolff displeased his boss, Reichsführer Heinrich Himmler, by requesting and being granted an audience with Pope Pius XII in Rome. The session had been arranged by the German ambassador to the Vatican, Ernst von Weizsäcker, after Wolff had shown his good faith by releasing from jail several prominent Italians whom the Vatican had expressed interest in helping.

During his hour-long audience with the pope on May 10, 1944, Wolff stated that he was willing to "do whatever is within my power for the rapid conclusion of the war, should an honorable opportunity present itself."

Meanwhile, U.S. and British forces had invaded Italy at Salerno, a third of the way up the boot. After months of savage fighting, the Americans captured Rome three weeks after Wolff's session with the pope.

Until Adolf Hitler's last-ditch offensive in the Battle of the Bulge was eventually smashed in January 1945, Wolff had believed strongly that a compromise peace could be negotiated with the Western Allies. Now he knew that defeat was inevitable.

In early February 1945 Wolff was contacted by two acquaintances: Major Max Waibel of the Swiss secret service, and an Italian industrialist, Baron Luigi Parilli. They advised the general that they would arrange for him to sneak across the Italian border into Switzerland for a clandestine meeting with Allen Dulles, chief of the American OSS station at Bern.

For his part, Dulles had been leery. Wolff might be playing some sort of trick. But Parilli had vouched for the SS general's earnest desire to end the war and halt the bloodshed and destruction in Italy. However, Dulles demanded that Wolff demonstrate both his good faith and his authority by releasing two Italian underground leaders, Antonio Usmiani and Ferruccio Parri, who had been captured by the SS police and were being held in jail and facing execution.

A wise old owl, Dulles knew that if Wolff carried out the request, it would be proof that the German could back his claim that he controlled forces in northern Italy. Four days later, Parri and Usmiani had been spirited out of northern Italy and taken to Zurich. Under fictitious names, they were admitted as patients at an upscale medical clinic in an elegant section of the city. It was judged to be the safest place for them.

Meanwhile, General Wolff, in civvies, and other members of the phony German-Italian trade commission arrived on the Milan express train in Zurich, and the SS officers were promptly secreted in a plush apartment belonging to Professor Max Husmann, who ran a private school on the Zugerberg. One of Baron Parilli's relatives had attended Husmann's school, and this was the link that had brought the educator to Parilli's attention.

At the same time, the OSS spymaster, Allen Dulles, had come to Zurich from his base in Bern and holed up at a rented apartment that was used only for meetings of the most delicate nature. Professor Husmann arrived and wanted to bring Wolff right over, but Dulles said he wanted to see the SS general alone. An hour later, Husmann and Wolff were in the secret apartment, and after the Swiss professor introduced the two men, he left, as planned.

Wolff's far-reaching proposals shocked even the hard-bitten Dulles. The war was lost, the German declared, and to continue it would be a crime against the people of the Third Reich. To help end the bloodshed, the general stated that he would put himself and his SS troops in northern Italy to do the bidding of the Allies. He assured the OSS chief that he was acting alone, without the knowledge of his immediate boss, Reichsführer Himmler.

Wolff referred to his friendship with Field Marshal Albrecht Kesselring, the German supreme commander in Italy, and said he felt sure that Kesselring would help in surrender negotiations. Moreover, the SS general later said he would free a few hundred Jews being held in Italy and send them to Switzerland.

After a third round of Scotch, it was midnight. Dulles thanked his visitor, remained noncommittal, and said he would get back in touch with the German.

A few hours later, the OSS spymaster radioed the substance of the conversation to Washington and to British Field Marshal Harold R. L. G. Alexander, Allied supreme commander in the Mediterranean, at his headquarters in Caserta, near Naples, Italy. Without waiting for a response from on high, Alexander, a man of action, informed Dulles that he was immediately sending two high-ranking aides, British Major General Terence S. Airey, his intelligence chief, and U.S. Major General Lyman L. Lemnitzer, his deputy chief of staff, to talk with Karl Wolff.

Now Dulles was confronted by the need to establish fake identities for Lemnitzer and Airey, who would be wearing civilian suits. Swiss border guards habitually grilled travelers closely, including American soldiers on leave. However, it was decided that the identification "dog tags" would be taken from two OSS sergeants, and Lemnitzer became Nicholson and "acquired" several children and a home on Long Island in New York, and Airey became McNeely, who would be from New York City but have a distinctive British accent.

At the Swiss border, the two generals, wearing the borrowed dog tags around their necks, knew that they might be exposed as imposters if they only briefly hesitated in reciting their serial numbers. Lemnitzer was first to be quizzed and, after having practiced countless times earlier, he rattled off his serial number faultlessly. Fortunately, Airey, with his telltale accent, was then waved on past.

Meanwhile, Allen Dulles had arranged to use a villa at Ascona, on Lake Maggiore, for the covert meeting among Wolff, Lemnitzer, Airey, and himself. The site was secluded and peaceful—a perfect place for the rendezvous.

When the meeting began at the lake house, Allen Dulles introduced General Lemnitzer and General Airey to Wolff merely as his military advisers—no names, no ranks. The situation was one of the most unique of the war: it was the first occasion when Allied and German generals met on neutral soil to discuss a surrender and talk peacefully while their respective armies were engaging in a bloody fight with one another among the towering mountains of Italy.

Early in the discussion, Wolff disclosed that his plan already had gone awry: Field Marshal Kesselring had been transferred to take command of the Western Front, where Allied forces were knocking on the front door of the Third Reich. Replacing "Smiling Al," as Kesselring was known to British and American leaders, would be General Heinrich von Vietinghoff, himself a capable officer.

Taking part in the secret surrender of German forces in Italy were, from the left, Gero von Gaevernitz, General Heinrich von Vietinghoff, and SS General Karl Wolff. (National Archives)

Wolff said he believed he could coerce Vietinghoff into cooperating, because Kesselring's chief of staff, Major General Hans Röttiger, had remained in the same job in Italy. Röttiger, Wolff explained, had indicated that he would help in peace efforts.

A day after Karl Wolff returned to his post in Italy, he received chilling news: Heinrich Himmler ordered him to come to Berlin immediately. Had the Gestapo learned of Wolff's dealings with the Allies? If so, he was a goner.

Himmler had learned that Wolff had been in Switzerland, but he expressed no objection. Intelligence services were expected to keep lines open to the enemy. But the Reichsführer had no comprehension of just how far Wolff's talks had gone or how high had been the rank of those he had met.

Himmler, an incessant schemer, instructed Wolff to keep his lines open in Switzerland but never again to return to that country. Just to make certain his strict order was obeyed, Himmler said he had placed the general's family under "my personal protection." That brutal threat meant that Wolff's loved ones would be murdered if he conspired with the Allies.

The threat was serious enough to keep Wolff from returning to Switzerland, but he pursued his quest for peace in Italy by calling on General von Vietinghoff. Dulles learned of the results of that meeting in a written report brought to him on April 8 by an Italian underground courier. Wolff, it seemed, had turned Vietinghoff around—but not far enough. The German commander in Italy indicated he was willing to sign an instrument of unconditional surrender provided the Allies agreed to some "points of honor."

German soldiers would stand at attention when the Allies arrived to accept their surrender, Vietinghoff insisted. The POWs would not be kept in England or the United States, but rather used for reconstruction of roads and railways in Italy. After the situation had stabilized, Vietinghoff's men were to return to Germany with belts and bayonets as proof of an "orderly surrender."

Now that Dulles felt that there was an excellent chance for a successful outcome of the surrender negotiations (now code-named Sunrise), he felt the need to establish much faster communications with General Wolff in Italy. The solution was to insert an OSS agent in an SS facility near Wolff's headquarters to serve as a radio operator.

Dulles selected for the perilous mission a German-speaking radio operator, Vaclav Hradecky, a twenty-six-year-old Czech who already had survived numerous life-threatening episodes during the war. He had escaped from the Dachau concentration camp in 1940, lived underground in Germany for three years, was arrested again, but escaped into Switzerland in early 1944.

After the Wehrmacht was driven out of France, Hradecky, a diminutive, soft-spoken man, crossed the Swiss border, signed up with the OSS, and was trained as a radio operator. Now Allen Dulles informed him that he was to be turned over to an SS officer at the Italian border, and he was given a suitcase radio, code pads, a signal plan—and a huge supply of cigarettes.

Dulles explained that he would be hidden in a building, that he couldn't leave his room, and that he was to transmit the messages the SS officer gave him and to listen for signals from Dulles's operation in Bern. He was to give Dulles's messages to the SS officer.

Hradecky would be acting on faith alone. Dulles gave him no clue to the reason for his going on the mission.

On April 13 the Czech was met at the Italian border by the SS officer, who drove him to Piedmont, where he was installed in a room on the top floor of a building that was the headquarters of SS counterespionage. Its job was to catch enemy agents—such as Vaclav Hradecky.

Twenty-four hours later, the Czech's first radio message was picked up at Field Marshal Alexander's headquarters at Caserta. Known to Dulles and his men simply as "Wally," the radio operator in the weeks ahead became perhaps the most important member of the Allies in Italy.

For two and a half weeks, Wally tapped out and received a blizzard of messages: Wolff to Dulles. Alexander to Wolff. Dulles to Eisenhower. Wolff to Dulles. Eisenhower to Dulles. Dulles to Alexander.

Then, on April 28, Lieutenant Colonel Viktor von Schweinitz, on behalf of General Heinrich von Vietinghoff, and Sturmbannführer (SS Major) Max Wenner, representing General Karl Wolff, signed the document of unconditional surrender in a low-key ceremony at Field Marshal Harold Alexander's headquarters in Caserta.

The capitulation took effect at 2:00 P.M. on May 1, 1945. The war in Italy was over.[7]

A Covert Plan to Seize Berlin

WITHIN DAYS AFTER ALLIED ARMIES stormed across the Rhine River, the ancient barrier to invasion of Germany, on March 24, 1945, General Dwight D. Eisenhower had American, British, and French armies preparing to launch an all-out offensive to end the war. A year earlier, when plans for the invasion of Europe had been drawn up, the ultimate objective was Berlin, some four hundred miles east of the Rhine.

Now, with Berlin in ruins after many raids by British and American bombers, a small band of anti-Hitler civilians hatched a scheme to take over the city. The core of this clandestine group was the Reichsbanner, a World War I veterans' organization.

Drawing on their military experience gained many years earlier, the Reichsbanner leaders drew up a detailed plan. They had scouted possible sites for drop zones for American and British paratroopers and chosen an area between Berlin and Potsdam, twenty miles to the south. Two large lakes, the Schlachtensee and the Wannsee, would serve as landmarks for guiding in the planes.

A group of guides was set up to lead the American airborne men around German defenses and into the heart of the sprawling city. So meticulously had the Reichsbanner leaders planned the operation that they even pinpointed a headquarters for the invading force. It would be at 28 Unter den Linden, in a large office suite belonging to Hans Bauer, a member of the conspiracy.

At the same time, U.S. Lieutenant General Lewis H. Brereton, commander of the First Allied Airborne Army, issued orders for the war's most audacious operation, code-named Eclipse. It called for a parachute assault by more than two divisions on Berlin, a metropolis with a peacetime population of some three million persons.

Brereton's orders read: "Be prepared to enter Berlin and quell disorders." These disorders, it was implied, could come from armed German soldiers, violence-prone civilian groups, or Soviet troops bursting into the capital from the east.

Eclipse called for Major General James M. "Slim Jim" Gavin's U.S. 82nd Airborne Division to seize the Tempelhof and Rangdor airfields; Major General Maxwell D. Taylor's U.S. 101st Airborne Division to capture the Gatow and

Staaken airfields; a British brigade to capture Oranienburg airfield; and one Polish regiment to remain in reserve for an emergency.

Within hours of receiving the Eclipse orders, Gavin's All Americans and Taylor's Screaming Eagles were conducting "dress rehearsals" under the strictest security. Everything about the mammoth parachute assault was to be top secret. Only those with an absolute need to know were privy to details, fewer yet to the target: Berlin.

Most officers and men in the Allied parachute formations thought they were undergoing the customary rigorous training. Because the war in Europe seemed to be winding down, there was much conjecture in the ranks that the practice assaults on Target A (Berlin) were actually preparations for an eventual invasion of the Japanese homeland.

While General Gavin was preparing for Eclipse, an old friend, Arie Bestebreurtje, unexpectedly appeared at the 82nd Airborne's camp near Sissone, France. A captain in the Dutch Army, Bestebreurtje had been a fabled underground fighter, and he was at Jim Gavin's side throughout the Allied airborne assault in the Netherlands the previous September.

"Captain Harry," as the Dutchman was known to the GI paratroopers, had conducted himself with valor and distinction in the Netherlands operation, so Gavin hoped to take him along on Eclipse because he had special knowledge of Berlin. During the early days of the war, Captain Harry had reached Berlin by way of Switzerland as a spy. He had lived in that city as a teenager and knew the Tempelhof airfield area intimately.

Early in March 1945 he had received secret instructions to rendezvous with an American staff car near Namur, Belgium, in the middle of the night. He was told to remove all insignia from his Dutch Army uniform, and the need for strict secrecy was impressed on him. Then he was taken to Sissone.

Now Captain Harry was escorted to the 82nd Airborne war room. Although the two heavily armed sentries knew the escorting parachute officer, they demanded to hear the day's password. Inside the structure, Captain Harry and his guide went through another door where, in great secrecy, planning for Eclipse was in full sway.

A heavy curtain covered the large wall map so it could not be seen through the door of the second room. Then the map was uncovered for Captain Harry, and he was briefed by a major.

After listening in silence, the Dutch officer impressed on the parachute officers, including General Gavin, the unique character of the buildings around the Tempelhof airfield, an area known as the Mietskasernen. Each structure was a minifortress. It seemed highly likely to Captain Harry that if the Germans resisted, the buildings' capture could be a bloody affair.

Before unleashing his mighty armies east of the Rhine, General Eisenhower began to have doubts about capturing Berlin. So he sought the views of his closest confidant, General Omar N. Bradley, who commanded most of the U.S. ground forces that would spearhead the drive.

"I think it will cost us one hundred thousand casualties to capture Berlin— a pretty stiff price for a prestige objective, especially when [President Roosevelt] has already conceded the eastern region of Germany to the Soviets," Bradley declared.

Unwilling to pay the monstrous cost in American and British blood to seize Berlin, a "prestige" objective, Eisenhower changed his orders. Allied spearheads plunged deep into Germany with orders to halt at the Elbe River, ninety miles short of the Nazi capital. This decision resulted in the cancellation of Operation Eclipse. Berlin would be left for the Soviet Army.

It would be nearly two decades before General Jim Gavin learned that, despite the intense secrecy around Operation Eclipse, Soviet dictator Josef Stalin had known about the plan to parachute troops of the Western Allies to seize Berlin. Cornelius Ryan, a British author, was interviewing Gavin in 1974 when Ryan mentioned that he had talked with several Soviet generals in 1963. They had told Ryan that Marshal Stalin had informed his top commanders to hurry and capture Berlin because two Allied airborne divisions, aided by the German underground, were making preparations to seize the city.[8]

Urgent: Pilfer One Hundred Huge Missiles

SOON AFTER DAWN ON APRIL 11, 1945, Lieutenant Colonel William A. Castille, an intelligence officer, was in his jeep heading eastward in a column of the U.S. 3rd Armored Division near Nordhausen, deep in Germany. His radio crackled and he received an urgent summons from another intelligence officer: "Come quick! You aren't going to believe this! A big mainline railroad track leads right into a mountain. Lots of railroad cars loaded with 'stuff.'"

Twenty minutes later, Colonel Castille was at the foot of a towering elevation he learned was called Kohnstein Mountain. Along with two other 3rd Armored officers, he walked cautiously into the entrance of the tunnel. The Americans were awestruck by what they discovered: a colossal underground factory containing two parallel tunnels, each 1 1/4 miles long, and a maze of 46 galleries, each 250 yards long, 14 yards wide, and up to 30 yards high.

The mammoth plant had belonged to Mittelwerk, a German company established for the mass production—safe from Allied bombing—of V-2 missiles, the secret weapons that Adolf Hitler had believed would bring England to its knees when he began raining them on London the previous September.

Prowling through the tunnels, Castille and his two companions found a number of V-2s that had been completed and were awaiting shipment to launch-

Entrance to the Mittelwerk plant, the huge underground factory in the Harz Mountains where V-2 missiles were assembled. (U.S. Army)

ing pads when American spearheads neared. These huge (for that era) missiles were 46 feet long, and each weighed 13 tons. Their speed exceeded that of sound. The world had never seen anything like this revolutionary weapon.

Within the hour after the American officers left the underground factory, Colonel Andrew Barr, G-2 (intelligence officer) for the 3rd Armored Division, radioed word of the unique find in Kohnstein Mountain to higher headquarters. The flash worked its way through the chain of command to Colonel Holger "Ludy" Toftoy, chief of ordnance technical intelligence, in Paris.

Only a few days earlier, Toftoy had received a copy of a top-secret memo written by Major General Hugh J. Knerr, deputy commander for administration of the U.S. Air Force in Europe:

> Occupation of German scientific and industrial establishments has revealed the fact that we have been alarmingly backward in many fields of research. If we do not take the opportunity to seize the apparatus . . . and put it to work promptly for us, we will remain [twenty-five] years behind.

Translation: Grab any V-2s that might be available before the Soviets seize them so that the missiles can be shipped to White Sands Proving Ground, in New Mexico, for scientific study and development. The Space Age had arrived.

Colonel Toftoy, a perceptive man of action, promptly formed a secret group to be known as Special Mission V-2. Its clandestine function was to rush to the Harz Mountains (which included Kohnstein), "liberate" (the GI term for steal) the one hundred missiles, and ship them to the Belgian port of Antwerp.

Toftoy knew that he had an especially delicate task on his hands. Earlier in the year, the Big Three—President Franklin Roosevelt, Prime Minister Winston Churchill, and Premier Josef Stalin—had agreed to divide a conquered Germany into four parts. Kohnstein Mountain was in the Soviet zone, so the U.S. First Army would soon have to pull back and relinquish that region to Stalin.

Another "sticky point" confronting Colonel Toftoy: The Big Three had also agreed that none of the Allied Powers would remove any German weapons or scientific advancements from another nation's zone of occupation. So not only would Special Mission V-2 be facing colossal logistics problems, it also would have to steal the missiles from under the noses of the Soviets.

Leader of Special Mission V-2 was twenty-six-year-old Major James Hamill, a graduate of Fordham University with a degree in physics. Serving with him were Major William Bromley, an ordnance officer and a Stanford University alumnus, and Louis Woodruff, an electrical engineering professor at Massachusetts Institute of Technology.

"Officially, I'm reminding you that the high-level agreement is that nothing is to be moved out of the Soviet zone," Toftoy told Major Hamill. "Unofficially, I'm telling you to get those damned one hundred V-2s out of Kohnstein Mountain—without making it too obvious that you are raiding the joint!"

Major Hamill and his men left Paris for Germany and set up a coordinating base at Fulda, fifty-eight miles west of Kohnstein Mountain. Hamill had embarked on one of the most bizarre clandestine operations of the war, although he did not grasp its monumental significance at that moment.

On May 7, a few days after Special Mission V-2 reached Fulda, a delegation of Wehrmacht brass arrived at the headquarters of the Allied supreme commander, General Dwight D. Eisenhower, in a red brick schoolhouse outside Reims, France. Within an hour the Germans had signed an instrument of unconditional surrender.

That historic event injected even more urgency into grabbing the one hundred V-2s. Colonel Toftoy, a dedicated and flexible officer, knew that the mighty struggle for postwar domination between the free nations of the West and the Soviet Union and its satellite nations already had begun. So to Toftoy, one hundred long-range missiles falling into the hands of the Soviets was an unthinkable specter.

When Major Hamill and his key officers inspected the subterranean factory, they discovered that their task of "evacuating" the missiles before the Soviets arrived was mind-boggling in scope. No date had been announced for the American pullback from the Soviet Zone, but Hamill believed it to be June 1.

A major obstacle was that only some of the missiles had been assembled. The Special Mission V-2 team would have to select components found in Mittelwerk and ship them out for later assembly in the United States. That would be an impossible task without the parts list and other V-2 technical documents that still had not been found by American intelligence officers.

A major railhead at the nearby town of Nordhausen had escaped destruction by Allied bombs, but hundreds of trucks would have to be rounded up to transport the hundreds of tons of V-2 parts from the underground factory to the railhead.

There were more depressing problems for Jim Hamill and his cohorts. Most of the main railroad bridges and large portions of track leading from Nordhausen to the Belgian port of Antwerp were twisted wreckage. It was estimated that 340 railroad cars would be needed to ship the components to Antwerp. Sixteen large cargo ships would then be required to haul the Mittelwerk loot across the Atlantic Ocean.

Although the Special Mission V-2 team had been operating on a hush-hush basis, Soviet intelligence officers, in civilian disguise, traipsed in and out of the subterranean factory. Then Major Bromley secured the services of a company of infantry, and a tight cordon was thrown around the premises. No one could enter without a pass from the Special Mission V-2 leaders. The GIs had been told only that "important technical items" were in the tunnels.

Now Louis Woodruff, the electrical engineering expert, was able to isolate most of the needed missile components based on his intense study of U.S. intelligence documents. However, the control systems that guided the V-2s were manufactured elsewhere in the region, and without these items it would be impossible to reconstruct the missiles in the United States.

Now Major Hamill and his team were ready to load onto railroad flatcars the many thousands of missile components and subassemblies, a job that would require some 200 men with a knowledge of machinery. That problem was solved when Major Bromley obtained the services of the 144th Motor Vehicle Assembly Company, which was rushed from Cherbourg, France, about 750 miles to Nordhausen.

Nearly 200 civilian laborers were hired and paid to haul away the tens of tons of earth, rock, and debris that clogged the tunnel through which the railroad tracks ran into the mountain.

On May 19 Hamill and Bromley received staggering news: Early the next day, the U.S. Army Transportation Corps would begin moving the hundreds of usable railroad cars in the region across the lone surviving bridge leading from Nordhausen westward into the American Zone. During the night, the crucial span had been blown up with dynamite, and the rolling stock could not be moved. It appeared to the Special Mission V-2 team that all the tedious work would go for naught, and the missiles and components would be taken over by the Soviets.

Hamill was not prepared to surrender, however. Armed with a fake card allegedly signed by General Dwight Eisenhower that authorized him to collect and ship German equipment, he quickly obtained the services of the U.S. 1186th Combat Engineer Company to repair the blown bridge. To operate the trains, Hamill and Bromley recruited former German railroad employees, who were happy to find a paying job in the chaos of the Third Reich.

Early in the morning of May 25, 1945—five days before the Soviets were expected to arrive—the first train, loaded with V-2 components, chugged out of Nordhausen. It rolled to Erfurt, Germany, where men of the U.S. Railway Service took it over and steered it on to Antwerp.

During the next four days, nine other trains, each averaging thirty-four cars, steamed out of Nordhausen. Altogether there were 341 rail cars carrying a cargo of some 1,300 tons.

Despite the gargantuan success of "liberating" the equivalent of 100 long-range missiles, it was still too early for Colonel Toftoy and the Special Mission V-2 team to rejoice over their coup. The components would be merely 1,300 tons of junk at White Sands Proving Grounds unless the missing blueprints and data could be located. It would be impossible to reassemble the V-2 parts and test-fire the missiles without this critical information.

During the time Hamill and Bromley had been evacuating the components from inside Kohnstein Mountain, another young American army officer, Major Robert Staver, had been scouring the region in search of the documents. Acting on a tip, he located Karl Otto Fleischer, former general manager of Elektromechanische Werke, who lived in Nordhausen. The German agreed to cooperate with the Americans, but he kept to himself the fact that he was the only person in the region who knew where the V-2 data were hidden.

A few weeks earlier, two rocket scientists, Bernhard Tessman and Dieter Huzel, along with a squad of SS troops under a captain, had driven at night in a heavy rainstorm to an abandoned mine outside the small town of Dörnten. Under heavy canvas covers on the beds of several decrepit trucks were the valuable documents relating to the research and development of the V-2—fourteen tons of paper. Men in the tiny caravan dismounted and began shouldering cartons of documents and stashing them away inside the dark mine. Then the entrance was sealed by blasting, and the Germans hurried away.

Before fleeing to Bavaria in southern Germany a few days later to escape the oncoming Allied armies, Dieter Huzel and Bernhard Tessman had confided the secret to Karl Fleischer.

As the days rolled past, Major Staver continued to grill Fleischer, who helped to locate many items of rocket equipment but remained silent on the burial site of the priceless materials. Staver felt that the scientist was holding back, so he decided to try to trick the German into revealing the hiding place of the papers.

The young major pulled a notebook from his pocket and began reading to Fleischer what seemed to be a report from U.S. counterintelligence agents, but actually it was wording created by Staver himself. "Our intelligence officers have talked to Wernher von Braun [the chief architect of the V-2] and other scientists who have fled to Bavaria and are interned at Garmicsh," Staver read from the phony report. "They told us that many drawings and important documents were buried underground somewhere near [Kohnstein Mountain]."

Otto Fleischer flinched like a raccoon caught at night in a flashlight beam, but remained silent. The major was now convinced that Fleischer knew the burial site.

Twenty-four hours later, Fleischer sent for Staver. The German, looking drawn and tired, admitted that he knew where the V-2 documents were concealed. Qualms that he would be a traitor to Germany had kept him from revealing this knowledge earlier, he explained.

Staver rushed to the old mine, about thirty miles from Kohnstein Mountain, rapidly rounded up a work force of Germans who were delighted to be on a payroll, and placed a platoon of infantry soldiers at the site with orders to shoot to kill anyone who tried to make off with any of the boxes in the mine. Around-the-clock work shifts were established.

Six days later, the hundreds of boxes of V-2 materials were loaded onto a pair of large semitrailers, bound for Antwerp and shipment to the United States.[9]

Notes and Sources

Introduction

1. Peter Young, *Rommel* (London: Collins, 1950), p. 32.
   Gerard M. Devlin, *Silent Wings* (New York: St. Martin's, 1985), p. 13.
   Pierre Accoce and Pierre Quet, *A Man Called Lucy* (New York: Coward-McCann, 1966), p. 23.
   Willi Frischauer, *The Rise and Fall of Hermann Göring* (Boston: Houghton Mifflin, 1951), p. 38.
   Edward V. Rickenbacker, *Seven Came Through* (Garden City, N.Y.: Doubleday, 1943), p. 104.
   John W. Wheeler-Bennett, *The Nemesis of Power* (New York: Macmillan, 1954), p. 96.
   Author's archives.

Part One—Heading Toward the Abyss

1. **Sinister Plots in the "New Germany"**
   B. H. Liddell Hart, *The German Generals Talk* (New York: Morrow, 1948), p. 21.
   Harold C. Deutsch, *The Conspiracy Against Hitler* (Minneapolis: University of Minnesota Press, 1968), pp. 20–22.
   David Irving, *Hitler's War* (New York: Viking, 1977), p. xxiv.
   Richard Brett-Smith, *Hitler's Generals* (San Rafael, Calif.: Presidio, 1976), p. 185.
   Rupert Butler, *Black Angels* (New York: St. Martin's, 1977), pp. 18–19.
   Author's archives.
   Anthony Cave Brown, *Bodyguard of Lies* (New York: Harper & Row, 1975), p. 182.

2. **"Burglars" Call on a Japanese Spymaster**
   Author interview with Vice Admiral John D. Bulkeley (Ret.), 1992.
   Ellis M. Zacharias, *Secret Missions* (New York: Putnam, 1946), pp. 78–79.
   Eddy Bauer, ed., *Illustrated Encyclopedia of World War II* (New York: Marshall Cavendish, 1966), p. 41.
   Ladislas Farago, *The Game of the Foxes* (New York: McKay, 1971), p. 31.

3. **Ten Moles in Hitler's High Command**
   Anthony Read and David Fisher, *Colonel Z* (New York: Viking, 1985), pp. 211, 223.
   Alexander Foote, *Handbook for Spies* (New York: Doubleday, 1949), pp. 32, 45.
   Anthony Cave Brown, *Bodyguard of Lies* (New York: Harper & Row, 1975), p. 22.
   Pierre Accoce and Pierre Quet, *A Man Called Lucy* (New York: Coward-McCann, 1966), p. 43.
   Author's archives.

4. **A Scheme to Declare Hitler Insane**
   John W. Wheeler-Bennett, *The Nemesis of Power* (New York: Macmillan, 1954), pp. 372, 411.
   Willi Frischauer, *The Rise and Fall of Hermann Göring* (Boston: Houghton Mifflin, 1951), pp. 38–39.

Karl Bracher, *The German Dictatorship* (New York: Praeger, 1970), p. 138.
Albert Speer, *Inside the Third Reich* (New York: Macmillan, 1970), pp. 373–374.
Anthony Cave Brown, *Bodyguard of Lies* (New York: Harper & Row, 1975), p. 184.
Author's archives.
Interrogation by U.S. Historical Section, Germany, of leading German generals, manuscript, December 1945, Modern Military Records, National Archives, Washington, D.C.

5. **The Blond Beast's Ruse Backfires**
Walther Schellenberg, *The Labyrinth* (New York: Harper, 1956), pp. 197–198.
Heinz Höhner, *Canaris* (Garden City, N.Y.: Doubleday, 1979), p. 226.
Author's archives.

6. **Did His Generals Sabotage the Führer?**
Eugene Davidson, *The Trial of the Germans* (New York: Macmillan, 1966), p. 380.
Harold C. Deutsch, *The Conspiracy Against Hitler* (Minneapolis: University of Minnesota Press, 1974), pp. 95–96.
Author's archives.

7. **Her Serene Highness Plots with Goering**
Don Whitehead, *The FBI Story* (New York: Random House, 1956), p. 233.
Willi Frischauer, *The Rise and Fall of Hermann Göring* (Boston: Houghton Mifflin, 1951), p. 38.
Lord Halifax, *Fullness of Days* (New York: Dodd, Mead, 1957), p. 186.

8. **A Bizarre Kidnapping Scheme**
Leon Turrou, *The Nazi Spy Conspiracy in America* (Freeport, N.Y.: Books for Libraries Press, 1969), pp. 46–47, 52, 56.
Reports of FBI interrogation of Günther Gustav Rumrich, February–March 1938, in author's files.

9. **The French Consul's Janitor**
Charles Wighton and Günter Peis, *Hitler's Spies and Saboteurs* (New York: Holt, 1958), pp. 107–108.
Ladislas Farago, *The Game of the Foxes* (New York: McKay, 1971), pp. 87–88.
Author's archives.

10. **A German General Spies on Himself**
John R. Angolia, *On the Field of Honor* (San Jose, Calif.: Bender, 1979), p. 82.
F. W. Winterbotham, *The Nazi Connection* (New York: Harper & Row, 1978), pp. 196–197.
Albert Kesselring, *A Soldier's Record* (Novato, Calif.: Presidio, 1987), p. 65.

11. **A Baseball Player's Foresight**
Author's archives.

12. **Tailing a Soviet Spy in England**
Ladislas Farago, *The Game of the Foxes* (New York: McKay, 1971), pp. 98–99.
Anthony C. Brown, *Bodyguard of Lies* (New York: Harper & Row, 1975), p. 73.
Author's archives.

Part Two—The Lights Go out in Europe

1. A Weird Hoax to Launch a War

William L. Shirer, *The Rise and Fall of the Third Reich* (New York: Simon & Schuster, 1971), p. 41.

John W. Wheeler-Bennett, *Nemesis of Power* (New York: Macmillan, 1964), p. 446.
Affidavit signed by Alfred Naujocks at Nuremberg trials of war criminals, November 10, 1945. National Archives, Washington, D.C.

2. **Most Secret: Defuse the Magnetic Mines**
   Eddy Bauer, ed., *Illustrated Encyclopedia of World War II*, vol. 1 (London: Marshall Cavendish, 1966), pp. 130–133.
   Author's archives.
   Edwin P. Hoyt, *The U-Boat Wars* (New York: Arbor House, 1984), pp. 47–48.

3. **Mystery Explosion in a Nazi Shrine**
   Herbert M. Mason Jr., *To Kill the Devil* (New York: Norton, 1978), pp. 85–86.
   Walther Schellenberg, *The Labyrinth* (New York: Harper, 1956), p. 107.
   André Brissaud, *The Nazi Secret Service* (New York: Norton, 1974), pp. 73, 256.
   Author's archives.

4. **Goering Hires a Rainmaker**
   David Irving, *The Rise and Fall of the Luftwaffe* (Boston: Little, Brown, 1973), p. 83.
   Willi A. Boelcke, ed., *The Secret Conferences of Dr. Göbbels* (New York: E. P. Dutton, 1970), p. 8.

5. **Churchill's Amazing Gamble**
   Eddy Bauer, ed., *Illustrated Encyclopedia of World War II*, vol. 7 (London: Marshall Cavendish, 1966), p. 878.
   John W. Wheeler-Bennett, *The Nemesis of Power* (New York: Macmillan, 1954), pp. 25–26.
   Field Marshal Alanbrooke, *Diaries* (Garden City, N.Y.: Doubleday, 1955), pp. 98–99.
   Reader's Digest, November 1955.
   Admiral Karl Doenitz, *Memoirs* (London: Weidenfeld & Nicolson, 1959), pp. 325, 341.
   Winston S. Churchill, *Their Finest Hour* (Boston: Houghton Mifflin, 1949), pp. 43–44.

6. **A Covert Weather War**
   History of the U.S. 21st Weather Reporting Squadron (Maxwell Air Force Base, Ala.: U.S. Air Force Historical Branch, 1948).
   The U.S. Coast Guard in World War II (Washington, D.C.: U.S. Government Printing Office, 1953), pp. 76–77, 91, 103.
   Dwight D. Eisenhower, *Crusade in Europe* (Garden City, N.Y.: Doubleday, 1948), pp. 240–41.
   Anthony Cave Brown, *Bodyguard of Lies* (New York: Harper & Row, 1975), pp. 292, 294.
   John M. Stagg, *Forecast for Overlord* (New York: Norton, 1972), pp. 186–187.

7. **Masquerade on the High Seas**
   Eddy Bauer, ed., *Illustrated Encyclopedia of World War II*, vol. 6 (London: Marshall Cavendish, 1966), pp. 741–742.
   New Zealand National Archives, Navy Intelligence Summaries, March 21–30, 1941.
   Edwin T. Layton, *Pearl Harbor and Midway* (New York: Morrow, 1985), pp. 418–419.
   Author's archives.
   John Campbell, ed., *The Experience of World War II* (London: Oxford University Press, 1989), p. 130.

8. **Nazi Spies in the U.S. Capitol**
   Testimony transcript of Phyllis Spielman at trial of George Viereck, National Archives, Washington, D.C., June 1942.
   Testimony of George Hill at trial of George Viereck, July 6, 1942.

New York Times, June 25, 1940.

Washington Post, June 27, 1940.

Leon Turrou, *The Nazi Spy Conspiracy in America* (Freeport, N.Y.: Books for Libraries Press, 1969), pp. 187, 206.

Author's archives.

9. **Two Tiny Tots Escape to England**
Maria Wilhelm, *For the Glory of France* (New York: Messner, 1966), pp. 101–102.
Author's archives.

10. **The World's Dumbest Spy**
Wilhelm Hoettl, *The Secret Front* (New York: Praeger, 1954), p. 71.
Ladislas Farago, *The Game of the Foxes* (New York: McKay, 1971), pp. 235–236.
John W. Wheeler-Bennett, *The Nemesis of Power* (New York: Macmillan, 1954), p. 429.
Karl Bracher, *The German Dictatorship* (New York: Praeger, 1970), p. 419.
Anthony Cave Brown, *Bodyguard of Lies* (Harper & Row, 1975), p. 234.
Author's archives.
OSS Report No. 2087, "An Introduction to the Irish Problem," May 23, 1944, Modern Military Records, National Archives, Washington, D.C.

11. **Global Celebrity a Secret Agent**
Author's archives.

12. **A POW's Wife Unlocks a Code**
Paul Brickell, *Search for the Sky* (New York: Norton, 1954), p. 127.
Raymond F. Toliver and Trevor J. Constable, *Fighter General* (Zepher Cove, Nev.: AmPress, 1989), pp. 150–151.
Edward H. Sims, *The Greatest Aces* (New York: Harper & Row, 1967), p. 93.
P. R. Reid, *Colditz* (New York: St. Martin's, 1984), pp. 167–168, 182.
Reinhold Eggers, *Colditz Recaptured* (London: Robert Hale, 1973), p. 158.
John Campbell, ed., *The Experience of World War II* (London: Oxford University Press, 1989), p. 122.

13. **Canada's Covert "Luxury Fleet"**
Author's archives.

14. **One Airplane Infuriates the Führer**
Charles Wighton and Günter Peis, *Hitler's Spies and Saboteurs* (New York: Holt, 1958), pp. 212, 214.
David G. McCullough, ed., *Picture History of World War II* (New York: Crown, 1966), pp. 59, 74.
Anthony Cave Brown, *Bodyguard of Lies* (New York: Harper & Row, 1975), p. 36.
Author's archives.

Part Three—Thrusts and Counterthrusts

1. **A Cunning Forgery Pays Off**
Author's archives.
William Stevenson, *A Man Called Intrepid* (New York: Harcourt Brace Jovanovich, 1976), p. 268.
Don Whitehead, *The FBI Story* (New York: Random House, 1956), pp. 214–215.

2. **Shopping for U.S. Secrets**
American Mercury, December 1944.

Stanley E. Hilton, *Hitler's Secret War* (Baton Rouge: Louisiana State University Press, 1981), p. 17.

Ladislas Farago, *The Game of the Foxes* (New York: McKay, 1971), p. 371.

Author's archives.

Alan Hynd, *Passport to Treason* (New York: McBride, 1945), p. 91.

3. **A Scientist on a Covert Mission**

Nigel West, *Encyclopedia of World War II* (New York: Simon & Schuster, 1971), p. 123.

William Stevenson, *A Man Called Intrepid* (New York: Harcourt Brace Jovanovich, 1976), p. 143.

4. **"Black Propaganda" Warriors**

Winston S. Churchill, *The Second World War*, vol. 1 (Boston: Houghton Mifflin, 1948), p. 498.

M. R. D. Foot, *SOE in France* (London: Her Majesty's Stationery Office, 1966), p. 12.

Author's archives.

Sefton Delmer, *Black Boomerang* (New York: Viking, 1962), pp. 15–16.

5. **A Trojan Horse Hoax**

Seymour Reit, *Masquerade* (New York: Hawthorne, 1978), pp. 52–53.

Ronald Wheatley, *Operation Sea Lion* (London: Cassell, 1959), pp. 161–162.

Author's archives.

6. **The *Bulldog* Bites the German Navy**

Winston S. Churchill, *The Second World War*, vol. 2 (Boston: Houghton Mifflin, 1949), pp. 493–494.

Author's archives.

Karl Doenitz, *Memoirs* (London: Weidenfeld & Nicolson, 1959), pp. 332, 341.

Anthony Cave Brown, *Bodyguard of Lies* (New York: Harper & Row, 1975), pp. 59–60.

7. **Keeno, King of the Robots**

Thomas Parrish, *Roosevelt and Marshall* (New York: Morrow, 1989), p. 201.

Edwin T. Layton, *Pearl Harbor and Midway* (New York: Morrow, 1985), pp. 107–108.

Al Blake, "Me Jap Agent—for Uncle Sam," *Official Detective Stories*, February–June 1942.

"The Magic Background of Pearl Harbor," Modern Military Records, National Archives (Washington, D.C.: U.S. Department of Defense, 1977).

8. **A German POW Makes History**

Don Whitehead, *The FBI Story* (New York: Random House, 1956), pp. 239–240.

Author's archives.

9. **A Kamikaze Plan Against Pearl Harbor**

C. L. Sulzberger, *Picture History of World War II* (New York: Crown, 1966), p. 146.

Gordon W. Prange, *At Dawn We Slept* (New York: McGraw-Hill, 1981), p. 21.

Author's archives.

10. **Hijacking Mussolini's Money**

St. Louis Post-Dispatch, July 2, 1941.

Time, June 7, 1941.

Ladislas Farago, *The Game of the Foxes* (New York: McKay, 1971), pp. 306–307.

Author interview with former FBI Assistant Director W. Raymond Wannall, 1998.

Declassified FBI files, 1940–1945.

11. **Hitler's Doom Seen in the Stars**

Author's archives.

12. **Abwehr Dupe: Vice President Wallace**
Mark M. Boatner III, *The Biographical Dictionary of World War II* (Novato, Calif.: Presidio, 1996), p. 596.
Ladislas Farago, *The Game of the Foxes* (New York: McKay, 1971), pp. 346–347.
C. L. Sulzberger, *Picture History of World War II* (New York: Crown, 1966), p. 132.
Author's archives.

13. **The Nazis' Most Unlikely Secret Agent**
Michael Bar-Zohar, *Arrows of the Almighty* (New York: Macmillan, 1985), pp. 107, 234.
Author's archives.

Part Four—Conflict Spreads Around the World

1. **A Batty Idea for Firebombing Tokyo**
Bradley F. Smith, *Shadow Warriors* (London: Deutsch, 1983), pp. 102–103.
Author's archives.

2. **The FBI Nabs a Honolulu "Sleeper"**
Declassified FBI files, 1940–1941. National Archives, Washington, D.C.
Don Whitehead, *The FBI Story* (New York: Random House, 1956), pp. 190–192.
Record of Trial of Bernard Julius Otto Kuehn, Clerk of Court, U.S. Army Court of Military Records, Falls Church, Virginia, pp. 41–57, 111–114.
"Hearings Before the Joint Committee on the Investigation of the Pearl Harbor Attack, Congress of the United States," Part 35, pp. 491–492.
Affidavit of Otto Kuehn, January 1, 1942. National Archives, Washington, D.C.

3. **A French Counterfeit Traitor**
Maria Wilhelm, *For the Glory of France* (New York: Messner, 1968), pp. 137–138.
Eddy Bauer, ed., *Illustrated Encyclopedia of World War II*, vol. 9 (London: Marshall Cavendish, 1966), pp. 1239–1240.
Patrick Beesly, *Very Special Intelligence* (Garden City, N.Y.: Doubleday, 1972), p. 124.
Author's archives.

4. **Their Weapons Were Words**
Author's archives.

5. **Peculiar Demise of a Captured Plane**
Jerrard Tickel, *Moon Squadron* (Garden City, N.Y.: Doubleday, 1958), pp. 43–45, 121–122.
Eddy Bauer, ed., *Illustrated Encyclopedia of World War II*, vol. 4 (London: Marshall Cavendish, 1966), pp. 758–759.
Author's archives.

6. **A Bishop in Disguise**
Wilhelm Winterhager, *Der Kreisauer Kreis* (Mainz: Hase & Kohner Verlag, 1985), pp. 235–236.

7. **The Mysterious Inspector Thompson**
Nebur Gulbenkian, *Pentaraxia* (London: Hutchinson, 1965), pp. 97–99, 105.
R. V. Jones, *Most Secret War* (London: Collins, 1976), pp. 212–213.
Author's archives.
Airey Neave, *Room 900* (Garden City, N.Y.: Doubleday, 1970), pp. 152–153.

8. **A Nazi Counterfeiting Plot**
Secrets and Spies (Pleasantville, N.Y.: Reader's Digest Association, 1964), pp. 507–508.

André Brissaud, *The Nazi Secret Service* (New York: Norton, 1974), p. 291.
Walther Schellenberg, *The Labyrinth* (New York: Harper, 1956), p. 297.

9. **A Chance Meeting in a Café**
Author interview with General Mark W. Clark, 1984.
Lucian K. Truscott Jr., *Command Missions* (New York: Harper, 1950), pp. 72–73.
Samuel Eliot Morison, *The Two Ocean War* (Boston: Little, Brown, 1961), pp. 127–128.
George F. Howe, *Northwest Africa* (Washington, D.C.: Chief of Military History, 1957),
    pp. 88–89.
American Legion Magazine, August 1946.

10. **Hitler's Evil Guardian Angel**
John W. Wheeler-Bennett, *The Nemesis of Power* (New York: Macmillan, 1954), p. 403.
Harold C. Deutsch, *The Conspiracy Against Hitler* (Minneapolis: University of Min-
    nesota Press, 1954), p. 372.
International Military Tribunal, vol. 31, T-175. National Archives, Washington, D.C.
John R. Angolia, *On the Field of Honor*, vol. 2 (San Jose, Calif.: Bender, 1979), p. 232.
Peter Hoffman, *The History of German Resistance* (Cambridge, Mass.: MIT Press,
    1977), pp. 136–137.

11. **Roosevelt's Guest a Nazi Spy**
Foreign Relations of the United States, *The Conference at Washington and Casablanca*,
    II (Washington, D.C.: U.S. Government Printing Office, 1968), pp. 506, 508.
George S. Patton Jr., *War As I Knew It* (Boston: Houghton Mifflin, 1947), pp. 11–12.
Charles Wighton and Günter Peis, *Hitler's Spies and Saboteurs* (New York: Holt, 1958),
    pp. 15–16.
Author's archives.

12. **Ruse in a Berlin Brothel**
Walther Schellenberg, *The Labyrinth* (New York: Harper, 1956), p. 107.
Eddy Bauer, ed., *Illustrated Encyclopedia of World War II*, vol. 1 (London: Marshall
    Cavendish, 1966), p. 54.
Galeazzo Ciano, *The Ciano Diaries*, ed. Hugh Gibson (Garden City, N.Y.: Doubleday,
    1946), pp. 123, 126.
André Brissaud, *The Nazi Secret Service* (New York: W. W. Norton, 1974), p. 26.

13. **A Spy Spies on the Spymaster**
Walther Schellenberg, *The Schellenberg Memoirs* (New York: Harper, 1956), p. 137.
Pierre Accoce and Pierre Quet, *A Man Called Lucy* (New York: Coward-McCann,
    1966), p. 193.
Author's archives.

Part Five: The Tide Turns

1. **A Female Resistant Tricks the Gestapo**
Author's archives.

2. **An Owner Blows Up His Factory**
Author's archives.

3. **A Plan to Bomb the United States**
Ronald H. Bailey, *The Air War in Europe* (Alexandria, Va: Time-Life Books, 1981), p.
    328.
Alfred Price, *Luftwaffe* (New York: Ballantine, 1969), pp. 267–268.

4. **The Princes and Seven Thousand Danish Jews**
   Anthony Cave Brown, *Bodyguard of Lies* (New York: Harper & Row, 1975), pp. 413, 518.
   Illustrated Story of World War II (Pleasantville, N.Y.: Reader's Digest Association, 1969), p. 72.
   Author's archives.

5. **Eisenhower's Secret Weapon**
   Richard Collier, *Ten Thousand Eyes* (New York: Dutton, 1958), pp. 138, 205.
   William Casey, *The Secret War Against Hitler* (Washington, D.C.: Regnery Gateway, 1988), pp. 29–30.
   "London Secret Intelligence Files," 1942–1945. National Archives, Washington, D.C.

6. **A Call for Nazi Suicide Pilots**
   Charles Foley, *Commando Extraordinary* (Costa Mesa, Calif.: Noontide Press, 1988), p. 103.
   John R. Angolia, *On the Field of Honor* (San Jose, Calif.: Bender, 1979), p. 32.
   Hana Reitsch, *Flying Is My Life* (New York: Putnam, 1954), p. 212.

7. **A Plot to Murder Two Allied Generals**
   Before his death in 1984, General Mark Clark told the author that he had been aware of the Gestapo hit squad, but added: "I was so busy trying to keep us from getting kicked off the Anzio beachhead that I had no time to dwell on who may have been trying to do me in."
   Author's archives.

8. **Hitler Warned by a Female Spy**
   General Dwight D. Eisenhower letter to General Brehon B. Somervell, April 4, 1944. Eisenhower Library, Abilene, Kansas.
   Author's archives.

9. **An Alarming Breach of Security**
   Norman Longmate, *How We Lived Then* (London: Hutchinson, 1970), p. 95.
   Anthony Cave Brown, *Bodyguard of Lies* (Harper & Row, 1975), p. 599.
   New York Times, March 27, 1944.
   Ralph Ingersoll, *Top Secret* (New York: Harcourt, Brace, 1946), pp. 103–04.
   Author's archives.
   Ladislas Farago, *The Game of the Foxes* (New York: McKay, 1971), pp. 548–549.
   Eisenhower Foundation, *D-Day: The Normandy Invasion in Retrospect* (Lawrence: University Press of Kansas, 1971), pp. 170–171.

10. **The Wizard and the Mushroom Man**
    David Irving, *The Mare's Nest* (London: Kimber, 1964), p. 236.
    Office of Air Chief of Staff, Intelligence, *Impact*. U.S. Department of War, September 1944.
    Author's archives.

11. **Warning: Your Submarine May Explode**
    Author interview with Mrs. Helge Janson, the American wife of the Swedish consul in Japanese-held Manila during the war, 1990. She and her husband were friends of Commander Charles Parsons.
    Courtney Whitney, *MacArthur* (New York: Knopf, 1956), pp. 144–145.
    Ira Wolfert, *American Guerrilla in the Philippines* (New York: Simon & Schuster, 1945), pp. 56–57.
    Author's archives.

12. **A Puzzling Episode in Normandy**
    R. G. Rupenthal, report, "Utah Beach to Cherbourg," 1947, Office of Chief of Military History, Washington, D.C.
    Drew Middleton, "The War as Rommel Fought It," *New York Times* book review, May 17, 1953.
    Report of Transfer of German Nurses, September 21, 1944, Hoover Institution of War, Revolution, and Peace, Stanford, Calif.
    Dr. Walter Bargatzky, "Personal Recollections," Hoover Institution, October 20, 1945.
    Author's archives.

13. **A Poison "Treatment" for Hitler**
    John Toland, *Adolf Hitler* (Garden City, N.Y.: Doubleday, Anchor Books, 1976), pp. 814, 827.
    Author's archives.

14. **Belgian Resistants Steal a Locomotive**
    Author's archives.

15. **A German General Cuts a Strange Deal**
    Author's archives.

Part Six—Allied March to Victory

1. **The Armée Secrète Saves Antwerp**
    SHAEF, G-2 Report, ETO Tactical Situation, August 23, 1944, National Archives, Washington, D.C.
    Forest Pogue, *The Supreme Command* (Washington, D.C.: Office of the Chief of Military History, 1954), pp. 263–264.
    Dwight D. Eisenhower, *Crusade in Europe* (Garden City, N.Y.: Doubleday, 1948), pp. 290–291.
    J. L. Moulton, *Battle for Antwerp* (New York: Hippocrene, 1978), pp. 24, 43.

2. **Machinations at a Dutch Hotel**
    Author interview with Colonel Barney Oldfield, USAF (Ret.), who had been staying at the Hôtel du Lévrier at the time the three Dutch detectives arrived, 1997.
    Author's archives.

3. **"Gift-Wrapping" a Kidnap Victim**
    Author's archives.

4. **An Ingenious German Deception Plan**
    Author's archives.

5. **Spies Swarm into the Third Reich**
    Allen W. Dulles, *The Craft of Intelligence* (New York: Harper & Row, 1963), pp. 214–215.
    William Casey, *The Secret War Against Hitler* (Washington, D.C.: Regnery Gateway, 1988), pp. 187, 198.
    Joseph E. Persico, *Piercing the Reich* (New York: Viking, 1979), pp. 322–323.
    Dwight D. Eisenhower, *Crusade in Europe* (Garden City, N.Y.: Doubleday, 1948), pp. 404–405.
    Author's archives.

6. **Blasting Doomed Resistants to Freedom**
    G. L. Sulzberger, *Picture History of World War II* (New York: Crown, 1966), p. 557.

Anthony Cave Brown, *Bodyguard of Lies* (New York: Harper & Row, 1975), pp. 413, 416.

William Stevenson, *A Man Called Intrepid* (New York: Harcourt Brace Jovanovich, 1976), pp. 452–453.

7. The Plot to Surrender a Nazi Army

Saturday Evening Post, September 22 and 29, 1945.

Tempo magazine (Milan), February 24, 1951.

F. W. Deakin, *The Brutal Friendship* (New York: Harper & Row, 1962), pp. 178, 196.

Author's archives.

8. A Covert Plan to Seize Berlin

Author interview with Lieutenant General James M. Gavin (Ret.), April 1988.

Author interview with Colonel Barney Oldfield (Ret.), June 1993.

James P. O'Donnell, *The Bunker* (Boston: Houghton Mifflin, 1978), pp. 91–92.

Chester Wilmot, *The Struggle for Europe* (London: Fontana, 1959), p. 690.

9. Urgent: Pilfer One Hundred Huge Missiles

Report by Major William Bromley, "Evacuation of V-2 Missiles from Nordhausen, Germany," July 7, 1945. U.S. Army Military History Institute, Carlisle Barracks, Pa.

Author correspondence with Colonel William A. Castille (Ret.), 1992.

Author interview with Colonel Andrew Barr (Ret.), 1991.

Index